Trends and Tools for Operations Management

An Updated Guide for Executives and Managers

Roy L. Nersesian

QUORUM BOOKS
Westport, Connecticut • London

Library of Congress Cataloging-in-Publication Data

Nersesian, Roy L.
    Trends and tools for operations management   :   an updated guide for
executives and managers / Roy L. Nersesian.
        p.   cm.
    Includes bibliographical references and index.
    ISBN 1–56720–225–X (alk. paper)
    1. Production management.   I. Title.
TS155.N34   2000
658.4′034—dc21   99–40349

British Library Cataloguing in Publication Data is available.

Library of Congress Catalog Card Number: 99–40349
ISBN: 1–56720–225–X

First published in 2000

Quorum Books, 88 Post Road West, Westport, CT 06881
An imprint of Greenwood Publishing Group, Inc.
www.quorumbooks.com

Printed in the United States of America

The paper used in this book complies with the
Permanent Paper Standard issued by the National
Information Standards Organization (Z39.48–1984).

10 9 8 7 6 5 4 3 2 1

TO THE STUDENTS
OF THE
SCHOOL OF BUSINESS
MONMOUTH UNIVERSITY
WHO MADE THIS BOOK POSSIBLE

Contents

Preface

Thoughts on what should be taught in operations management have entered my mind at the start of each semester for nearly 15 years. I abandoned conventional textbooks early in my teaching career over concern about what material would be most beneficial to students. It was not what was included but what was excluded. In the mid-1980s textbooks virtually ignored the fact that the Japanese were gaining market share at the expense of American companies through their adoption of Deming's concepts. American companies seemed mired in the concepts of Taylor, already discarded by progressive companies. As an example, a textbook discussion on work design was based on dividing a task into its simplest elements and assigning a worker to each element. Students were expected to take completion times for each individual task in order to calculate daily output for each production line and then the number of production lines to handle daily demand. No mention was made of the possibility of assigning some or all the elements to a single person, or a group of people, as espoused by Joseph Juran and others. I performed a survey on a number of operations textbooks at that time and found that some had no, and others virtually no, mention of Deming, his Fourteen Points, the quality revolution, the industrial ascendancy of Japan, and the economic decline of the United States. In many respects, the textbooks mirrored the sentiment of American management at that time—what, me worry?

Not covering the competitive threat of Japan started me on a long trek of developing my own set of notes. I must admit that today's operations management textbooks do not lack in dealing with quality in all its manifestations. But by the time publishers became convinced that there should be a change in format, my notes were long since completed. This book is an expansion of those notes to reach a new audience: practicing operations managers who desire a refresher course. The book contains material omitted in my lectures because of classroom time constraints; in particular, problem solving. The traditional applications of linear programming to operational problems are illustrated using What's Best spreadsheet software. Evolver and RISKOptimizer spreadsheet software are introduced to handle operational problems that cannot be solved by linear programming.

These are the "tools" mentioned in the title. "Trends" are also part of the title. Trends infer a discussion about the future of operations management. This is a tall order. Unlike Alice in Wonderland's looking glass, the future is not translucent. Unfortunately, the perception of what an operations manager or any professional will need to know in the future is not only mired in the present, but also firmly entrenched in the past. The 1939 World's Fair typified perceiving the future as an extrapolation of what was already happening. For instance, appliances were already reducing kitchen drudgery. Therefore, the future, as an extrapolation of an existing trend, would remove kitchen drudgery through automation. This concept was then generalized and applied to all forms of work. The resulting forecast was a plethora of leisure time from advances in automation technology.

Now, 60 years later, kitchen drudgery has been dramatically reduced, and automation technology is thoroughly embedded in modern society. But we do not have much in the way of leisure time. Today's harried professional, married and not-so-married couples microwave ready-prepared frozen meals as they dash from door to bed to rest up for the next grueling 12 to 15-hour day that has become the norm for the up-and-coming. We no longer have the leisure to prepare and enjoy a home-cooked meal.

The 1939 World's Fair predicted a television in every room, but a lab model of a television already existed. The future airplane was still propeller-driven. Future cars had a distinct 1939 appearance, but they were driven on congestion-free, gravity-defying roadways spread like ribbons among magnificent skyscrapers. Today, the jet has replaced the propeller-driven aircraft, and automobiles are still based on 1939 technology other than advances in fuel economy and pollution controls. Our roadways are not ribbons suspended in air nor congestion-free and are modeled after the 1930s-built German autobahns. The fair's implication that mankind would eventually rid itself of poverty and war needs no comment.

So, too, am I perplexed as to what present-day trends mean for the future of an operations manager. Certainly, more of what is apparent today will be required, but what about factors that are not apparent? That's a tough call. With my perspective firmly mired in the present and entrenched in the past, surely global competition will continue to threaten production jobs in North America and Europe. Global competition will also threaten jobs in any nation that succeeds in raising workers' pay such as Japan and, perhaps Korea, Taiwan, and Singapore. Decent-paying manufacturing jobs will be threatened more and more by workers who are not paid enough to buy the output of their labor. This is not good news and is just the reverse of the trend that existed the last time a century passed.

A case in point was the recent exposé on Malaysian women employed making sneaker-wear for about $1.37 per day plus room and board to ensure continuous production. The sneakers sell for over $100 per pair in the United States. This is equivalent to about three months' gross pay for a woman to buy what she makes in minutes. The only difference between this arrangement and slavery is $1.37 per day, no beatings, and Sunday off. Where did the sales price of $100 plus come from? Could it be related to the highest possible price that could be charged that still makes it unattractive to build a sneaker-wear factory in the United States manned by Americans? Generally speaking, prices of imports from low labor-cost nations do not reflect low labor costs but high profit margins. The end result is that U.S. workers, who do not have jobs making sneakers, buy sneakers from those who cannot afford to buy the sneakers they make. This paradigm for commercial success has feet of clay.

I was once engaged in a conversation with a president of a company who had moved nearly all production to Mexico. I asked him if the Mexican workers could buy the products they made. He laughed and said that the workers were glad to get one square meal a day and free health care at his factory; forget about the pay. I then asked him the hypothetical question of what would happen if all the world's manufacturing were moved to nations such as China and India where pay is one dollar per day—"To whom do you sell?" His response was a shrug of his shoulders. Then he added parenthetically that had he not exported his labor requirements to Mexico, global competition would have driven him out of business.

Yet, has not exploiting the world's poor been a success? Following World War II, a Japanese worker received $1 per day and now makes $15 per hour. Only a couple of decades ago, a Korean worker received $1 per day and is now up to $10 per hour. Today, millions of workers in Southeast Asia, China, and India are paid a few dollars per day. Their hope is to somehow bootstrap themselves up to a higher standard of living just like workers in other Asian nations, most notably, the Far East Tigers (Singapore, Taiwan, Hong Kong, Korea) and Japan. Yet, all the while, we are losing manufacturing jobs where workers, who once made $20 per hour, become security guards for something close to minimum wage.

Does it really make sense to insist that U.S. workers receive a minimum wage that guarantees a labor cost savings if production is moved elsewhere? Does it make sense to open our doors to a flood tide of products made by workers whose remuneration is a tiny fraction of the minimum wage? I'm not espousing doing away with the minimum wage. Real wages have been falling in the United States for more than 20 years. But I'm beginning to wonder why goods made by workers under conditions that violate a whole host of national laws are given free access to our markets. A possible answer may be a minimum wage for goods entering the United States.

How, then, do these observations relate to the future of operations managers? Operations managers will be taxed to the limit of their abilities to ensure the efficiency, effectiveness, and productivity of the workforce to save what remains of our manufacturing base. Technological change in the nature of products and in the processes for making these products is an effective barrier against erosion. Another barrier is a greater intellectual contribution on the part of the workforce in the production process. Educated workers making a decent wage ought to be able to contribute intellectually to help create a competitive advantage for their firms. This is the secret to success of the Japanese workforce. The Japanese workforce is expected to make intellectual contributions to improve the product or the process making a product, in addition to manning machines. The intellectual capacity of the U.S. workforce remains largely untapped. This means that the vestiges of the Taylor system of "managers think and workers do" must be obliterated. More than this is going to be needed to ensure that operations managers have something to manage in the twenty-first century. What form that "more" may take is part of this book.

A number of steps have to be taken from forecasting product demand to delivering finished goods to customers. These include forecasting itself, the transformation process from labor and raw materials to finished goods, scheduling production, determining material and capacity requirements, locating facilities, enhancing productivity, achieving quality goals, and managing inventory and distribution. Unfortunately, operations management books treat these as isolated and individual topics for individuals who must integrate these disparate areas of expertise in the course of doing their jobs. It would be advantageous to avoid a piecemeal presentation, but I have not figured out how to present so much material in an integrated fashion. However, I am mindful of the need for practitioners to integrate many different concepts in order to be effective. I will attempt to synthesize material whenever possible.

This book emphasizes Japanese production techniques and the contribution made by W. Edwards Deming and others in transforming Japan from a third-rate, war-ravaged economy to world domination in consumer and industrial goods. Those who still adhere to the principles of Taylor in thinking and practice are still around. Stories from former students are sufficient in number for me to repeat the oft-told tale of total quality management (TQM), Deming's Fourteen Points, just-in-time (JIT) philosophy, and differences between American and Japanese production and operation techniques. *Out of the Crisis* by Deming, published in 1986 by the Center for Advanced Engineering Study at MIT, transformed my course when I discovered it. It remains a mainstay of this book.

There are others whose "pen is mightier than the sword" writings have been instrumental in creating the world that exists today for the production of goods and services. The contributions of Adam Smith, Eli Whitney, Frederick Taylor, Henry Ford, W. Edwards Deming, Joseph Juran, Philip Crosby, and Arnold Feigenbaum are covered. With the exception of the English economist Adam Smith, the rest are Americans. Deming, Juran, Crosby, and Feigenbaum are primarily responsible for teaching the Japanese a new approach to operations management that nearly sank the United States to the status of a second-rate industrial power. Indeed, in the late 1980s some were ready to write off the United States as an economic power. Japanese ownership of valuable Hawaiian properties, major Hollywood studios, a major interest in Rockefeller Center, and prime office space in leading U.S. cities symbolized to many the beginning of the end of America.

Ironically, these have become symbols of the beginning of the end of Japan. Certain of the Hawaiian properties, Hollywood studios, and Rockefeller Center have been liquidated at tremendous losses. Much of Japan's vaunted investments in prime real estate properties throughout the United States are, in the late-1990s, up for sale. Losses in liquidating these properties will be monumental. Japan is certainly not free of problems, but the problems do not stem from adopting Deming's principles but from their success. By applying Deming's principles, Japan bootstrapped itself to a high labor-cost society. The Japanese must now compete against low-cost Asian companies that have learned Japanese mean and lean production techniques for high quality products. Much of this learning has come from Japan's transplant factories that have spread the word on the secrets of Japanese success, including the United States. In addition to high labor costs, Japan suffers from a weak internal financial structure overrelying on bank debt as a source of capital. Whatever financial problems beset Japan and whatever their eventual outcome, the point is that Japan bootstrapped itself to become the world's second largest economic power. We are still first primarily because we have twice the population of Japan. This book is concerned with our remaining in first place.

To be fair, the transformation of Japan was not totally American-inspired. Among the Japanese making important contributions to production of quality products were Ishikawa, Toyoda, Ohno, Nakajima, Shingo, Taguchi, and others. Japanese emergence as a world industrial power was more than a few American and Japanese voices singing a new tune. Japanese executives, as choir directors, had to make a strategic decision to switch from Taylor to Deming. The transformation still would not be complete until the choir of untold thousands of operations managers learned the new tune. The responsibility for the United States' nearly losing its preeminence as a world economic power lies squarely on the shoulders of U.S. executives and operational managers who stayed with the tried-and-true way of doing things, long after the tried-and-true way was shown to be lacking. The story of America's resurgence as an industrial power started when U.S. executives and operations managers began listening to the same Americans that the Japanese listened to decades before.

I hope the reader has patience with my occasional use of hyperbole to emphasize a point. I stress Deming at the expense of Taylor and teamwork at the expense of destructive competition, although I am well aware of the contributions of Taylor and the beneficial aspects of competition. I realize that the world is not all one thing or the other. One former student of mine told me that the nature of the workers and the work at the company where he was employed was such that Taylor reigned supreme and Deming and everything else that I taught were irrelevant. I had to agree with him when I heard the circumstances, but I was a little uneasy about the concept that there was no way for the workers to contribute in the form of suggestions for improving the process. Other students have informed me that the team concept that I espouse in class was as dead as a dodo bird in their extremely competitive work environments where assignments are kept narrow and specialized. I hereby acknowledge to the reader that Taylor is apparently alive and well in our workplace. As long as a Taylor-type workplace is relatively immune to global competition, there is a place for Taylor. But I'm not convinced that Taylor provides the sure way to victory for companies that face global competition. Let me be a little more assertive. There is no way that a Taylor-run company in an industry with a modicum of technology can sustain the competitive onslaught from a Deming-run company. After all, isn't that what Japan's industrial resurgence and America's economic decline are all about?

I hope the reader also has patience with my occasional excursions from what is contained in traditional texts on operations management. It works to my advantage that the market for business school textbooks in operations management is well served, if not saturated. This forced the publisher to look elsewhere for a market and, as a consequence, gave me the freedom of expression that would not have been possible if business professors were the primary audience.

I would like to take the opportunity to thank Lynn Taylor and Eric Valentine of Quorum Books, Nina Duprey production editor, and my wife and family for their continual support.

Chapter 1

Transformation Process and Feedback Systems

Operations management is all about transforming raw inputs in the form of labor, material, and capital into useful goods and services. While output of enterprises is normally depicted as goods and services, there is also waste. Waste adds to costs and detracts from a company's competitive advantage. Waste can be reduced greater efficiency in the production process and by improving quality. If a process has a 10 percent defect rate, then 900 units of output require 1,000 units of input. If the defect rate is reduced to 1 percent, then the output increases 10 percent to 990 units with no change to input.

Transforming waste into something useful is another way to enhance a company's competitive position. In the United States, heavy users of hot water may install cogeneration plants to produce electricity rather than purchase electricity from electric utilities. Excess electricity production can be sold to public utilities at their average cost. Generally speaking, the rate of return on the investment in selling electricity does not justify a company's dedicating scarce capital resources for a cogeneration plant. The primary advantage of a cogeneration plant to industry is in capturing waste heat in the form of hot water. The savings in not having to purchase energy to heat water swing the economic calculation in favor of cogeneration plants.

Companies have learned that environmentally desirable actions may also be profitable. Glass and aluminum products made from recycled glass and aluminum waste require 90 percent less energy than making glass and aluminum from sand and bauxite. Recycled paper and plastic products are far less costly to manufacture than paper products made from trees and petrochemicals, plus the added benefit of reducing landfill requirements. Reverse logistics is a formal methodology for upgrading outmoded equipment as an inexpensive substitute for new equipment and to transform waste into useful products. These actions enhance a firm's competitiveness.

FEEDBACK MECHANISMS

The transformation process needs a feedback mechanism to measure a manager's performance. Traditional books on operations management state that profit is the appropriate feedback mechanism. And indeed it is. Profit means, by definition, that the output of goods and services exceeds the inputs of labor, material, and capital. I have no argument with that concept other than noting that profit is not a universal signal for success or failure in operating a company.

The mid-1980s had three feedback systems in operation. While the profit feedback mechanism was predominant in the Western world, it certainly did not apply to the communist world, which, at that time, accounted for about a quarter of the world's population (Mainland China, Soviet Union, Eastern Europe). More importantly, it was not being followed by the one nation responsible for creating the "Midwest Rustbelt": Japan. While the Soviet Union no longer exists, it is still interesting to examine its feedback mechanism if for no other reason than to realize how a poorly designed feedback mechanism can lead to adverse results. Another reason is to show that profit is not the only feedback system. The risk of having more than one feedback system is that the selected feedback system may not be the best.

	USSR	U.S.	JAPAN
Feedback Mechanism	Satisfy a quota: 500 tons of bathtubs	Maximize short-term profit	Maximize long-term market share via quality products

Under the old Soviet system, a manager would receive an order from central planning in Moscow (GOSPLAN) to manufacture, say, 500 tons of bathtubs. The sole responsibility of the Soviet manager would be to satisfy the quota. He or she did not have to be concerned with raw materials, as that was GOSPLAN's responsibility. Nor was the bathtub manufacturer responsible for marketing and distribution, as GOSPLAN dictated who was to receive bathtubs, along with both assigning labor to the factory and determining daily pay. A Soviet manager's only concern was making 500 tons of bathtubs. For doing this, he or she received a "gold star" for performance.

The traditional American manager was, and in many cases apparently still is, the quintessential short-term profit maximizer. Everything is measured in terms of what it means for next quarter's bottom line. If an action or decision cuts costs or increases revenue, then it is the right action or decision; if not, it is wrong. Thus, the way to maximize shareholder wealth, the whole purpose of a corporation, is to focus exclusively on the bottom line.

Japanese managers, once profit maximizers who were doing a poor job at it, learned a new concept from Deming. It is elegant in its simplicity: success to maximizing bottom-line profits can be accomplished by maximizing "top" -line market share, and the sure way of capturing market share is to sell competitively priced products of superior quality. Traditional American managers focus on short-term profits; Japanese managers focus on long-term market domination. While a traditional American manager's planning horizon barely extends beyond the next quarter, Japanese managers think in terms of decades. There are supposedly business plans covering the next 200 years.

The nature of the feedback mechanism reaches deep into the decision-making process. Take, for instance, a shipment of components of marginal quality selling 75 percent off list price. What might a traditional, short-term, profit-maximizing American manager decide to do? By accepting the shipment, costs drop, and near-term profits rise. With a time horizon of three months, the repercussion of poor quality products on future sales will not be felt. The decision is automatic: accept the shipment.

The same situation for a long-term, market-share maximizing Japanese manager will be handled differently. His (there are virtually no female managers in Japan) focus is on the long-term impact on sales as marginally acceptable products circulate about the market creating negative word-of-mouth advertising. The Japanese manager does not consider the near-term impact on profits because near-term profits are not controlling his decision making process. The only thing that matters is the long-term impact on market share. On that basis, the decision is automatic: reject the shipment.

The feedback mechanism is the puppeteer controlling a manager. Once a feedback mechanism is selected, a whole array of decisions is automatically made. Managers think they are making independent decisions, but these decisions are actually under the control of the feedback mechanism puppeteer. This is what makes the choice of a feedback mechanism so critical—it finalizes the nature of many decisions. Moreover, the decision maker is not even aware that decisions have been, in effect, removed from his or her discretion. This discussion can easily be generalized for all decisions made by human beings. Our core value beliefs strongly affect the nature of our decisions without our being aware of their role. Much of what follows is a consequence of the choice of feedback mechanism.

	USSR	U.S.	JAPAN
Financial Results	Checkbook approach: no real meaning attached to accounting principles or the concept of profit	The be-all and end-all of being in business	Financial results are the results of an operation and the pursuit of a business strategy

Financial results for the extinct Soviet manager were of no relevance. The price of the bathtubs was fixed by GOSPLAN, as were the price of raw materials and the number and pay of the workers. Under these conditions, financial management was reduced to something akin to a personal checking account where checks are deposited and written. Only it was better because there was no need to balance the checkbook. If deficits occurred because of the nature of government-mandated pricing on goods, raw materials, and labor, the checking account was subsidized by a cash infusion by the government. If a surplus developed, the government took it. There was no presentation of accounts in terms of income statements and balance sheets. Knowledge of basic accounting principles and budget preparation was not needed. Profit was not calculated because profit was the sin of capitalism made void by communism. As a matter of fact, the cost of labor was considered, in the convoluted thinking of Marx, as the true source of profits. The more workers assigned to a factory, the greater the "profit," irrespective of their output.

There is no need to discuss the importance of financial results for traditional American managers, but more than a few words are appropriate for the Japanese attitude on financial results. Financial results are taken literally: financial results are the results of business decisions on operating a company and pursuing a business strategy. If a business strategy and making it operative are correct, then the financial results will be positive. Financial results are of secondary importance. Having the right business strategy and the right operation is of primary importance. If the business strategy to maximize market share through quality products is the right business strategy, and the nature of the operation is such that it can produce competitively priced, high-quality goods, then the financial results will be positive.

Apparently, making competitively priced, better quality products must have been the correct business strategy, as judged by the financial results of Japanese companies and Japan's positive balance of trade. Also just as apparent, the U.S. manager's single-minded focus on the bottom line must not be the correct business strategy, as seen by the Midwest Rustbelt, a wide swath of abandoned factories in the heartland of the United States and our enormous balance of trade deficit with Japan. The Midwest Rustbelt became the visual proof of the failure to maximize profits by maximizing profits. The Japanese learned how to maximize profits by not focusing on profits but by focusing on taking over the market with quality products.

	USSR	U.S.	JAPAN
Marketing	What marketing? make tubs and ship	Very important	Very important, also concept of product sells itself

A Soviet manager did not have to market his or her output. As a matter of fact, the manager did not know who the buyer was. Most of the output was eventually shipped to "rabbit coop" apartment complexes being built throughout the Soviet empire. With the manufacturer not responsibility for marketing, one might ask how an individual purchased a bathtub. First of all, there probably were no bathroom fixture retail outlets and no advertisements in the Sunday papers or yellow pages in the phone book to find one. Even if there were a retail outlet, the chances are that it would not be stocked. An order might not be filled for months or years.

The solution to marketing for the consumer was ultimately theft: organized theft. A buyer of a bathtub had to know someone who knew someone who knew someone who worked at a construction site. A bathtub could be procured for vodka, the real medium of exchange in the Soviet Union. Today's commentary on the corruption in Russia is nothing new, and it certainly did not stem from the adoption of capitalism. Corruption and theft have been the primary functioning elements of Soviet society for over 70 years to satisfy consumer demand. The only difference now is that it is in the open.

Marketing is obviously as important in the United States as in Japan. However, the Japanese added an element to marketing: the concept that a high-quality product sells itself. That concept was incorporated some years ago in a series of Honda commercials featuring Danny, a Honda car salesman. Danny was frustrated because he could not sell a car. Buyers came in already convinced to buy a Honda because of its reputed quality, leaving a frustrated Danny with nothing to do but take an order.

Positive word-of-mouth advertising during the 1970s and 1980s made Americans aware that superior products at less cost that lasted longer and required less service were available. Positive word-of-mouth advertising comes from satisfied customers and it doesn't cost a company a penny. A satisfied consumer extolling a product's virtues to his or her friends and acquaintances is the most effective, and cheapest, advertising. On the other hand, clever commercials and cute advertising cannot sidetrack the negative impact of dissatisfied consumers bitterly criticizing a product's performance. Studies have shown that negative word-of-mouth advertising is four times more effective in causing sales to fall than positive word-of-mouth advertising in causing sales to rise. One student of mine berated a particular U.S. make of car for 20 minutes of class time. There was no way to stop her once she started venting her ire. When she was done, there was not a single potential customer for that make of car in the class. As instructor, I was too embarrassed to admit owning one.

Once it became apparent that Japanese products performed better, lasted longer, required less service, and cost less than U.S.-made products, there was little that U.S. companies could do to prevent positive word-of-mouth advertising for their competitors' products and counter negative word-of-mouth advertising for their own. Eventually, some companies decided that maybe they ought to take action against companies producing superior products by producing superior products themselves. Our quality had slipped to such a low level in the 1970s that it had been noted that were it not for Japan, the United States would have had to invent Japan to improve quality.

	USSR	U.S.	JAPAN
Customer requirements	What customer requirements? make tubs and ship	Very important	Extremely important

A Soviet manager was not concerned with style, color, or size or whether the plumbing attached to the bathtubs fitted the plumbing where they were to be installed. This was simply not within his or her purview. Feedback ended with the manufacture of 500 tons of bathtubs.

As important as satisfaction of customer requirements is to American managers, the Japanese elevated customer satisfaction to a higher rung on the ladder of corporate objectives. If long-term market share rather than short-term profits is the puppeteer governing management actions, then there will be a greater emphasis on satisfying customer requirements in terms of performance, quality, reliability, and price. Moreover, the Japanese expanded the concept of customer satisfaction to include the internal, in addition to the external, customer. External customers are those who buy a company's products. Internal customers are work teams within factories. If work team A makes part X that is consumed by work team B, then the basic relationship between the two would be as though work team A was an independent factory selling its output to work team B. Work team B becomes an external customer. If work teams assume the same set of values that exist between sellers and buyers concerning customer satisfaction, then there is going to be a major difference in attitudes among work teams that will enhance their productivity. And where did the Japanese arrive at such a quaint idea of the internal customer? From an American, Arnold Feigenbaum, the originator of total quality control (TQC), now known as total quality management (TQM).

	USSR	U.S.	JAPAN
Management style	Assign blame and punish (shoot)	Assign blame and punish (fire)	Identify source of problem and resolve

Stalin best exemplified the Soviet form of management by fear. He was unique in the hall of tyrants in having killed so many of his own. There is an apocryphal story about Stalin in his quest to spread the word of atheism among those clinging to the old ways. He had one of the most famous Moscow cathedrals publicly blown up and then asked the people why God had not punish him. Good question. Stalin was then left with what to do with the vacant site. Seeing that he was building the workers' paradise, Stalin could have built a factory, apartment house, hospital, or school. But he didn't. Instead, he decided to build a colossal statue of himself, something on the order of the Statue of Liberty. This statue required a massive foundation, which, when laid, was swallowed up by the spring mud. One or two other foundations met a similar fate before Stalin employed his favorite method of management control: he had the architects shot. Today, Stalin is dead, and the cathedral has been rebuilt. Good answer.

We, as a society, are more humane with managers and executives whose plans and intentions have gone awry. They are simply fired rather than being fired upon. The Japanese, on the other hand, tend to ban together, identify the nature of the problem, and attempt to resolve it.

The Japanese are humans just as Russians and Americans are, yet their cultural reaction to the same stimulus of corporate failure is so different. An explanation may lie in the way they make decisions. Decision making by consensus, practiced by the Japanese and other Asian nations, has been criticized as slow and inefficient. Yet once a decision is made, who's to be blamed if it turns out to be wrong? No single person can assume sole responsibility because all those involved in the decision had to "buy-in" before the decision was made. There have been rare occasions when Japanese managers have atoned for a poor business decision by taking their own lives. Talk about dedication of purpose.

	USSR	U.S.	JAPAN
Management results	Capture workers' brawn inefficiently	Capture workers' brawn efficiently	Capture workers' brawn and brains

The Soviet system was notoriously inefficient. Workers were simply assigned to factories whether or not the factories needed workers. There was no unemployment in the Soviet system, although there were underemployed workers. A Soviet manager who advocated doing the same work with half the workers would find himself in trouble with the GOSPLAN bureaucrats. As a matter of fact, cutting the workforce in half would be equivalent to halving the "profitability" of the factory. With the fall of communism, one factory in the now Czech Republic had 80 people assigned to clerical and supervisory functions for 20 workers. It is a wonder how such an inefficient system so unresponsive to the needs of the people could have lasted as long as it did.

The U.S. productive system is notoriously efficient. The reason for this is that we scrupulously follow the teachings of Taylor, and Taylor is known for efficiency. But efficiency is no longer sufficient to guarantee commercial success or even survival. The Japanese, in switching from Taylor to Deming, have been successful in capturing both the workers' brawn (the strength in their arms) and the workers' brains. Suggestions are an act of the brain, not the brawn of a worker. The proof that the Japanese have succeeded in capturing the brains of their workers is seen by the millions of suggestions made by Japanese workers versus virtually nil for American workers. U.S. worker suggestions have not only been few in number but spurious in nature. "Can we shut the factory down on Friday–it's the first day of deer-hunting season" is an actual and unfortunately typical U.S. worker suggestion. Moreover, the Japanese method for soliciting suggestions is not a suggestion box conveniently located near the toilets. It is a highly organized effort, described later in the book.

Capturing the brain power of workers in addition to their brawn power is a serious matter for American managers. Imagine two production managers, each with a workforce of 30 workers. One group comes to work and does exactly what it is told, and the other group not only performs the necessary physical work but remains after work to come up with suggestions on how to improve the product or the process for making the product. Which manager is at a competitive disadvantage?

	USSR	U.S.	JAPAN
Problem solving	Non-systematic	Nonsystematic; "if it ain't broke, don't fix it"	Systematic; "if it ain't being fixed, it is broke"

A nonsystematic approach simply means that problem solving is done when and if desired. It is epitomized by the saying, "If it ain't broke, don't fix it." The Japanese version, "if it ain't being fixed, it is broke," means that if a product is not being continuously improved, then the system of continuous improvement has broken down. Put another way, the Japanese are never satisfied with the status quo. Their cultural approach to production is that something can always be improved, whereas our cultural approach is that everything is fine as is. In viewing these cultural disparities, we should not be misled into thinking that the Japanese approach to continuous improvement stems from time immemorial. It is actually only a few decades old, beginning with Japanese adoption of Deming's and Juran's management principles.

Our approach to improvement is voluntary in that we may decide to, or not to, take an action to improve a product or the process of making a product. The Japanese approach is formally institutionalized to ensure that *kaizen*, never-ending improvement, never ends. In addition, we tend to deal with a problem directly, whereas the Japanese are prone to focus on the system that created the problem. These are fundamentally different approaches to problem solving. Multiple approaches to problem solving mean that one may be better than the other and that it is possible that the better way may not be our way.

	USSR	U.S.	JAPAN
Supplier	Deliver sufficient raw materials for manufacturer to satisfy quota	Adversarial relationship between buyer and seller based on price	Partnership based on the buyer's and seller's mutual benefit

It is interesting that Soviet quotas were usually in terms of weight, not number. After all, making 500 tons of bathtubs does provide an incentive for making rather heavy bathtubs. The advantage of measuring everything in terms of weight is that it allows GOSPLAN bureaucrats to more easily administer raw material requirements. If a number of bathtubs were specified, then the bureaucrats would have to know how much material is consumed in making a bathtub in order to be able to issue orders to raw material suppliers.

This uncomplimentary analysis of the Soviet system does have a purpose. Centralized planning for a national economy has been proven to be unworkable. This raises the question of whether the efficacy of centralized planning works for large, integrated corporations. It appears that, generally speaking, medium- and small-sized companies are more responsive to changing market conditions than their larger rivals. In response to this, large companies are setting up internal organizations that mimic medium- and small-sized companies where decision making is done close to the operating level by those most closely involved with a problem. The old General Motors administrative system of a request moving up through several layers of management in one department before it crosses over to another department and works its way down through several layers to the appropriate level is now being short-circuited with direct communications between the affected groups. Rather than permanent organizations to deal with a multiplicity of problems, temporary teams made up of individuals of several disciplines are created to deal with a specific problem. When the problem is resolved, the team is dissolved. Then another team is organized, tailor-fit to handle another problem. Problem resolution by those closest to the operating level augmented by specialists with the required technical expertise has been shown to be more productive than administrative deliberation involving multiple layers of management. This discovery has led to the pruning of unnecessary layers of managers, the "great white-collar slaughter." While this certainly has social costs, trimming "deadwood" has made American industry more responsive, productive, and competitive with remaining jobs being more meaningful.

Purchasing practices in the United States and Japan are fundamentally different. In reviewing these practices later in the book, one will be amazed at the impact of culture on a mundane operational function. The differences have nothing to do with Deming. Deming's espousal of single sourcing based on mutual trust between buyer and seller was practiced in Japan long before Deming arrived. Purchasing practices in Japan and the United States illustrate that when there is more than one approach for doing something, a manager must now face the perplexing question of whether his or her approach is best.

	USSR	U.S.	JAPAN
Job content	Narrow and specialized	Narrow and specialized	Broad and generalized

The Taylor system calls for workers to be given narrow and specialized assignments. Managers also tend to specialize in finance, marketing, or operations for most of their careers. In Japan, work teams are expected to learn each other's jobs to become sufficiently conversant with the various functions of a group in order to be able to offer suggestions. Managers in large Japanese corporations are often given rotating assignments in finance, marketing, operations, and even the exclusive preserve of accounting.

This system affects the nature of top management. Suppose that a U.S. manager and a Japanese manager of 20 years of experience are candidates for becoming presidents of their respective firms. Suppose that the U.S. manager has 20 years in marketing. Everything about marketing is known, but little is known of operations or finance. While the Japanese manager may lack depth of understanding in any single functional area, a series of assignments in all the functional areas does provide a candidate with a broad appreciation of what a company does. Which system should breed more effective presidents?

THE CAPACITY FOR MANAGERS TO CHANGE

What is the capacity of humans to change? For Soviet managers, the transition is monumental. Now they must ensure that workers are being productively employed, that the output of their effort is fit for sale, and that revenues exceed costs. They must learn to make decisions rather than follow orders, survive without subsidies, and perform capitalistic functions such as preparing budgets and financial statements. If the alternative is starvation in the cold and dark, one can glibly conclude that Soviet managers can and will adopt Western-style capitalism.

The evidence suggests otherwise. Only Poland and the Czech Republic have made visible progress in adopting Western economic practices. Other East European nations have reverted to a form of communism. Russia is on the verge of abandoning democracy and capitalism. Part of the problem is the inability of Russian managers to differentiate between creating wealth and making money. An individual can make money through stealing but is not creating wealth. Creating wealth is accomplished by producing goods and services that consumers are willing to buy. By so doing, jobs are created, adding to the number of consumers and to the demand for the company's products. Managers of ex-Soviet enterprises, for the most part ex-communists, seem more interested in enriching themselves than in creating national wealth. Another contributing factor is that most Russians and Eastern Europeans have not benefited from the fall of communism. To them, having nothing in a communist society is preferable to having nothing in a capitalist society: at least they don't starve in the cold.

Can American managers change their attitudes from maximizing profits to maximizing market share through quality products? Yes, but with great difficulty. It appears that firms must be brought to a point of crisis before change can be instituted. The automobile industry is a case in point. Ford was the first company to get into financial trouble because of loss of market share to Japanese imports and the first to adopt Deming's teachings. Chrysler was the second to get into financial difficulty and the second to change. General Motors took longer to get into financial difficulty and, after losing billions of dollars per year in the late 1980s, decided to bite the bullet and change, that is, build a car that people wanted to buy. Why did management wait so long? The threat of Japanese automobile imports was apparent in the early 1970s, when Toyota seized the West Coast market. Yet the top managers of GM wasted nearly 20 years before instituting change, and then only when bankruptcy loomed over the horizon.

Reluctance to change is a characteristic of American managers; yet, we live in a world of accelerating change. The great advantage of the Japanese is their apparent ease to adapt to change while simultaneously preserving their culture and traditions. The Meiji Restoration in the 1860s signaled Japan's decision to abandon feudalism and accept Western values, a major shift in direction, to say the least. The Japanese searched the world to see who did what best and then adopted that approach. They modeled their railroads after Britain's and their education system after Germany's. They had no problem dropping the old and accepting the new while maintaining the essentials of their culture and traditions. Japanese ability to adapt is seen in their religious practices. Two-thirds of the Japanese belong to two religions. They marry as Shintos and are buried as Buddhists. There are major differences in beliefs between these two religions, yet the Japanese seem to exhibit no difficulty in reconciling the two. Less than 1 percent of the population is Christian, yet Christmas is universally celebrated. The Japanese watched Americans play baseball and golf and became enthusiasts of both. Once they saw the advantages of Deming over Taylor, they shed Taylor as easily as a snake sheds its skin. Meanwhile, American managers clung to Taylor far too long. Thousands of companies went out of business, creating the Midwest Rustbelt rather than switch and win. Why change is so difficult for one culture and easy for another is left for sociologists or anthropologists to ponder.

Chapter 2

Quality under Taylor and Deming

FREDERICK TAYLOR—FATHER OF SCIENTIFIC MANAGEMENT

I do not wish to denigrate the achievements of Taylor, although I already have. For his time, he was the right person. That is the essential problem: his time is past for companies with some degree of technological sophistication and high labor costs facing global competition.

Much of what goes on in management had its beginnings in running military campaigns and railroads, the first major industry of the Industrial Revolution. At the start of the nineteenth century, an owner personally ran a workshop, attending to all details. This was fine as long as workshops remained workshops; but, as the century progressed, many workshops evolved into large, complex organizations with owners still trying to personally control every activity. Thus, factories tended to become disorganized. It was not unusual for a worker to wake up in the morning not knowing whether he had a job that day; or if he did, what he would be doing. Early each morning, he would mill around with others in front of a factory waiting for the shop foremen to appear. If selected by a shop foreman, a worker had a job for the day. He did not know what the job would be, but he was about to find out.

Taylor introduced basic organization into factory life whereby a worker going to sleep at night knew that he had a job and what the job would be when he awoke. He accomplished this by creating a new profession called managers. Tasks previously performed by an individual owner were split up and assigned to managers. The basic organization chart of a president assisted by vice presidents in marketing, finance, and operations and these, in turn, assisted by others is the work of Taylor. Managers were to plan and organize activities within their respective spheres of responsibility. Managers then told the workers what to do. Taylor separated planning from doing. Managers plan, workers do; managers issue orders, workers obey; managers think, workers don't–no feedback was expected or desired from the workers.

Taylor's organization of factories did not stop at the top. He examined work to be accomplished by those at the bottom. Every task was broken down to its simplest elements, and each element was assigned to an individual worker. The very essence of Taylor is embodied in assembly line production, invented by Ford, where one worker attaches nuts to bolts, and the next worker tightens them. The Taylor system was extremely successful because Taylor was dealing primarily with immigrants with scant knowledge of English, limited education, and few skills. There would come a time when workers spoke English, were educated, and had skills yet were employed in a system that assumed they had none.

Taylor was the first to bring the stopwatch into the factory. His purpose was altruistic. He believed that there was no reason for a worker to be in a factory other than to feed his family. Worker productivity was low because pay was poor. Taylor felt that productivity would rise if a worker were paid enough to decently support a family. To accomplish this, Taylor used a stopwatch to time the work being done by an individual. He developed what is today called cost accounting in order to be able to calculate incremental profits from enhanced production. From this he created a sliding scale. If a worker's output remained below a certain point, his pay remained low. If a worker exceeded this point, then the piece rate would escalate. Taylor set up a sliding scale for piece-rate work whereby if a worker worked hard, it would be physically possible for him to earn decent pay to support a family. Roughly one-third of incremental profits from enhanced productivity went to the worker, and the rest went to the owner. Both workers and owners liked Taylor.

In time, Taylor died, and the altruism associated with the stopwatch followed him to the grave. The stopwatch was no longer welcomed, but became feared by the workers. Timing workers resulted in quotas, and performance was measured in terms of meeting quotas. Suppose that a group's average output is 100 units per day per worker. Now a quota is assigned for each worker to produce 100 units per day. How many workers will fail to meet the quota? How about half? If performance is a normal distribution with a mean of 100, then half of the workers are below the mean, and half are above, excluding those exactly on the mean. First-line supervisors threatened those below the quota with loss of employment. Fear gripped the workforce, as it was continually being culled of its poorest performers. As the average performance of the group rose, the quota was vamped upward to replenish the supply of workers to be culled. Workers had to work harder and harder simply to keep a job without the benefit of increased pay from the sliding scale invented by Taylor.

It has been observed that the devil himself could not have invented a better system to guarantee worker dissatisfaction than what eventually became of the Taylor system. Work content became monotonous, tedious, and stripped of all meaning as tasks were divided into their simplest elements and workers assigned to each element. Stress and fear of losing one's job accompanied each hike in performance quotas. The rise of the labor movement was spurred not just by poor pay and poor working conditions, but also by poor work design that robbed a worker of job satisfaction and created a work environment of stress and fear.

The Taylor system also bred an attitude that a worker was merely an extension of a machine. Owners loved machines because machines can work 24 hours a day, never stopping to eat, rest, powder one's nose, or be paid. Too bad a worker had to be attached to a machine to make it run because a worker couldn't function 24 hours a day without eating, resting, and powdering his or her nose. Moreover, unlike a machine, a worker had to be paid. The point that paid workers were also the buyers of the products they were making and what other factory owners were making and therefore the ultimate source of profits was generally lost on factory owners.

Taylor had many disciples. The Gilbreth husband-and-wife team developed time-motion studies to enhance worker productivity. A series of photographs were taken of a worker performing a task–later a film was made. Each photograph or frame of a film was studied to fully appreciate hand, wrist, and arm motions. Then the work would be redesigned to simplify these motions. This enhanced a worker's output without a concomitant increase in effort. Lillian Gilbreth, a psychologist, also wrote the first book on management.

Gantt was another disciple whose contribution was in devising bar charts as an aid in project management. A Gantt chart visually displays starting and completion dates for individual activities as horizontal bars. The start of activity B is dependent on first completing activity A, and starting activity C is dependent on first completing activity B, and so forth, until the completion of the last activity marks the end of the project. By comparing actual progress with that shown on a Gantt chart, a manager knows where he or she stands in meeting a deadline and is in a position to take action to ensure that an activity is completed on time. In addition to these individuals, generations of efficiency experts sprang from Taylor, whose guiding principle was that busy machines manned by busy people pointed the way to profits.

TAYLOR AND QUALITY CONTROL

Prior to the Industrial Revolution, owners of workshops, as master craftsmen, inspected a product before it left the shop. Often a product bore the name of the master craftsman. There was a preexistent "top management commitment to quality" long before Deming espoused such a principle. Planning and doing were in the hands of the worker-craftsmen who were personally responsible for the quality of their work. The Industrial Revolution drastically changed this arrangement. Under the Taylor system, quality was implied in that a worker completing 100 units meant 100 units fit for use. Taylor separated planning from doing, with managers responsible for the former and workers for the latter. In time, not only were planning and doing separated, but so were production and quality. Production workers were responsible for making goods, and quality inspectors were responsible for the goods meeting prescribed standards.

QUALITY BY INSPECTION

Quality was inspected into the product, which meant that quality was achieved by removing defects. A quality control or assurance department was set up separate from production. In time, the quality control or assurance department became a dumping ground for those who would not, or could not, succeed on the production floor. Assignment to quality control carried the stigma of failure. Few, if any, individuals rising to top management began with a stint in the quality control department. This, perhaps, best exemplified the relative importance of quality in the general scheme of things.

Inspectors examined the output of the workers. If the item was good, it was passed on to the next station. If the item could be salvaged, rework was performed, and the item was reinserted into the production process. If it could not be reworked, the item was scrapped. This process of inspection to remove defects was carried out at every step of the production process and then repeated on the finished product. A finished product was not passed to the consumer unless it passed inspection or was reworked to make it fit for purchase. If, by chance, a defective product escaped notice and was discovered after purchase, the consumer was protected by a warranty.

Actually, the system worked in protecting the consumer from defective products, but it was very costly. The enormity of the labor input of rework can be appreciated by imagining an inspector giving a defective part to a worker. The worker walks back to a workbench examining the part for what may be wrong. After some tinkering, the worker discovers the fault. Correcting the fault requires either more tinkering or perhaps replacing a component. For the latter, the worker removes the defective component and obtains and installs a substitute component. Then the worker saunters back to the inspector, who, after inspecting the part, reinserts it into the production process. All the while, the clock has been ticking away, escalating the labor cost component for a part that, for the most part, is made by machine. Then the worker is given another part for another round of labor-intensive tinkering. Of course, the inspector may sense that rework is too expensive and decide to scrap the part. Now the cost is the total loss of labor and material up to that point.

When the product is completed, there is a final round of inspection leading to rework or scrapping of defective products before being passed to the consumer. As a final measure of protection against a defect, the consumer is granted a warranty. If anything goes wrong with the product within a prescribed time period, the consumer can return the product for free repair or replacement. Up to this point, the cost of the system of quality by inspection is the cost of the inspectors, rework, scrapping and the "goodwill" costs of a warranty program, which include administration, shipping, and repair or replacement of a defective product. All this can be quantified. While a warranty program is designed to ensure customer goodwill, there is also customer "ill will" associated with the circumstances surrounding the exercise of the warranty. A scenario can illustrate the ill will aspect of a warranty.

You're driving your new car over the Rocky Mountains in winter. You notice a loss of power, and as you casually glance out the rearview mirror, you see the transmission scattered all over the road. After coming to a stop, you get out of the car in below-zero weather. Luckily for you, there is only a five-mile walk to the nearest town. Luckily for you again, there is a dealer. You tell him your problem, and he is both sympathetic and responsive. He puts you up in a motel at no cost and retrieves your car. You discover that you are the only guest in a motel designed for the summer tourist season. The room's heater can barely keep the temperature above freezing. The television doesn't work. The only place to eat in town is a food-vending machine outside a gas station. You devour untold numbers of frozen chocolate cupcakes for the next four days waiting for the arrival of a new transmission. Finally, the dealer is at your door with a long list of accomplishments with a "No Charge" at the bottom and a great big smile on his face. Are you really happy as you look in the back seat of your car and see the frozen body of your pet cat? When it comes time to buy another car, will this episode affect your decision on what to buy? Will you tell your friends of your horrific experience? Will this impact their buying decisions?

During the 1980s there were a number of recalls on U.S. made cars. Owners of U.S.-made cars were honored with a letter inviting them to return their cars to the dealer to install a strap around the engine to keep it from falling out when the car goes over a bump at high speed. Another letter asked owners to return their cars for a minor alteration to ensure that the accelerator does not depress itself against the floorboard, driving the car and its occupants headlong into the nearest tree. Then another letter to have the ignition system checked out to ensure that the motor does not burst into flames when the car is started, incinerating the occupants. How many owners are eager to buy the same make of car after receiving such letters? How do these owners feel about the make of a neighbor's car that did not have to be recalled? How does the better quality performance of a neighbor's car affect their purchasing decision when it is time to buy their next car? The cost of ill will is the loss of future sales caused by poor performance or the circumstances surrounding the exercise of a warranty.

Arnold Feigenbaum quantified the direct and indirect costs of quality by inspection. Direct costs include the inspectors, rework and scrapping of parts, and the goodwill aspects of a warranty program. The indirect cost is the loss of future sales from the ill will generated by poor performance or the circumstances surrounding the exercise of the warranty. He estimated that the cost of quality by inspection was 30 to 50 percent of manufacturing costs. He talked about the "hidden" factory, a factory within a factory, where workers do nothing but correct defects made by others. It is ironic that the Taylor system, known foremost for efficiency, would contain a quality assurance system that added so much to manufacturing costs–a grossly inefficient way to ensure quality.

The problem of quality by inspection was the absence of a feedback system. It is hard to believe that a system designed to remove defects had no mechanism for removing the causes of defects. An inspector from the quality assurance department would throw away the output of a worker from the production department with no feedback to the worker that his or her output was being scrapped. Separating quality from production institutionalized the inefficiency of quality by inspection. But no company was at a competitive disadvantage as long as quality by inspection was universally practiced. The problem materialized when the Japanese, taking their cue from Deming, began to drive out not defects but the causes of defects.

Once a company accepts Deming's teachings to aim at making a product right the first time, the hidden factory begins to disappear, lowering production costs. Not only are higher-quality goods more attractive to customers, but their prices can be lowered by passing a portion of the savings of the disappearing hidden factory to the consumer. As an example, suppose that a company has a defect rate of 1 percent. That means that 99 percent of the output is fit for sale. On the surface, that sounds pretty good. Now consider what this means in terms of producing a million units. One percent defect rate translates into 10,000 defective products. Now 99 percent defect-free doesn't sound so good. Ten thousand defective products cannot be passed on to the consumer without creating a great deal of negative word-of-mouth advertising. The company has to hire inspectors who have to be paid plus pay the costs of rework and scrapping. For those defective products that escape the inspectors' scrutiny, a warranty program has to be set up to ensure customer satisfaction. But as noted, one cost of a warranty program designed to generate goodwill with customers is the associated ill will arising from the circumstances surrounding the exercise of a warranty. This leads to a loss of future sales along with poor performance.

Further suppose that this company is competing against a company like Motorola. Motorola, with its six-sigma quality program, has reduced the defect rate to three or four in a million. Suppose that the cost of inspection is $1 per unit. A company may pay $1 million to hunt out ten thousand defects in a million, but not three or four. What is the cost of rework and scrap if nothing is reworked or scrapped? What is the cost of a warranty program when the extremely few defects are discovered at the point of sale? How can a company with 99 percent defect-free products relying on quality by inspection hope to compete against Motorola and survive? Answer: it can't.

U.S. companies initially accused Japanese companies of price dumping when they began selling higher-quality products at lower prices. It was thought impossible to sell higher-quality goods, which must cost more to produce, at a lower price. The critical point missed was not that higher-quality goods cost more but that there were offsetting savings in reducing the size of the hidden factory. As the number of defects fell by eliminating the causes of defects, so did the factory that did nothing but correct defects. As the hidden factory disappeared, the resulting savings could be passed on in the form of lower prices. The Japanese were not price dumping but were passing the cost savings of getting rid of the hidden factory to consumers. U.S. manufacturers were stuck with the full cost of the hidden factory and could not match the price cuts. American consumers had the choice of buying superior Japanese products at a lower price or mediocre U.S. goods at a higher price; or was it a choice?

W. EDWARDS DEMING—FATHER OF QUALITY MANAGEMENT

Deming's background was in mathematical physics, or what is today called applied mathematics. He learned about applying statistics to enhance quality from Walter Shewhart of Bell Labs, one of the founders of the American Society for Quality Control (ASQC). Deming began to develop his quality management principles while observing experiments being conducted at the Hawthorne Works of Western Electric, the manufacturing arm of AT&T. Another individual observing these experiments was Joseph Juran, the second luminary in the quality heavens. Apparently the two never met. The Hawthorne experiments acknowledged for the first time that a worker was something more than an extension of a machine. Experiments were run on the number and length of rest periods, the number of working hours, different equipment and working conditions. Productivity was measured along with recording workers' attitudes toward their assignments and the nature of their supervision.

One experiment was on how lighting affected worker productivity. A small group of women were taken from the thousands assembling telephones in a warehouse-type setting and placed in a separate room. While the room was being prepared for running the experiment, their output was measured to establish a base for comparing output with different lighting intensities. Output was not constant, but rising. Then the experiment began by increasing the intensity of lighting, and worker productivity continued to rise. The room was ablaze in lights, with productivity still climbing. Then someone thought of dimming the lights, and productivity kept going up even when the room was barely lit. Clearly, something else was happening besides changing the lighting.

That something else was small group dynamics. The women were honored in being singled out from thousands. They interpreted this as a form of recognition, even though recognition had nothing to do with their selection. As a small group, they got to know one another on a personal basis and developed interpersonal relationships. When one woman saw another having difficulty, she would give helpful suggestions. If another learned of a better way of doing a task, she would spread the word and teach the others. Improved job satisfaction led to higher morale and increased productivity. Changing the lighting intensity had nothing to do with the increase in productivity. These observations formed the basis for Deming's and Juran's views on managing workers. The Hawthorne Works experiments eventually led to the idea of quality circles, now more commonly known as work teams or groups. A work team is given responsibility for performing a task and is held accountable for its performance rather than assigning individuals a mandatory quota to perform monotonous and tedious elements of a task.

During World War II, Deming worked for the government to improve the quality of munitions. Bombs did not explode on impact because firing mechanisms were defective. Torpedoes fired from submarines went full circle rather than straight, striking the submarines. Not only was the gyro defective, but, fortunately, so was the firing mechanism. The submarines limped back to port to have a torpedo extracted from their ballast tanks. Deming taught manufacturing personnel in war munitions companies to use statistical process control charts to improve quality. These charts were displayed on U.S. factory walls during World War II. As long as Deming stayed with statistical aids to enhance quality, he was welcomed. However, when Deming strayed from statistical aids to espouse his management principles to enhance quality, both management and labor pulled the welcome mat. Taylor-trained managers could not psychologically accept the principle of worker participation in running a factory. Union leaders wanted to maintain the traditional adversarial relationship between workers and management to give weight to the threat of a strike during labor negotiations.

Following World War II, U.S. managers actually made a correct decision when they threw away the statistical process control charts. The only nation capable of producing consumer goods was the United States, as Europe and Japan lay in ruins. It didn't matter what the quality was for consumer products when there were no other companies making consumer products. U.S. manufacturers switched to mass-volume production, which was, at that time, the right thing to do. Who cared if a consumer product was of mediocre quality when no others were available? Any washing machine was better than no washing machine. Unfortunately for U.S. manufacturers, circumstances changed. The market was no longer infinite after Japan and Europe rebuilt their industries. The Japanese, in particular, learned that they could gain market share by producing better-quality consumer products. Meanwhile, U.S. manufacturers stayed with the tried-and-true formula for success: mass-volume production of mediocre goods. Some of the firms that tossed Deming out of their factories in the 1940s begged for his return in the 1970s and 1980s, when they began to realize that times had indeed changed.

JAPAN AS A VULNERABLE COUNTRY

Japan and vulnerability are synonymous. It has no sources of raw materials and energy, grows half its food, and sits on a geologically active zone where earthquakes, volcanoes, and tidal waves are relatively common. Japan has half the population of the United States stuffed in a total area slightly larger than California. While placing half of the population of the United States into California may sound congested, much of Japan turns out to be too mountainous for settlement. Its arable and livable land is about the size of Connecticut. Now this is real congestion, the reason why Japanese land values are so high.

During the 1930s Japan advocated the Southeast Asia Co-Prosperity Sphere to solve the problem of not having sufficient raw materials, energy, and food. Southeast Asian nations were to export raw materials, energy (oil), and food to Japan in return for manufactured goods. To the Japanese, the benefits were too good to be left to chance, and they attempted to set up the Southeast Asia Co-Prosperity Sphere through military aggression. After the Japanese lost the war, they still had the same problem of starving to death in a cold, dark room.

Military conquest was no longer an option. At this time, General MacArthur, as virtual dictator during the U.S. occupation, wanted to communicate to the Japanese people directly, but Japanese radios were unreliable. One can reasonably ask how a nation that conquered much of Asia, obviously capable of building battleships, tanks, and aircraft, could not build radios, actually vacuum tubes, that worked. As already discussed, the Soviet Union, as a great military power, could not satisfy consumer demand for bathtubs or anything else. Several U.S. aerospace and military equipment companies have had notable failures in attempting to penetrate the consumer product market.

General MacArthur brought in quality experts to teach the Japanese how to make better-quality radios. But the problem was far deeper than defective vacuum tubes. "Made in Japan" was just another way of saying that something was a piece of junk. The principal Japanese export item in the 1930s was toys with a well-deserved reputation for shoddiness. After World War II, Japan's survival depended on making manufactured goods of sufficient quality that they could be sold in the world markets to generate the funds necessary for the purchase of raw materials, energy, and food. This responsibility ultimately fell on the Japanese Union of Scientists and Engineers, which brought in U.S. quality experts to help Japan reform its manufacturing processes. Deming and Juran were among those invited. Deming's assignment was to teach Japanese engineers about statistical tools to improve quality. Juran's assignment was to teach Japanese managers on how to improve quality. Deming strayed from the narrow confines of statistical control and lectured about his chain reaction to Japanese engineers. Ichiro Ishikawa, chairman of the Japanese Union of Scientists and Engineers and father of Kaoru Ishikawa, professor of engineering and Japanese quality guru, recognized that Deming was talking to the wrong audience. He ought to be talking to top executives and managers, not scientists and engineers. Ichiro Ishikawa arranged for Deming to deliver his talk to the right audience.

DEMING'S CHAIN REACTION

Deming's chain reaction starts with making a better quality product.

Isn't that an illuminating objective, an absolute revelation? The Deming chain reaction is so grounded in good common sense that one wonders why it has to be taught. Yet, apparently, it does.

A better-quality product will initially cost more. It is here that the Deming chain reaction dies in many U.S. companies. For bottom-line profit maximizers, increasing costs reduces profits and the Deming chain reaction is dead at the point of conception, never mind birth. One of my students was an assistant to the production manager at a plumbing fixture manufacturer. He invited me to the factory and at the first opportunity, showed me a pile of recycled zinc costing about 11¢ per pound. It was stained blue to separate it from virgin zinc costing about 40¢ per pound. How much recycled zinc was used in the manufacturing process? For a profit-maximizing company, the answer was as much as possible. The company would have preferred using only recycled zinc, but then the faucets and other products wouldn't work. Therefore, they used as much as possible to supposedly maximize profits by minimizing costs. The unavoidable side effect of profit maximization was a product of mediocre quality. The student knew that sales were slipping and that the company had to resort to price discounting to keep the slide in sales volume from becoming a free fall. As sales volume and price fell, so did revenue and profit. The company was in a downward spiral not unlike what happens when a toilet is flushed. The student could plot declining profits against time on a graph and get a fix on when the company would be flushed out of existence. He went to the purchasing manager, who worked in the finance department, for permission to use more virgin zinc to enhance quality.

One can hear the purchasing manager's response, "Aren't we having enough problems? Every quarter, sales volume is going down in spite of our giving out greater and greater price discounts. Our revenue is falling like a rock. Our profit is rapidly slipping from black to red, and you want to quadruple material costs? Do you have any idea what this is going to do to our bottom line? Have you gone mad!?"

"Perhaps, improving the quality would improve sales."

"Oh? By how much?"

"How do I know how much sales would improve for something we haven't done?"

"Then you don't know?"

"No."

"Well, then I'll tell you how much: none."

The student did not want to see his firm fail, yet it was failing. He made his attempt to change the direction of the *Titanic* away from the looming iceberg and was thrown out of the purchasing manager's office for his effort. He asked me what he should do. I sensed his helplessness. There was no commitment from top management to make a quality product, and he was only an assistant too low on the corporate totem pole to count for much. He was neither in a position to initiate change nor was top management receptive to change. I thought about suggesting that he get his résumé up to date and begin looking for another job. I might have thought about something else, but he received a call, and I didn't have to answer the question.

Nevertheless, he was correct. A better-quality product would increase sales. The purchasing manager was also correct. On day one, a better-quality product would cost more. But a better-quality product also reduces the cost of the hidden factory by having less rework, scrap, and warranty expenses. If the benefits of higher quality in terms of getting rid of the hidden factory and improving sales equal the cost of higher quality, then, as described in Philip Crosby's book, *Quality Is Free*. But the Japanese learned that the benefits of higher quality exceed its costs; therefore, quality is not free but profitable.

Continuing with the Deming chain reaction, a better-quality product will result in more satisfied customers, more repeat business, and greater market share.

More satisfied customers will increase sales through positive word-of-mouth advertising. How much marketing has to be invested in a satisfied customer who intends to buy the same product? I have listened to a Honda car owner state that he will never own another make of car for the rest of his life. When I heard this proclamation of eternal faith in Honda, I couldn't help but think of Danny's plight in not being given an opportunity to sell a Honda. Danny will forever be an order-taker.

This leads to higher profits and ...

No one is against making profits, not Deming, not the Japanese. Profits are absolutely essential for survival. A company that does not make enough revenue to pay its bills eventually goes out of business. In Deming's chain reaction, profits are a consequence of capturing a greater market share by improving the quality of the product. Thus a manager can either pursue maximizing the bottom line or pursue the right business strategy. The financial results of successfully pursuing the right business strategy are profits. Thus profits are of secondary consideration–the primary consideration is identifying the right business strategy and setting up an organization and operation to put it into effect. The two approaches to generating profits are fundamentally different.

... greater job security.

Traditional American managers are not concerned with job security. Labor is a cost to be minimized—an unneeded worker is simply laid off. The Japanese are much more concerned about providing security for their workers. Their attitude is that labor is an asset to be maximized, another major difference in values between the two cultures. Japanese managers were attracted to the job security aspect of the Deming chain reaction because this was what they wanted to provide to their workers; U.S. managers were not

If a company is experiencing an ever-increasing market share, it can promise its workers lifelong job security because an increasing market share means an expanding workforce. A company not only can promise workers lifelong security but may have to depend on them to recruit their friends and relatives. Promising lifelong job security does not cost a penny if the company needs workers for the rest of their lives. But to the Japanese, lifelong job security means lifelong job security. If workers are no longer needed to perform some task, they are retrained and reassigned to the greatest possible extent. In the poor economic environment of the 1990s, smaller Japanese firms did not have the opportunity to retrain and reassign workers. These companies were forced to lay off workers, breaking their social contract. The Japanese take job security very seriously—there were a few instances of factory owners and managers taking their lives after laying off their workers. The Deming chain reaction is repeated by making an even better quality product. It is part of the concept of never-ending improvement. Deming's chain reaction has an aura of being "good for God and country" as a company strives to improve its product to better satisfy consumer expectations. In serving the market with better-quality products, the company creates employment opportunities for more and more workers, raising the living standards of a nation.

TOYODA'S FATEFUL DECISION

Among those accepting Ishikawa's invitation to listen to Deming's chain reaction was Kiichiro Toyoda, president of Toyota Motors. He faced a particularly difficult situation: few would buy his cars. In the 1930s, when Ford and GM had factories in Japan, the order of preference for Japanese car buyers was first U.S. imports because of their higher quality, then cars made in U.S. "transplant" factories in Japan, and in last place, cars made by Japanese companies. The irony of the situation is that in the 1970s, Americans wanted first Japanese imports because of their higher quality, then cars made in Japanese transplant factories in the U.S., and in last place, cars made by American companies.

The idea that the Japanese have always dominated the world's automobile market is dead-wrong. Toyoda, realizing that the Japanese would not buy his cars, decided to test the export market and sent a shipment of Toyotas to California. This was a historical shipment in automotive folklore. Turning the door handle had three possible outcomes: the door opened, the door did not open, the handle came off the door. Assuming that the door opened and the driver got in the car, grabbing the inside handle to shut the door had three possible outcomes: the door shut, the door did not shut, the handle came off the door. Settling back in the seat had only two outcomes: the spot welds holding the seat did or did not fail. If they did, the driver was left staring at the car roof. Never mind the excitement of turning the ignition key—the shipment was scrapped.

Not being able to sell domestically or overseas, Toyoda was at the brink of bankruptcy. Crisis breeds change. In desperation, Toyoda, after listening to the Deming chain reaction, made a fateful decision for Japanese and American manufacturers: drop Taylor, adopt Deming. Taiicho Ohno, production manager of Toyota, began a slow and deliberate 20-year conversion of Toyota from Taylor to Deming. As soon as the rest of Japan saw the initial benefits accruing from adopting Deming's principles, they, too, joined Toyoda in dropping Taylor and adopting Deming. Meanwhile, U.S. automobile manufacturers stuck doggedly with Taylor even after Toyota took over the West Coast market in the early 1970s. As mentioned, GM management did not respond to change until the late 1980s, when they were losing billions. If top executives are supposed to sense business trends and position their firms to take advantage of, or deal with, these trends, what performance grade would one assign to GM management and the management of many other U.S. companies? While GM transformed itself from making billions to losing billions in the late 1980s, Toyota went from near-bankruptcy to one of the world's richest companies, the "Bank of Toyota." GM attempted to maximize profits by concentrating on the bottom line and failed, whereas Toyota attempted to maximize profits by capturing market share with quality products and succeeded.

ECONOMIC DECLINE OF THE UNITED STATES

Up to some years ago when the minimum wage was increased, there was a 10-year hiatus during which the minimum wage remained unchanged. There were tens of millions of Americans whose pay was at or near the legal minimum wage. They experienced a decline in living standards as the cost of living escalated by over 50 percent. Middle-class families maintained their living standards largely by wives' joining the workforce. Untold numbers of workers lost their $20 per hour manufacturing jobs and moved into the so-called service industry as security guards or hamburger flippers at a fraction of what they were previously making. Clean service jobs were touted as a worthy substitute for dirty manufacturing jobs. Some economists believed that the service industry was the wave of the future and that losing the nation's manufacturing base was a visible sign of progress.

True, there are many high-paying service jobs in information technology, computers, communications, marketing, finance, and so forth. But what about those whose natural proclivities are to be machine operators rather than computer programmers, financial deal makers, and advertising account executives? Untold numbers of workers are employed by Burger-Barf fast-food franchises on a part-time basis near the minimum wage with no medical and retirement benefits. Labor laws stipulate that a part-time worker employed for a certain length of time automatically becomes a full-time worker entitled to such benefits. When this is about to happen, Burger-Barf restaurants lay off their workers. The workers walk across the street and are hired by another fast-food restaurant to maintain their benefitless part-time status. For many, the much heralded service industry has failed to live up to its expectations. Even in Japan, service jobs are paid much less than manufacturing jobs.

In the early 1970s U.S. workers were the highest paid workers in the world. The following table is the cost of labor, including benefits, in the early 1990s.

	$/Hour
Germany	$27
Norway	25
France	22
Great Britain	20
Italy	19
Japan	15
United States	15
Korea	10

U.S. labor costs have fallen and Japanese labor costs have risen to the same level. However, U.S. workers still have a higher standard of living because food and living quarters are much more costly in Japan. The higher pay in Germany has to take into consideration higher taxes. Nevertheless, from the point of view of what labor costs a company, U.S. labor costs are far from being the highest in the world. In fact, the United States has become a relatively low labor-cost nation with a stable and educated workforce. The decision for a German car manufacturer to build an assembly plant in the South to serve the U.S. market makes a whole lot of good economic sense once one realizes the relative wage scales between German and American workers.

KONOSUKE MATSUSHITA'S DECLARATION OF WAR

When Japan was at its peak as a threat in unseating the United States, Konosuke Matsushita, founder of Matsushita Electric, the world's largest consumer electronics firm (Panasonic and other brands), delivered the following speech.[1] It is interesting to judge this speech with the passage of time.

We are going to win and the industrial west is going to lose out: there's nothing much you can do about it, because the reasons for your failure are within yourselves.

Khrushchev delivered the same speech before the United Nations long before Matsushita, pounding his shoe on the table. To Khrushchev, communism would inevitably assign capitalism to the dustbin of history. To Matsushita, Japanese industrial invincibility would inevitably consign us to the dustbin of economic history. Matsushita tells us why our failure is inevitable.

Your firms are built on the Taylor model; even worse, so are your heads. With your bosses doing the thinking while the workers wield the screwdrivers, you're convinced deep down that this is the right way to run a business.
For you, the essence of management is getting the ideas out of the heads of the bosses into the hands of labor.

Matsushita believed that we were incapable of abandoning the system of "managers think, workers do." Unfortunately for Matsushita, globally oriented U.S. firms have abandoned Taylor in favor of Deming. We do build quality goods. Worse yet for Matsushita, low labor-cost Asian nations have learned Japanese production techniques and now compete against high labor-cost Japanese producers. Many of these factories were built with Japanese funds. The Japanese taught their production techniques to the Asians to ensure the success of their investments. The Japanese have hoisted themselves on their own petard much as U.S. had done a few decades before in building factories overseas only to create new competitors in their home market.

We are beyond the Taylor model; business, we know, is now so complex and difficult, the survival of firms so hazardous in an environment increasingly unpredictable, competitive and fraught with danger, that their continued existence depends on the day-to-day mobilization of every ounce of intelligence.

This is an interesting insight into the mind of the founder of the world's most successful company in consumer electronic products. Matsushita realizes that being on top is not permanent, but a laurel of victory that can be easily lost. Eternal vigilance is a necessity. Top executives of U.S. corporations may ensconce themselves in plush offices attired in the accoutrements of power and prestige, but Matsushita's office is spartan and located in a factory. Matsushita visits the company's factories regularly, giving talks to managers and workers. He urges them to strive to higher levels of performance in order for the company to maintain its preeminent position. Only by maintaining its position can the company guarantee employment to the workers and offer advancement opportunities to management. Matsushita expects everyone to contribute intellectually to improving the product or the process for making the product. So important is this intellectual contribution that he repeats it:

> For us, the core of management is precisely the art of mobilizing and pulling together the intellectual resources of all employees in the service of the firm. Only by drawing on the combined brainpower of all its employees can a firm face up to the turbulence and constraints of today's environment.

And again:

> This is why our large companies give their employees three to four times more training than yours, this is why they foster within the firm such intensive exchange and communication. This is why they seek constantly everybody's suggestions and why they demand from the educational system increasing numbers of graduates as well as bright and well-educated generalists, because these people are the lifeblood of industry.

The Japanese view labor as an asset to be maximized. Since they promise lifelong job security, training that upgrades the proficiency of the workers ultimately benefits the company. We tend to think of training as a cost to be cut when profits decline. Moreover, we may deny training to an individual in the belief that training would enable the individual to leave the firm for a higher-paying job.

> Your socially-minded bosses, often full of good intentions, believe their duty is to protect the people in their firms. We, on the other hand, are realists and consider it our duty to get our people to defend their firms which will pay them back a hundredfold for their dedication. By doing this we end up being more social than you.

Here, Matsushita clearly does not understand the situation. We do not have socially minded bosses, although there were companies who made an honest attempt to provide a secure source of employment for their workers. IBM, AT&T and banks were once "socially minded" in the sense of protecting their employees, but no more. To Matsushita, managers and workers are to "defend their firm" by contributing to the process of making a better product. If they succeed, the corporation can maintain its competitive edge and be in a position to repay them a hundredfold by providing lifelong employment. Lifelong employment is earned by the workers own efforts; it is not a gift from the corporation.

The age of consumer electronics was started by RCA (Radio Corporation of America). At the end of World War II, RCA was the world's largest consumer electronics firm and Panasonic a dream in Matsushita's mind. Top U.S. executives are paid roughly 10 times more in terms of seven-figure incomes than their six-figure Japanese counterparts. Assuming that top RCA executives were paid 10 times more than Matsushita, what, then, have the shareholders, workers, and the nation gained by a group of highly paid executives who have effectively overseen the liquidation of the world's largest consumer electronics company? Some have blamed the U.S. government policies for the decline in our economic prowess. In my opinion, the decline of RCA and a host of other companies no longer in business or a shadow of their former selves can be rightfully blamed on executives and managers unwilling or unable to deal with changing business conditions.

ENDNOTE

1.   Jim Warren, "We Have Found the Enemy, It Is Us!," *43rd Annual Quality Congress Proceedings* (1987).

Chapter 3

A Touch of History

The way we do things and the organization of our institutions are not from time immemorial; rather, they stem from the writings or actions of individuals. Individuals such as Adam Smith, Eli Whitney, Isaac Singer, and Henry Ford played important roles in developing the process by which labor, material, and capital are transformed into goods and services.

ADAM SMITH

Adam Smith, the world's first economist, laid the foundation for the free enterprise system in *An Inquiry into the Nature and Causes of the Wealth of Nations*, published in 1776, an intriguing coincidence with the publication of the Declaration of Independence. Two centuries later in the 1980s, three economic systems coexisted: those of Karl Marx and Adam Smith and socialism, the latter being a mix of the former two. In the 1990s Karl Marx was consigned to the dustbin of history, and many socialized and previously nationalized companies in Europe and South America were returned to the private domain through privatization. While socialism is still a powerful force in Europe and elsewhere, Adam Smith provides the principal working framework, or paradigm, for transforming capital and labor into goods and services.

Adam Smith differentiated between creating wealth and making money. One can get rich selling drugs or stealing, but that is not creating wealth. Forming a company to produce goods and services epitomizes wealth creation in the modern world. Goods and services provide consumers with something to purchase. Providing goods and services generates jobs that add to the number of consumers. The mark of wealth creation is a rising standard of living.

Adam Smith was critical of government's ability to manage economies and their involvement in the production of goods and services. He maintained that businesspersons with their feet firmly held to the fire of a profit-and-loss statement would be far more responsive to the market than a government agency. Profits are absolutely necessary to ensure the survival of a firm and are contingent on a company's making goods and providing services that consumers are willing to buy. Adam Smith also differentiated between productive and unproductive labor. He used as an example a customs inspector who, though very busy, was not productive in the sense of providing useful goods or services. It does not take a great deal of imagination to think of a busy person who feels that he or she is productive; but in actuality, not only is nonproductive but may also be obstructing others from being productive.

ATTACK ON GUILDS

Adam Smith attacked the guild system whereby an individual had to be the son of a guild member to become, say, a glassblower in Venice. The closed membership of the guild permitted the guild to exercise total control over the nature of the output, prices charged, wages paid, and advancement of a member from apprentice to journeyman to master craftsman.

Suppose that a guild-member glassblower has been instructed to blow red vases, and he senses that consumers want blue plates. Under the guild system, the glassblower would not think in terms of blowing blue plates after work in his backyard, of going into business with, or hiring, other glassblowers to blow blue plates. He would not think of opening a store to market blue plates or selling financial interests in a new company to build a glassblowing facility. The social milieu of the guild system did not permit independent or entrepreneurial activity.

Adam Smith did not attack the guilds directly but attacked their closed membership. Smith realized that opening up the membership to anyone who wanted to be a glassblower would strip the guild of its primary means of control. Sooner or later, a non-guild member glassblower would begin blowing blue plates in response to market demand. Guild members would be forced to either respond to market demand for blue plates or drown in an inventory of red vases.

The primary legacy of Adam Smith in his attack on the guild system is the free enterprise system. The free enterprise system gives individuals the freedom to form a new company and make key decisions without obtaining permission from a government or a guild. These decisions include the nature and characteristics of a product, choice of manufacturing technology, location of production facilities, price of the product and volume of production, marketing, distribution and service, and financial arrangements. Success depends solely on consumers' buying a company's products or services. A consumer's purchase grants a company the right to exist in business for another increment of time. Without consumer purchases, a company no longer has a grant to exist–the hallmark of the free market.

The commercial life of a nation is to operate with a minimum of interference from government authorities–the hallmark of *laissez-faire* economics. Adam Smith was not against the government playing a vital role in the lives of its citizens in what he considered its proper sphere of activity such as education, fire and police protection, national defense, and building of roads and ports, but not the production of goods and services. Here, businesspersons responsible for a profit-and-loss statement would be far more responsive to consumer needs than government bureaucrats. In the two centuries since Adam Smith, governments have become involved with the conduct of business in ways not anticipated by Adam Smith. Laws have been passed concerning child labor, minimum wage, safety and health of workers, and protecting the environment. These laws were in response to blatant abuses. For instance, British textile mills employed children at an extraordinarily young age to cart work about the factory for scant wages. Other industries imposed working conditions that were hazardous to the safety and health of workers. Industrial waste was disposed in a manner dangerous to the community and the environment. Something had to be done to curtail these abuses, and that something was government intrusion in the conduct of business. Nevertheless, government intrusion rarely involves the key decisions of running a business, rather, the manner in which businesses are run.

While Adam Smith recognized the inherent productivity of the free enterprise system's responding to market demand where profit and loss determined winners and losers, he was not particularly enamored with businesspersons.

People of the same trade seldom meet together, even for merriment and diversion, but the conversation ends in a conspiracy against the public, or in some contrivance to raise prices.

This thought, embodied in the Sherman Anti-Trust Act, makes it illegal for competitors to join together to fix prices, control output, or do anything that can be considered a restraint of trade.

The guild system is very much alive today. A young lawyer is initially an apprentice assisting others. After a while, he or she is assigned simple cases virtually impossible to lose. Cases become increasingly complex as the young lawyer gains experience. Based on performance, he or she may become a junior partner and eventually a senior partner with the responsibility for guiding the firm in addition to handling the most difficult cases. This is the essence of the guild system. The difference is that a lawyer need not be the son or a daughter of a lawyer to become a lawyer.

ATTACK ON MERCANTILISM

Under mercantilism, a word coined by Adam Smith, the winner in international trade was the nation with the largest horde of gold. Gold, the international medium of exchange, accumulates when there is a positive balance of trade. In order for exports to exceed imports, the government intervenes in commerce to encourage domestic industry, regulate production, and control trade. Domestic industry is protected from competition when a king or queen or a government awards a legal monopoly to a noble family or company accompanied by the erection of barriers of trade against imports of competing products in the form of quotas and tariffs. Thus, a company is protected from both domestic and international competition, assuring its success. In return, a company is expected to repay the favor by exporting goods, contributing to a positive balance of trade, which allows a king or queen or nation to accumulate gold. The winner in international trade is whoever has the largest horde of gold.

The importance of gold was particularly evident in Spain's conquest of the New World. Britain was less fortunate in that most of its colonies had no gold. But mercantilism was present in Britain's insistence that manufacturing be done in Britain for export to the colonies in exchange for raw materials. Britain correctly identified that a positive trade balance can be achieved in value-added manufacturing, not in producing raw materials. Under mercantilism, the British colonies were to be the market for British-made goods. Mercantilism was enforced by the presence of the British army to monitor manufacturing activities and by requiring that exports and imports be carried on British flag vessels to monitor trade.

The paradigm of mercantilism was to protect industry from domestic competition by awarding a monopoly and from international competition by erecting barriers to trade. Then the government encouraged domestic firms to export in order for the government to be able to accumulate gold. Like so many paradigms, this one, too, had an inherent flaw. As enticing as it might sound to a king or queen or government, it could not succeed. In fact, it guaranteed failure because one nation's exports were another nation's imports. World trade under mercantilism suffered from the universal erection of trade barriers against imports.

Adam Smith advocated scuttling mercantilism in favor of free trade based on the exchange of goods, not the accumulation of gold. Whereas mercantilism erected barriers to trade, Adam Smith's free trade tore them down. In Adam Smith's mind, the wealth of nations would increase if each nation specialized in what it did best and trade the rest. For whatever reason, Venice is excellent in making glass products and Britain in making steel goods. Hence, it is a suboptimal allocation of scarce resources for Venice to make steel goods and Britain to make glass products. Instead, Venice should export glass products to Britain in exchange for steel goods to satisfy domestic needs, not gold to satisfy a ruler's greed.

This idea of specialization was to be applied to communities. If one community was good at making wheelbarrows, and another at making baskets, then each community should specialize in what it did best and exchange those goods for everything else. Moreover, within communities, labor should specialize. If an individual, for whatever reason, is good in making wheelbarrow handles, then that individual should specialize in making wheelbarrow handles. Since the number of workers and working hours is finite, if every individual does what he or she does best, then the wealth of nations should increase.

Adam Smith encouraged the use of money as a medium of exchange rather than barter. Barter is an inefficient way to exchange goods; for instance, how many baskets is one wheelbarrow worth? Specialization can be better achieved if goods and services were sold for money. Money received in providing goods and services can then be spent buying goods and services. Interestingly, the practice of barter is growing. Of the nearly 200 nations in the world, only about three dozen have globally acceptable or hard currencies such as the U.S. dollar, British pound, Japanese yen. Most nations have soft currencies that cannot be readily converted into hard currencies. To avoid accumulating soft currencies, companies exporting products or investing in soft currency nations may enter into bartering arrangements where products sold in soft currency nations are exchanged for something that can then be sold in a hard currency nation. For example, soft drink exports to Russia are not paid in rubles but bartered for vodka and tankers, which when sold for hard currency, completes the business transaction.

The concept of free trade is embodied in the General Agreement on Tariffs and Trade (GATT), now incorporated in the World Trade Organization. GATT has been very successful in dismantling barriers to trade since World War II throughout the world with the exception of, you guessed it, Japan. With certain exceptions such as commercial aircraft, Japan has historically made it difficult for businesses to export manufactured goods into Japan. For instance, U.S. ski equipment is in demand in Japan but cannot be imported because U.S. ski manufacturers cannot demonstrate that their equipment meets the specifications of the snow that falls on Mt. Fuji. How would the Japanese react if their automobiles are prohibited entry into the United States on the basis that their headlights do not meet the specifications of the night that falls on the Western Hemisphere?

Japan does not permit importing American-made wooden baseball bats because of the fear of termites but does permit importing logs. The real reason why Japan imports logs and not baseball bats is not the fear of termites but to ensure that value-added manufacturing of converting logs to baseball bats and other lumber products is done in Japan. This is the same mercantilism practiced by colonial powers centuries ago to ensure that value-added manufacturing was reserved for the mother nation.

Toys-R-Us spent years trying to open up a store in Japan. It is ironic that the first company to penetrate the barriers to trade erected by Japan to protect its domestic market was a toy store, toys being the chief Japanese export item before World War II. To make things more difficult for those trying to penetrate the Japanese market, a Japanese retail outlet carries only the brand associated with its respective *keiretsu*, one of the several galaxy of corporate entities in which all Japanese business activities are concentrated. To do competitive price shopping in Japan, a consumer must visit several retail outlets representing each *keiretsu*, whereas in the United States and elsewhere, a single retail outlet carries a variety of domestic and overseas brands. Thus the nature of the Japanese retail and distribution system makes it difficult, if not impossible, to obtain shelf space.

Mercantilism is alive and well in Japan. It was embodied in the Southeast Asian Co-Prosperity Sphere of the 1930s, where Asian nations were to supply Japan with raw materials in return for manufactured goods. This same relationship continues to exist between Japan and the rest of the world. In the 1980s Japan was considered the greatest mercantilist nation on earth except that it did not accumulate gold, but foreign reserves. In the 1990s this observation is less true. Japan is now a high labor-cost nation. There are intense economic pressures within Japan to outsource some of the manufacturing of components to low labor-cost Asian nations in order for Japanese products to remain price competitive in the world market. Many of the new plants in Asia were built by the Japanese to supply parts and components to Japanese factories. Nevertheless, Japan still cannot be considered an open market for finished goods.

PRICE, THE INVISIBLE HAND

Price is the invisible hand guiding the decisions of factory owners and managers on whether to produce more (rising prices) or less (falling prices). Price, in turn, reflects the relationship between the supply of, and demand for, goods. If demand exceeds supply, prices increase while inventories decline, and businesspersons react by increasing production. If a factory is at capacity, rising prices are the signal to add capacity by building another factory. If the supply of goods exceeds demand, prices fall while inventories climb, and businesspersons react by cutting production. The invisible hand controls production without any intrusion by governments or guilds; it is elegant in its simplicity, yet it is responsible for the business cycle.

The Business Cycle

Adam Smith did not live through a business cycle. Had done so, he might have had some second thoughts. The business cycle contains the Achilles' heel of Adam Smith's economic system. A businessperson should not treat the business cycle as a purely economic phenomenon but should seek to understand the business cycle in order not to become its victim. Moreover, assessing where an industry is in the business cycle is necessary for forecasting sales, the first step in production planning.

The business cycle has to be described using the price of something. For reasons to be mentioned later, the business cycle is described in terms of the price of pigs or pork. A cycle has to start somewhere, and the place to start is low pork prices and high inventories. A pig farmer has a farm with breeding stock. Suppose that the cost in feed to raise a piglet to a 250-pound pig ready for slaughter is $150. The market price for pigs is $50. How many pigs does a pig farmer send to market? This should not be a difficult question.

To ensure that none are going to market, the pig farmer separates the boy and girl pigs by building a wall down the center of the pigpen. No pigs are going to market, and the price of pork is cheap. When do prices begin to rise? Only when the excess inventories have been liquidated, in this case, eaten up.

At some point, the slaughterhouse boys desire to buy some pigs to replenish falling inventories and offer $50, the market price. There are no takers. They offer $60, no takers; then $70, no takers; $80, still no takers, and so forth until the price is up to, say, $120. There are still no takers, but each pig farmer is intently watching rising prices and falling inventories. They begin to draw trend lines, at least mentally, of when they can clear their costs of $150 per pig. They are all looking at the same database and thinking the same thoughts. The price is now up to $130, and some start tearing down the wall running through the center of the pigpen. At $140, walls are being torn down in earnest. At $150, the walls are gone, and the boars are in pig-heaven. At $160, the boars are recuperating from making all the sows pregnant.

Each pig farmer thinks that he is an independent businessperson making an independent business decision. However, all businesspersons are making the same business decision at the same time because they are all looking at the same database of price and inventory. If they are all making the same decision at the same time, are they making independent decisions? If their decisions are not independent, are they independent businesspersons?

Eighteen months separate pig honeymoons from fully grown pigs ready for slaughter. This hiatus provides ample opportunity for prices to soar. A pig farmer can't wait for the alarm to go off at four in the morning. Slopping the hogs is a lot of fun because the pig population may have risen during the night, they certainly weigh more, and the price of pork has risen. Pig farmers do a mental calculation of their net worth as they slop the hogs. They are richer and the feeling of being richer pervades the pig-farming community. The business cycle moves into the euphoria or greed stage.

A pig farmer looks at this truck and tractor. Both are in need of replacement. He needs new farm implements along with expanding and repairing the barn so he can raise even more pigs. He thinks of his wife who has remained faithfully by his side through thick and thin. She certainly deserves a new cotton dress. Where does he get the money, since the pigs are not ready to be slaughtered? The bankers—the bankers are eager to make loans when the collateral exceeds the amount of the loan and, to make it even better, is gaining value daily. They visit the farmer, see the collateral, hear the collateral, smell the collateral. The loan application is approved on the spot. Tens of thousands of pig farmers spend the loan proceeds on new trucks, new tractors, new farm implements, and new barns. The euphoria of the business cycle spreads to other industry sectors such as truck, tractor, and farm implement manufacturers, barn builders, and, of course, cotton dress manufacturers as orders pour in from the pig-farming community.

Finally, those who were a little early in tearing down the wall through the middle of the pigpen deliver the first welcomed shipments of pigs to the slaughterhouses desperate to replenish their exhausted inventory. As more pigs show up at the slaughterhouses, price continues to escalate, but not as fast. The number of pigs arriving at the slaughterhouses keeps on expanding until inventory is restored to a desired level. A stable price signals equilibrium between supply and demand, but equilibrium does not last long. As even greater numbers of pigs arrive at the slaughterhouses, supply gets ahead of demand, plain for all to see as the price of pork begins to decline.

Now the euphoria of the business cycle begins to wane, along with the fun of getting up at four in the morning. The farmer is now becoming poorer rather than richer when he slops the hogs. True, there may be more pigs, and true, they certainly weigh more, but prices have fallen since the day before. The pig farmer is poorer, not richer. As an independent businessperson, he looks at the downward trend in the price of pork and the upward trend in pork inventories and arrives at an independent decision. Later in the morning, he fills his brand-new truck to the brim with pigs and rushes down to the slaughterhouse before prices fall further. Too bad when he arrives that he finds himself in a three-mile queue with other pig farmers, who in scrutinizing the same database of price and inventory, have arrived at the same independent decision. Fear supplants greed, the market is flooded with pigs, prices plummet, and inventories go out of sight, taking us back to the starting point of the business cycle.

The pig cycle has been studied for 150 years by the U.S. government. During the nineteenth and early twentieth centuries, farming was the nation's largest business, and advances in technology had caused agricultural output to exceed what the city folk could eat. The farmers, representing a large portion of the electorate, pressured their representatives in Congress to do something about wild swings in agricultural prices. Just as it is possible to study the structural breaking up of the *Titanic* as an intellectual exercise, ignoring the plight of those stuck on board, so, too, can one study the business cycle, ignoring the human plight when price no longer covers costs. Pig farmers caught in the downward swing of a business cycle lose their capacity to earn a living and if up to their ears in debt, possibly losing their farms. Government attempts to assuage the worst of the business cycle for farmers have failed repeatedly. Price supports only encourage further excess production. The reason for the failure of government farm programs is that they do not attack the true cause of the business cycle: excessive additions to productive capacity. Price tells farmers to breed more pigs, but does not tell them how many pigs to breed. Invariably, they breed too many pigs. The mistake is not known until it is too late; too many pigs are in the pipeline to the slaughterhouses. Only if the government bureaucrats were to take control over when and how many pigs to breed would the business cycle be subdued. This is called socialism. Under socialism, there is no such thing as an independent businessperson. The most critical decision made by pig farmers as independent businesspersons is when and how many pigs to breed. If this is taken away, who's going to get up at four in the morning to slop the hogs?

There are two principal observations concerning the business cycle that every manufacturer should realize. One, a depressed price cannot rise until excess inventories are liquidated. Two, price tells manufacturers when to build new factories, but does not tell them how many factories to build. Invariably, they build too many factories.

Inventory liquidation must take place before price can rise. Liquidation can take the form of selling inventory at a discount or placing the inventory on a ship, going out to sea, and throwing it overboard. It doesn't matter as long as the inventory is liquidated. If excess inventory is in the form of too many new office buildings, and if it takes 10 years to fill these buildings with occupants, then price in the form of office rentals will not increase for 10 years.

Price, the invisible hand, is elegant in its simplicity but also flawed. As price increases, manufacturers produce more. That is what they are supposed to do in Adam Smith's world. Price continuing to rise with factories at full capacity is the signal that there is insufficient productive capacity. Manufacturers, each looking at the same database of price and inventory, make the same independent decision to build another factory. According to Adam Smith, that is what they are supposed to do. But they get so caught up in the euphoria of the business cycle that they build too many factories. They become seemingly blind to what will happen in 18 months or so when all the factories are completed. Bankers and governments exacerbate the situation by making sure that money, in the form of debt, is readily available for capacity expansion.

After about 18 or so months have passed, the first of a wave of new factories begin operating increasing the supply of goods. Eventually, price stabilizes, but not for long. Price begins to decline as the first of the excess factories come on line, pushing more goods into the market than can be absorbed. The new factories cannot sell their full output because the market is flooded, and what is sold is at declining prices. Revenue falls, profits turn to losses, debts acquired in building new productive capacity cannot be serviced, and the friendly bankers are not quite so friendly. They withdraw credit that they had previously provided. Firms unable to generate enough cash for debt service may be forced into bankruptcy. Workers lose their jobs, shareholders lose their investments, and bankers have bad loans. There are no winners when business conditions turn sour other than the scavengers who can pick up assets for 10¢ on the dollar.

Just in case anyone feels that business cycles are a thing of the past, the Asian Contagion is a consequence of building too many factories to serve the European and North American export markets. Factories built in China, India, and Southeast Asia, where labor costs are a few dollars a day, sold their products into markets where prices for domestically made goods reflected wages of $15-25 per hour. By definition, factories in developing Asian nations had to be profitable as long as their goods were salable. If 1 factory was profitable, another was built. Two profitable factories led to the construction of 4. With 4 profitable factories, 8 more were built. As prosperity continued, 16 more factories, then 32, then 64, and so forth until the Asian skyline was cluttered with construction cranes, all financed by debt provided by the friendly bankers.

This continued right up to the moment when the export markets in North America and Europe became saturated. Factories could no longer operate at full capacity as their aggregate output exceeded what the export markets could absorb. Prices were cut to attract more customers, but to no avail. Revenues and profits began their downward spiral, causing friendly bankers to start worrying about their loans. Actions taken by bankers to protect their loans, which enabled the overexpansion of capacity during the upswing of the business cycle, made matters worse during the downswing. The real estate and stock market bubbles burst as factory owners scrambled to liquidate assets to raise funds to service their borrowings. Unfortunately, their borrowings were mainly in U.S. dollars and their funds from liquidating assets were in local currencies. Converting local currencies into U.S. dollars brought about a currency collapse. Construction workers building new factories were laid off followed by production workers. In some instances, as in Indonesia, social chaos ensued.

The Asian Contagion started in Thailand in mid-1997 and in about six months had engulfed much of Southeast Asia, threatening to bring down economies elsewhere. The cause of the Asian Contagion was that Europe and North America were unable to absorb the output of too much productive capacity. The Asian Contagion will continue until there is a market for the output of a bloated inventory of factories. While Adam Smith's invisible hand is supposed to ensure that production aligns itself with the desires of the market, it is unable to control additions in productive capacity. The mistake of adding too much productive capacity is discovered too late to correct the situation. The system is intrinsically unstable.

ELI WHITNEY AND COPYING

In 1794 Eli Whitney, a mechanical genius, was visiting a classmate from Yale in the South. The classmate made a passing remark that cotton growing would be quite profitable were it not for the enormous labor required to remove seeds from the cotton balls. Slave labor is not free; slaves must be purchased, fed, clothed, and housed.

Whitney returned to the North and, in about two weeks, invented the cotton gin, which he patented and began manufacturing in New Haven, Connecticut. He should have made a great deal of money, as the cotton gin virtually eliminated labor in removing cotton seeds. Unfortunately for Whitney, when the first cotton gins arrived in the South, the cotton growers opened them and peered inside. What they saw was simple to copy at a fraction of the cost of buying Whitney's patent-protected cotton gin. Whitney's sales collapsed, and he traveled to Washington to have the Patent Office enforce his patents in the South. Since no patent lawyers were willing to take a horseback ride into the Deep South, Whitney was forced into bankruptcy.

THE IMPORTANCE OF COPYING

Since Whitney was an early victim of copying, this may be a good point to talk about copying. Copying is a way of life in the free market environment. If a competitor is doing something better than you, either you must copy or adapt in some manner or be driven out of business. Copying has been institutionalized in reverse engineering, benchmarking, and to some extent, reengineering.

Reverse Engineering

Reverse engineering is an engineering approach to copy a patent protected product or method of manufacturing without infringing on the patent. It may seem curious that copying can be elevated to a formal field of study called reverse engineering. However, if a competitor has a patented process that is better than yours, what else can be done to ensure your survival?

Benchmarking

Benchmarking is a process of continuously comparing and measuring an organization with business leaders anywhere in the world to gain information which will help the organization take action to improve its performance.[1]

Companies have always taken a competitive product and dismantled it to examine each part to compare with their own. If a part made by a competitor has some advantage, then the advantage is copied or adapted. Benchmarking extends this concept to every business process. Competitive benchmarking is comparing performance between competitors, whereas process benchmarking is comparing performance of a business or production process, not necessarily among competitors. If another company has a better operation or process, then a benchmarking company either copies or adapts it to its own needs.

Xerox institutionalized benchmarking in the 1970s, when it faced competition for the first time with the expiration of many of its patents. While Xerox originally thought that Japanese copiers would have a higher price and be of lower quality, reality was just the opposite. Xerox realized that it was in danger of going out of business if it did not revamp its operations from top to bottom, not just manufacturing. Benchmarking requires establishing measures of performance in order to perform a comparative analysis. One of Xerox's first benchmarking exercises was with its Japanese affiliate Fuji Xerox, where it was discovered that Xerox (U.S.) took twice as long to develop new products and needed twice as many people to produce comparable products at twice the cost, twice the number of defects, twice the inventory, and twice the overhead.

The benchmarking process involves:

- determining what is to be benchmarked,
- forming a benchmarking team,
- identifying and forming an agreement for the mutual exchange of information with a benchmarking partner,
- collecting and analyzing information,
- determining gaps in performance,
- communicating findings within a company to build internal acceptance,
- formulating functional goals for the company,
- developing and carrying out action plans to improve performance,
- monitoring progress in filling performance gaps, and
- recalibrating benchmarks with the passage of time.

Robert Camp, Xerox manager and pioneer in benchmarking, launched benchmarking in his book *Benchmarking: The Search for Industry Best Practices That Lead to Superior Performance.* Xerox established the International Benchmarking Clearinghouse, whereby companies can query other companies about their business operations and the nature of the information to be exchanged. Xerox also established the Council of Benchmarking to set up a code of conduct for benchmarking. The code ensures a fair exchange of information between the participants (if I can copy you, you can copy me) that is to be respected and kept confidential. Benchmarking should not infringe on the restraint of trade provisions of the Sherman Anti-Trust Act, generally not a problem as long as benchmarking is confined to a company's operation and business processes. The Council of Benchmarking provides advice on how to:

- organize benchmarking teams with properly motivated individuals having the requisite cross-functional expertise with good communication and interpersonal skills,
- establish an internal network to plan and carry out benchmarking activities, and
- identify individuals to champion benchmarking by effectively communicating the process to others and creating awareness among employees.

Benchmarking is essentially a networking tool that shares information among organizations. Exchanging information saves time and money by presenting a company with a tried and successful solution to a business operation without having to reinvent the wheel. Other organizations are active in benchmarking.[2]

Reengineering

Reengineering may not involve copying but, like benchmarking, is an agent for change.

The fundamental rethinking and radical redesign of business processes to achieve dramatic improvements in critical contemporary measures of performance, such as cost, quality, service, and speed.[3]

An example is the reengineering of the IBM Credit Corporation. Originally, work design followed the principles of Taylor in that a credit application had to pass through a number of specialists in different departments, each completing a portion of the application. The credit approval process required seven days, negatively impacting sales.

In response to complaints from marketing, two senior managers decided to take a novel approach to problem solving and walk through the steps before taking any action. They discovered that the entire process actually took a few hours to complete, and most of the effort was routine. The managers decided to design a new system rather than fix an existing system. They were guided by how this function ought to be organized were they starting anew, the essence of reengineering. In the end, generalists completing the entire process replaced specialists handling separate steps of a process. An expert computer program guided the generalists step-by-step through the credit approval process. Generalists could handle most, but not all, of the credit applications. Some of the specialists were retained as a resource for more difficult credit applications.

In this example of reengineering, the original work design followed the Taylor model of breaking a task down to its essential elements and assigning an individual to each element. Reengineering followed the Juran model of assigning the whole task to an individual or a small group of workers. Whereas the specialist saw only a single step of the process and probably became quite bored, the generalist was responsible for the entire process. This enhanced his or her self-esteem and job satisfaction, leading to improved morale and productivity. Credit application turnaround time collapsed from seven days to four hours. The new system was able to handle over 10 times the number of applications with the same number of people—another ironic example where Taylor, the paradigm for efficiency, was not the most efficient way of doing something.

Business process reengineering (BPR) is driven by the three Cs of customers, competition, and change. Customers want products and services that fit their unique needs delivered to fit their schedules and priced to fit their budgets. Once a customer becomes acquainted with a higher level of quality or service, there is no going back. Competition is becoming more intense, with successful companies offering a superior package of price, quality, and service. Change is inevitable, and the pace of change in technological innovation is quickening. This means that companies have to move faster just to stand still.

Success in reengineering depends on:

- a willingness to make a major change, not just fix a problem,
- a full buy-in by management,
- a reengineering team made up of employees from diverse backgrounds to get different perspectives on the process, and
- team members who have a sense of usefulness to the company, think creatively and communicate effectively, and are rewarded based on performance.

Strategic reengineering takes the concepts of reengineering up to the boardroom to introduce fundamental change to the "business as usual" attitude to the corporate strategic mission. The goal of strategic reengineering is not to reduce cost, whose benefit is transient, but to refocus employees on overall business growth. Top management must identify those business processes critical in carrying out the corporate strategic mission, communicate these to the rest of the company, and set performance goals backed by the requisite capital and human resources. The focus on strategic reengineering is growth in profits, as this is the ultimate measure of success for companies and managers.

Deming stands for continuous change in small, incremental steps to improve an existing system. Benchmarking and reengineering accelerate the rate of change to large, discrete steps. In benchmarking, an old system is replaced by a new system copied or adapted from another existing system. In reengineering, an old system is replaced by a newly designed system based on how an activity would be organized if the company were setting it up for the first time. Benchmarking and reengineering have institutionalized a much more rapid rate of change involving new systems, much to the discomfort of those who prefer to stay with the old. Unlike Deming's method of incremental change relying on the same workers and managers to initiate and carry out change of an existing system, many workers and managers have been "reengineered" out of a job.

WHITNEY ON THE COMEBACK TRAIL

In 1765 General Gribeauval of the French army desired to rationalize armaments by advocating standard weapons with standard parts for ease of repair in battle. Thomas Jefferson picked up this concept in 1785 as minister to France. He wrote to John Jay, "He presented me with fifty locks in pieces. I put several together taking pieces at hazard (random) and they fitted in the most perfect manner. The advantages of this, when arms need repair are evident."[4]

In 1798 Whitney received a contract to manufacture 10,000 muskets with interchangeable parts that did not have to be fitted or filed when putting together a musket. As a result of this contract, Whitney is credited with:

- the first factory for the manufacture of a product with interchangeable parts,
- maximum use of laborsaving machines (powered by belts attached to a shaft of a water-driven mill wheel),

- specialization of labor to machines (the idea is Adam Smith's, but Whitney put it into action),
- beginning of "quality control" by inventing measuring devices to ensure that parts had the same dimensions to be interchangeable, and
- beginning of "assembly" of a product by randomly picking out a set of interchangeable parts and, without further filing and fitting, "assemble" the finished product.

The words "quality control" and "assembly/assemble" were not used by Whitney; they came later. But the concepts were his. While Whitney is credited with the first factory, his critics maintain that the factory never really worked as he intended. Whether the factory succeeded or not is immaterial; the point is that Whitney started the factory system that spread throughout New England. He launched the American system of manufacture that emphasized technology and machinery versus the European system of manufacture that emphasized hand craftsmanship.

Before leaving Whitney, a few words ought to be mentioned about the impact of technology on society. Whitney invented the cotton gin to become rich, or so he intended. The cotton gin made it possible to grow cotton with far fewer slaves. With fewer slaves needed for cotton growing, the price of slaves ought to have dropped, right? Wrong. The invention of the cotton gin made cotton growing immensely profitable. The South was literally plowed under and converted into the world's largest cotton-growing region. Cotton became America's number one export item and enriched the plantation owners. Overall demand for slaves skyrocketed for planting and harvesting cotton, as did the price of slaves.

Slavery was a dying institution before the invention of the cotton gin. With the invention of the cotton gin, the institution of slavery was given new life, and the South became an agrarian society based on slave labor. Meanwhile, Whitney's next venture into moneymaking created the factory system, which led to the industrialization of the North based on what has been described as "wage-slave" labor. Whitney inadvertently set the stage for the Civil War.

ROLE OF GOVERNMENT

The concept of interchangeable parts and the uniformity system to make products from interchangeable parts was brought into being by the government, not by factory owners. Private industry did not like interchangeable parts because relatively expensive machines were substituted for incredibly cheap labor. The concept was kept alive by government contracts for military goods stipulating interchangeable parts. Moreover the government itself manufactured armaments at its Springfield and Harper's Ferry armories, which became centers for the development of the technology for making interchangeable parts. Besides technology, these armories were also repositories of technical expertise which industry could turn to when making the transition to interchangeable parts. In

1835 Samuel Colt patented the revolver and won government contracts to make revolvers that stipulated interchangeable parts. Colt tapped the government armories for the necessary personnel and technology.

The government played a key role in encouraging several industries such as the railroads and airlines. The computer is a government-inspired product opposed by IBM from fear that its tabulating machines would become technologically obsolete. The Internet was originally developed by the government to assure a means of communications during the Cold War and was subsequently turned over to the public domain. Other examples can be cited on how private industry benefited by government policies and programs.

ISAAC SINGER

Singer was a winner among three competing sewing machine companies. His eventual success is credited to his innovations in marketing. Singer was the first industrialist to resort to advertising and demonstrations to let the public know about his product. He organized traveling training teams to teach women how to sew. Those trained on a Singer sewing machine were more apt to buy a Singer sewing machine. This same idea can be seen in Apple Corporation's providing personal computers to elementary schools. Students trained on an Apple computer are more apt to buy an Apple computer.

Singer once asked a housewife why she had not bought a sewing machine and was told that she could not afford one. He asked her if she could spare so many dollars for so many months, and she said yes. He then entered into the first "hire purchase" contract where ownership of the sewing machine was transferred on receipt of the last payment, marking the beginning of credit sales.

While Singer was more into marketing than production, his success in marketing led to problems in production. His first factory (Mott Street) produced 10,000-20,000 sewing machines per year. They were built without interchangeable parts. This meant that the workers had to file and fit parts to produce a workable sewing machine. This is incredibly inefficient but supports the contention that interchangeable parts were more of a goal than an actuality during the nineteenth century. This practice also hints at how cheap labor was. Nevertheless, this state of affairs could not last when, in 1873, Singer opened the Elizabethport factory, the largest in the world for making a single product. A company brochure describing plant operations used the word "assembly" for the first time. Some have opined that this factory could have been described by the words "mass production," but these would be reserved for Ford. Initial annual production of 200,000 sewing machines expanded to 500,000 units by 1880. Assembling this volume of sewing machines without interchangeable parts would have been a production manager's nightmare. Singer was forced to switch to interchangeable parts; and to do this, he drew on the resources of the armories.

Singer also launched the first global company. He viewed his market as not just the United States but every hamlet in the world from the remotest parts of Siberia, to Africa, to the Amazon. Sewing machines were often prominently displayed in the front window of dwellings for passers-by to see as they reflected favorably on an owner's standing. Singer also built factories overseas to service the world market. As with all the giants of history, he also had a personal side. Singer was married to five wives, simultaneously, without each knowing about the others until late in his life. He had over 20 children and named the eldest daughter in each family Mary, perhaps as a memory aid. Considering his private and public life, Singer would be an apt subject for a study in time management.

CYRUS McCORMACK

McCormack was another marketing promoter for his invention, the reaper. The horse-drawn reaper cuts grain and ties it in bundles, drastically lowering the labor input in harvesting grain. His production volume was far below Singer's, about 10,000 per year in the 1860s, 20,000 in the 1870s, and 30,000-50,000 in the 1880s. He did not achieve a uniformity system for manufacturing interchangeable parts because improvements to the reaper necessitated manufacturing a different model every year. Not having interchangeable parts meant that factory workers would have to file and fit a part to install it in a new reaper, and farmers would have to file and fit a spare part to install it in an existing reaper. This is another example of the reluctance of private industry in the nineteenth century to adopt interchangeable parts.

Farmers became accustomed to annual model changes. One year, McCormack had no improvements to make and did not change his model. Sales plummeted. McCormack did not hire a marketing research firm or send a memo to a marketing vice president to find out why. Like Singer's asking a housewife why she didn't buy his sewing machine, McCormack visited farmers and asked why they weren't buying his reaper. When he found out that the farmers wanted a model change before they would buy a reaper, he returned to his factory and made a superficial change that revived sales. After that, he always had an annual model change, something to be copied later by the automobile industry.

BICYCLES

The degree of advances in manufacturing technology during the nineteenth century can be seen in bicycles. In the 1890s productive capacity of bicycle factories had risen to a point of saturating a market for the first time in history. Manufacturers, who had never experienced such a phenomenon, continued producing bicycles long after sales slumped. By 1897 their unbridled conversion of cash into inventory that could not be sold bankrupted the industry.

The bicycle industry is also known for the first single-purpose machines to install spokes in wheels. Single-purpose machines cannot be adjusted–change the design of the wheel or the spokes and throw away the machines. However, as long as there were no changes, single-purpose machines were cheaper than flexible machines that could accommodate product design changes. The bicycle industry also originated the practice of stamping parts. The European system of manufacturing called for cutting and shaping metal to make a fender with a high degree of handcraftsmanship. The American system of manufacturing called for placing flat sheet metal in a press and stamping out fenders willy-nilly. Stamping parts was a sore point of contention between advocates of the two systems.

CONVEYOR BELT SYSTEMS

Conveyor belts were used as early as 1795 in the Evans Automatic Flour Mill in Virginia for transforming wheat to flour. In 1873 slaughtered animals were placed on a chain that carried the carcass from one butcher to the next, where the carcass was "disassembled." In 1895 the Norton Automatic Canmaking Manufacturing Company made tin cans on a moving belt line. As will be seen, the story of the origin of the moving assembly line suggests that Ford may not have been aware of these precursors to his most important innovation to manufacturing.

HENRY FORD

Henry Ford is still considered a giant among those responsible for the way things are made. Although a giant, he stands on the shoulders of others such as Adam Smith for espousing the free enterprise system whereby Ford could form his own company and run it free of government interference. Ford is indebted to Eli Whitney for the uniformity system to make interchangeable parts and the American system of manufacturing. Whitney, in turn, is indebted to the U.S. government for a contract that funded the development of the uniformity system. Ford is indebted to the U.S. government for keeping the concept of interchangeable parts alive throughout the nineteenth century in its armament contracts and the activity of its armories.

Singer gave Ford the concept of large-scale assembly. The bicycle industry gave Ford the concept of single-purpose machines and the stamping of parts. In addition, Ford did not invent the automobile. Others invented the gasoline engine and pneumatic tires in the 1880s. The pneumatic (air-filled) tire was actually a critical invention for the development of the automobile. Think what the cost of a tire made of solid rubber would be. Among the first commercial automobiles available to the public were those made by the Germans Daimler and Benz (the Mercedes is named after Benz's daughter). In the United States the Duryea brothers and Olds of Oldsmobile made important contributions to the development of the automobile, as did others.

But the laurels belong to Ford. In 1903 Ford made his third attempt to manufacture a commercial automobile with the formation of the Ford Motor Company. His objective was a "light, low priced car with ample horsepower capable of going where horse drawn carriages can go." He wanted to make a car for the people to be driven on dirt roads rather than making automobiles for the rich (Pierce Arrow, Mercedes Benz, and others) to be driven on city streets. In succession, Ford produced the Model A, B, C, F, K, N, R, and S, and finally, in 1906 he met his objectives in the Model T. In 1907 he opened up the Piquette Avenue factory capable of producing 10,000 Model Ts per year at a cost around $700-900 per car. He realized the inefficiency inherent in not having interchangeable parts by his pithy remark "no fitters shall be hired." He gathered a team of highly talented mechanics, as he was, and his factory was a scene of intense experimentation for high-volume, low-cost production.

Ford's first cars could not be considered cheap. With workers making two dollars a day, a Model T represented something of the order of a year and a half's pay. Ford knew that he had to lower his price to enable the common people to buy his car; and to do this, he originated the Ford cycle:

- build a car with a low profit margin (this is strange behavior for a capitalist)
- improve the efficiency of operations (all capitalists do this, although Ford was especially proficient)
- pass all cost savings on to consumers in the form of a lower price (another instance of strange behavior)
- lower price allows more people to buy, increasing volume
- higher volume leads to economies of scale
- lower costs from economies of scale passed to consumers in the form of a lower price
- when the factory is at capacity, build a new factory with even greater economies of scale
- pass these savings to consumers and repeat the cycle

Economies of scale played an important role in the Ford cycle. Suppose that there are two machines available for producing a part. Machine A has a productive capacity of 1,000 units per day with a daily fixed cost of $1,000 for capital and labor. Material cost is $10 per unit. At full capacity, the unit cost is fixed cost ($1,000) divided by 1,000 units plus $10 in material costs for a total of $11 per unit. If demand grows to 10,000 units per day, 10 machine A's would be necessary, and the total unit cost would remain at $11 per unit.

Machine B has a total productive capacity of 10,000 units per day, fixed cost of $6,000 per day, and material cost of $7 per unit. For sales of 1,000 per day, the fixed cost of $6,000 can be spread over only 1,000 units of production, or $6 per unit plus material costs of $7 per unit for a total of $13 per unit. For production of 1,000 units per day, a manufacturer should use machine A. Now suppose that sales increase to 10,000. Rather than buy 10 machine As, the job can be handled by one machine B. Its fixed cost of $6,000 is spread over 10,000 units or $0.60 per unit plus material costs of $7 per unit for a total of $7.60 per unit.

Ford knew that by expanding sales, he would be able to achieve economies of scale by being able, in this instance, to switch from machine A to machine B. The cost savings of $3.40 per unit would be passed on to the consumers in the form of a lower price. A lower price would expand volume. If the volume grew large enough, Ford could switch from machine B to machine C introducing even greater economies of scale whose savings were then passed on to consumers, further expanding his market. He simply kept on this cycle until he saturated the market in the 1920s just as the bicycle manufacturers did in the 1890s.

Ford did not become rich by focusing on becoming rich. Unlike the typical businessman of his day and ours, he intentionally maintained a low profit margin. He pursued a particular business strategy and had an operation that put this strategy into effect. The financial results, his becoming rich, showed that he had made the correct choice of business strategy. Does this sound familiar? While we're at it, it was noted earlier that when the Japanese adopted the teachings of Deming and began to get rid of the hidden factory, they passed the cost savings to the consumers rather than pocket the savings as incremental profits. Consumers had little choice when confronted with superior Japanese products selling at a lower price than mediocre U.S. products. Does this too sound familiar? There seems to be a connection between Deming, Ford, and Japanese business practices.

While Ford charged a low profit margin on the Model T, he did not have a low profit margin on repair parts. Why should he? The customer was trapped. Defense and aerospace companies often bid low for a government contract and then make their profits on change orders. Polaroid sells cameras at a low profit margin and makes its profits on the film. A razor company some years ago gave away the razors and made its money on the blades.

Only three years later, in 1910, Ford opened his second factory (Highland Avenue) with an initial capacity of 200,000 cars per year. Photographs taken inside the factory showed no moving assembly line system as late as 1913. Cars were pushed by workers from one station to the next to install more parts. The origin of the moving assembly line is associated with magneto coil assembly. At first, a worker sat at a workbench assembling 16 magnets, bolts, nuts, supports, and clamps into a magneto coil in 20 minutes. Ironically, this is the same work design espoused by Joseph Juran and others in order to provide some sense of job satisfaction in making a worker or a small group of workers responsible for the entire assembly of a component.

Then someone, and it was not Henry, decided to break the task of assembling a magneto coil into its simplest elements and assign a worker to each element. One Monday morning, the workers came to work and saw their workbenches removed. They were instructed to stand behind a moving belt, with each worker doing a single element in the task of assembling a magneto coil. This reorganizing of work design reduced the labor content for assembling magneto coils from 20 to 13 minutes. Further improvements to the moving assembly line reduced the labor content to 6-7 minutes, then finally to 4-5 minutes per coil. This was Taylor without Taylor because Ford made it a point to respond to anyone who mentioned that he was applying Taylor's principles in the moving assembly line by adamantly insisting that he had never read a word of Taylor and never would.

But Ford was not concerned about copying Taylor. All he knew was that the moving assembly line offered cost savings that could be passed to the customer, allowing more to buy his product. Once Ford saw the efficacy of assembly line operations, it was introduced to other components, and finally to the automobile itself. In short order, the Model T was assembled on a moving belt from parts carried on other belts from their point of manufacture to their point of installation. The Ford factory became a symphony of movement.

In 1914 Ford became world-famous, that is, far more famous than he already was. To appreciate what Ford was about to do, he has to be compared to other factory owners, typified by the eighteenth- and nineteenth-century British textile mill owners. Driven by the profit motive, British textile mill owners strove to maximize revenue by charging the highest price for textiles that the market could bear. Costs of labor and material were minimized, which the mill owners were especially talented in doing. They succeeded not just in minimizing the cost of labor but in crushing labor. Labor wages were so low that entire families had to be employed in the textile mills to eke out a living. Women tended to have large families, and the children were put to work as soon as they were able to cart clothing between workers. Labor was indeed crushed: hospital records show instances of child starvation, and photographs show workers wearing rags. The one exception was Robert Owen, who provided his workers with adequate food, shelter, and medical care. His textile mill, now a museum, is today a mandatory visit for British schoolchildren. He is treated as a secular saint, which gives a pretty fair idea of what the other mill owners must have been like.

Anyway, maximizing price to maximize revenue coupled with minimizing costs ought to be a perfect paradigm for maximizing the difference between the two, profit. Superficially, it looks as if it ought to work, but the paradigm contains a fatal flaw just as the paradigm for international trade in accumulating the largest horde of gold. The flaw is obvious for us peering into the past. If labor is crushed and must wear rags, to whom do you sell your textiles? To the rich and well-off, all 5 or 10 percent of the population? The British textile mill owners could not envision their workers being their market because for the workers to be a market, they would have to be something more than wage-slaves. According to the commonly accepted paradigm, both past and present, giving workers more pay would increase costs and, therefore, depress profits. Rather than increase their workers' pay, the British textile mill owners and other industrialists appealed to the government to acquire colonies. The colonies would be a market for their products and a source of raw materials. Sound familiar?

Ford had demonstrated to the world that he was a maverick twice over by selling a product with a low profit margin and passing all cost savings to the customer in the form of a lower price. He was about to become a maverick thrice over when he sat down with his accountant and, with no outside pressure, posed the question of what would happen if he increased the pay of his workers. Ford began the process of increasing the daily rate of pay of $2.30 a day by 25¢ without changing the price of the car. The accountant calculated how higher worker pay would affect sales by allowing more workers to be able to buy the output of their labor. Then he figured out how this higher volume of sales would introduce greater economies of scale, which, in turn, would allow for a lowering of the price and another round of the Ford cycle. When informed of the results, Ford upped the ante by another 25¢ and the accountant repeated the calculations. At $4.90 a day, the accountant told Ford that he had reached the limit. Ford sensed the public reaction to what he was about to do, rounded the $4.90 up to $5, and, on his own volition, did what no capitalist has done before or since: he doubled the pay of his workers.

In the short term, he did expect to lose money because he had doubled his labor costs without changing the price of the Model T. In time, these losses would be compensated from profits from increased sales. But his losses were far less than what he had anticipated. Working for Ford became highly desirable, and workers' productivity increased to make sure that they continued working for Ford. More importantly, other manufacturers were forced to raise wages to keep their workers. These workers were now able to purchase Model Ts adding to the volume of sales. The benefit of increased sales quickly erased Ford's anticipated short-term losses. Ford is credited with single-handedly creating the blue-collar, middle-class worker who could afford a home, a car, and the better things of life. Indeed, Ford needed a new class of consumers because he was making huge numbers of the Model T. By 1915 the Highland Avenue factory was up to 500,000 cars per year.

Critics have pointed out that Ford had to increase his workers' pay because his factories were noisy and dirty. Assembly work was extremely monotonous, plaguing Ford with high absenteeism and worker turnover. He cured these industrial ills by doubling his workers' pay. As sales continued to soar, he built the River Rouge plant in 1920, the world's first vertically integrated factory.

Vertical integration essentially means absorbing suppliers, such as steel manufacturers. Ford wanted to integrate steel production in his plant rather than purchase steel from an outside firm. He did not stop at simply building a steel mill in the River Rouge plant; Ford purchased iron ore and coal mines and the steamship and rail lines needed to move the raw materials to the plant. Molten steel was immediately poured into molds to produce engine blocks and other components. Steel shapes were made for the automobile frame and sheet metal for stamping out body parts. It took Ford 48 hours to convert iron ore and coal entering one end of the plant into a completed Model T car leaving the other.

Ford had a glass factory in the River Rouge plant for producing windshields and windows. He even attempted to manufacture his own tires, but his rubber venture in Brazil was a financial failure (a story in itself). Production ballooned in the 1920s to 2 million cars per year and the price of a Model T fell to about $330. At $5 a day, a worker could buy a car with 3 to 4 months' pay, down considerably from the initial year and a half. The world was astounded by Ford's achievements, coining the words "mass production" to describe what was going on in the River Rouge plant and "mass marketing" for selling what had been a rich man's toy to the common folk.

FORD'S OPERATING PHILOSOPHY

Ford's operating philosophy is to examine every step in a process. Every step costs money but may not add value. If a step does not add value, eliminate the step.

An example of this was Ford's buying steel from an outside supplier before building the River Rouge plant. Steel is produced hot, but delivered cold. This meant that Ford had to reheat the steel to pour it into molds to make engine blocks. Reheating is a step in the process that costs money but does not add value. Ford eliminated the step of reheating steel by building a steel plant in the River Rouge plant and pouring molten steel directly into the shapes and forms needed for manufacturing the Model T. Another example was receiving supplies on wooden pallets, which Ford threw away. He recognized these wooden pallets as a cost not adding any value. He made suppliers ship goods on mahogany pallets to be recycled as trim for the dashboards.

TAIICHO OHNO

Taiicho Ohno, production manager at Toyota Motors, was instrumental in originating Japanese lean production techniques. Interestingly, in a televised interview, Ohno did not mention Deming, only Ford. Ohno's opening remarks were Ford's operating philosophy. He gave the example of a worker intently watching an automated process. The worker thought that he was adding value to the company by continually keeping an eye on something that did not have to be watched; and so, too, did his fellow workers. Ohno watched him and asked about his function, which confirmed his suspicion that the worker was a cost not adding value. When I ask my class what Ohno did, the nearly unanimous response is, "Fired him!"

This is the American gut-response of what to do about a worker who is no longer needed. It is ingrained in our culture. The Japanese gut-response was given by Ohno, "Retrain and reassign." This reaction is ingrained in their culture. The Japanese culture holds that a worker is an asset to be maximized, while our culture holds that a worker is a cost to be minimized.

Ohno's second example of the Ford operating philosophy was the movement of work in process between two workstations. At workstation A, a worker places his or her output in boxes that are stacked on a pallet. When the pallet is full, a forklift truck moves the pallet to workstation B located in another building, where the next step of the manufacturing process is completed. Ohno pointed out that the movement of the pallet load of work-in-process (WIP) inventory costs money but does not add value. The obvious solution is to place the two workstations next to one another eliminating the forklift truck.

Interestingly, in Japan the forklift truck operator might actually make a suggestion to place the two workstations together. The operator is willing to do so because the operator not only realizes that he or she will be retrained and reassigned, but also realizes that he or she will be rewarded for making the suggestion. An American forklift truck operator and coworkers would not make such a suggestion because of the fear of losing a job. Our paradigm for minimizing labor costs may not actually minimize labor costs.

PUSH VERSUS PULL MANUFACTURING

Placing the two workstations together presents a good opportunity to discuss push and pull manufacturing. In push manufacturing a person makes something that is pushed into a warehouse or a storage area. The worker at the next step of the production process draws down from this work-in-process (WIP) inventory. Pull manufacturing is the immediate consumption of an item in the next step of the manufacturing process. This occurs when the two workstations are side by side whereby the downstream workstation consumes the output of the upstream workstation. Pull manufacturing prohibits any accumulation of WIP inventory between the two workstations other than some minimal number to ensure continuity of production. If there is a slowdown in any part of the factory, the entire factory slows down because upstream workstations are not allowed to accumulate WIP inventory above these minimal levels.

Eliminating the forklift truck generates savings in not having to finance, maintain, and operate it along with less chance of damage to parts and injury to workers by not having to move WIP inventory about the factory. However, the savings of placing two workstations together or savings going from push to pull or just-in-time (JIT) manufacturing, far exceeds the savings in eliminating the forklift truck. When the workstations were separated, about two forklift trucks of WIP inventory were necessary to keep both workstations continuously employed. As workstation A was making a forklift truckload of parts, workstation B was consuming a forklift truckload of parts. Another forklift load of parts had to be delivered to workstation B before the prior one was consumed.

If the output of workstation A was placed in a storeroom or warehouse, WIP inventory may number in the hundreds or thousands. By placing the two workstations close together, workstation B immediately consumes what workstation A produces with perhaps a few items in-between the workstations to ensure operational continuity. Thus, WIP inventory is virtually eliminated along with its carrying costs. Moreover, defects are detected almost immediately when the two workstations are together. If the output of workstation A is placed in a stockroom or warehouse, hundreds or thousands of defective units could be made before discovery by workstation B.

These are the two largest sources of savings when converting from push to pull or JIT manufacturing. Other savings include reduced management input when workstations are located close together. It is easier to manage an operation located in one area rather than spread over different buildings. A manager who can view his or her entire range of responsibility need not rely as much on computer printouts to figure out what is going on. Moreover, factories can be smaller in size as there is no need for warehouses, stockrooms, or extra-wide aisles for forklift trucks.

It is amazing that just-in-time (JIT) or pull manufacturing, supposedly a post-World War II concept originated by Ohno, was fully developed in the River Rouge plant. The only WIP inventory was on conveyors moving parts from where they were made to where they were consumed. Ford innately recognized that excess inventory was a cost that did not add value. He eliminated WIP inventory and practiced JIT manufacturing long before WIP and JIT were acronyms. He also had workers continually inspect what they were handling for rapid discovery of defects. That is why Ohno maintained that all he did was update Ford. However, in updating Ford, Ohno was instrumental in converting a nearly bankrupt company into the Bank of Toyota.

In push manufacturing, workers make a part that is pushed into a warehouse. Their view of the manufacturing process is truncated to supplying a warehouse or stockroom. Moreover they tolerate operational problems. Suppose that 800 units of a part are being consumed daily in the manufacturing process. A worker experiencing operational problems makes only 600 units. As there is a mountain of WIP inventory available in the warehouse, the factory keeps on running as though the worker had made 800 units. At some point, the worker will have to produce 1,000 units to make up for lost production, which generates overtime costs. The operational problems and their associated costs are tolerated in a just-in-case inventory system since the chief purpose of just-in-case inventory is to act as a buffer to cover operational problems just in case they occur.

The comfort provided by just-in-case inventory to compensate for operational problems is lost when a factory converts to pull, or JIT, manufacturing. Operational problems must be corrected because they can no longer be hidden by WIP inventory. Solving these operational problems adds to the savings of pull manufacturing, in this case, eliminating the need for overtime to make up for lost production. But these savings are dwarfed by the realization on the part of a worker that his or her poor performance can no longer be hid by just-in-case inventory. Poor performance is immediately revealed to all when the entire factory slows down. If a worker's output is reduced from 800 to 600, so, too, is the factory's output. For this reason, U.S. managers resisted converting from push to pull manufacturing. They thought that unreliable and unmotivated employees, disassociated from the process, hating their work, and counting their days to retirement, would utterly destroy a factory if factory performance depended on their individual performance. As seen at the end of this chapter, this paradigm, too, fell victim to reality.

TOM PETERS

Tom Peters, a famous management guru, gave a series of televised talks. One particularly noteworthy talk was on the Union Pacific Railroad.

The Union Pacific Railroad got a new president who called in the managers and asked them their opinion on the level of service provided by the railroad. They told him that service "couldn't be better." When asked how they measured service, the managers replied that service was determined by freight train departure time. If a shipper was told that the next freight train would leave Omaha at 6 P.M., and if it left at 6 P.M., service was given a high grade.

Then the president did something unexpected. He asked the railroad's customers, the shippers, about the level of service and was told that "service couldn't be worse." Satisfaction with the railroad's service was a rock-bottom 20 percent. In querying his customers, the president was following the advice of Arnold Feigenbaum, originator of total quality control (TQC), now called total quality management (TQM). Feigenbaum advocates letting the customer determine what constitutes a high-quality product or service.

The president continued his investigation on why the railroad had such a poor level of service. He asked a conductor what he did when he learned about a shipper's need to move goods. He was told that if an empty boxcar was available, it would be set aside for the shipper. If not, the conductor would request that a boxcar be added to the next arriving freight train from Mr. A in accordance with company directives. The president learned that Mr. A would act on the request and then pass it to Mr. B, then on to Mr. C, Mr. D, Mr. E, and finally Mr. F, all in accordance with company directives. If approved by Mr. F, then a dispatcher would be instructed to find an idle boxcar and add it to the train. By the time all six signatures were obtained, it was too late to get the boxcar on the next freight train. While it was true that freight trains left on time, they did so without the shippers' shipments.

Like the worker intently watching an automated process and not realizing that an automated process need not be watched, the six managers took their responsibilities very seriously. They came home exhausted from a day's work of adding their signatures to untold numbers of requests for boxcars to be added to freight trains. They viewed themselves as making a positive contribution to the functioning of a major railroad line. The Ford operating philosophy can be applied not only to blue-collar workers but also to white-collar managers. The step in the process is to obtain six levels of managerial approvals. Did the six managers cost money? Yes. Were they adding value? No. In fact, they were adding negative value. The delay in time to obtain the requisite signatures was sufficient to ensure that boxcars were not available for the next departing train.

These managers were destroying the Union Pacific Railroad without realizing it, a good example of Adam Smith's concept of unproductive labor. The president's solution can best be described as reengineering. He saw no point in fixing the existing system. He took the approach of what would be done if the railroad were just starting up in business. The solution was to set up a telecommunications system that linked the conductor directly to the dispatcher responsible for finding a spare boxcar. No management approval was necessary except for major changes, and that was limited to a single signature. When the new system was up and running, the old system was simply discarded. Almost immediately, the service approval rating jumped to 60 percent. At the time of Tom Peters' talk, it was 80 percent, with the objective of improving to 90 percent and beyond.

How many times did Mr. A say no to a simple request to add another boxcar? If none, then this is a telltale sign that his approval was not necessary. How many times did Mr. F say no when viewing five signatures saying yes? If none, then this is a telltale sign the Mr. F's approval was not necessary. White-collar managers should apply Ford's operating philosophy to themselves, the organizations that they are part of, and those who are reporting to them:

- Am I adding value to the organization?
- Is the organization adding value to the company?
- Are those working for me adding value?

If an individual is discovered not to be adding value, perhaps a manager should partake in a new cultural experience of retraining and reassigning rather than firing.

THE UNDOING OF FORD

Henry Ford believed in centralized management, which meant that Ford made all key decisions. His executives were expected to carry out his directives, not originate them. Alfred Sloan, head of General Motors, believed in decentralized management. This partly stemmed from General Motors' being a conglomerate of once-independent firms. Thus, the brain of Henry Ford was pitted against the brains of Sloan plus all his top executives running GM's various divisions, ultimately a losing proposition for Ford. Ford was primarily interested in how to run a factory more efficiently. Sloan was primarily interested in how to best coordinate the activities of many factories to enhance system productivity. Ford was production-driven and the Model T remained essentially unchanged from its birth in 1907 to its demise in 1927. Sloan was market-driven and instituted annual model changes (shades of Cyrus McCormack) to attract buyers. To accommodate annual model changes, GM plants invested in flexible machines that could be adjusted to accommodate a design change. Annual model changes were accomplished in only two weeks. Ford stayed with single-purpose machines that, though cheaper, could not accommodate a change in the design of the Model T.

Annual model changes gave GM the opportunity to make improvements such as adding a heater, a self-starter, and styling. GM also provided its customers with a choice of color. With time, the Model T began losing market share to GM. It took several years for the so-called Ford executives to build up their courage to face Ford and voice their opinion. They decided to focus on the matter of color and pointed out to Ford that Sloan offered his customers a choice of color, and Ford didn't. From Ford's perspective, a single color was easier for production, while from Sloan's perspective, a choice of colors was easier for marketing. Ford retorted that if the consumers wanted color, then "give them color, give them fourteen shades of black!"

In 1927 the fifteen-millionth Model T was appropriately bedecked and driven by Ford and his son Edsel from the assembly line straight to the Ford museum. Some commented that the museum was exactly where the car belonged; it had become an antique while still in production. The market for the Model T was first-time buyers, who subsequently would trade up to a GM product. Shortly after the celebration of the fifteen-millionth car, sales collapsed. Ford had run out of first-time buyers. As with the bicycles in the 1890s, Ford had saturated the market and was forced to abandon the Model T. It took six months to switch models, which entailed throwing away all the single-purpose machines and laying off most of his workforce. This was quite unlike the two weeks for GM to make a model change by adjusting the same flexible machines without any layoffs.

Much has been left unsaid about Ford and what subsequently happened. But one point deserves mentioning: the Asian Contagion. As mentioned, the Asian Contagion stems from building too many factories in the developing nations of Asia to serve export markets in North America and Europe. Like the British textile mill owners, the Asian factory owners missed a market about three times larger than North America and Europe combined: their own workers. For their workers to buy the output of what they make, they would have to be paid more than a few dollars per day. But increasing workers' pay would increase labor costs and depress profits.

The Asian factory owners became rich by paying their workers a few dollars a day and selling into a market where domestic products were made with labor costing $15-25 per hour. Unfortunately, they built too many factories and saturated the market. Ford solved this problem when he doubled the pay of his workers and created a new market. This option is no longer available for the Asian factory owners, as many of them are already bankrupt. Too bad that they did not see a much larger market for their goods coming to work at their factories every morning. However, even if they did, they lacked the intestinal fortitude to raise their workers' pay. When Ford is viewed in this light, his true greatness and uniqueness shine forth.

THE UNDOING OF THE ASSEMBLY LINE

The first break with the Taylor-inspired, Ford-invented assembly line was at Volvo in the 1960s. A highly educated workforce was not suited for the monotonous, self-esteem-destroying assembly line work. Absenteeism was 20 percent, meaning that 20 percent more people had to be hired than necessary to man the lines. Annual turnover was one-third of the work force, equivalent to a new work force every three years. Something had to be done.

Volvo switched to assembling a car in one location by a team of workers where parts flow to the workers. Each worker is expected to be able to assemble a significant portion of the car. This requires a costly commitment to training and education and is the one great disadvantage of work teams over the moving assembly line. New Volvo workers receive 16 weeks of training before being assigned to a work team. This is followed by 12 months of on-the-job training in order for each worker to learn at least one-seventh of all the operations, the minimum necessary for effective job rotation to break the monotony. The objective is for each worker to learn half of the operations in the total assembly of an automobile. This is quite different from Ford's Model T assembly line, where any job could be learned in just a few minutes of observation without a worker knowing a word of English.

Being Sweden, the Volvo work teams are made up of both sexes with a spread in age to promote social harmony. Each team assembles four cars at a time. The team is responsible for checking out the car and taking the necessary steps to ensure quality. There is no direct supervision of the work teams by management. Does this mean that managers have lost control over their workers?

First of all, managers do have the requisite information needed to manage. There is no way for the work teams to hide their output. Cars are big items easily counted. Therefore, output is known. Work teams are also responsible for the quality of their output. Quality is known from feedback from dealers when warranties are exercised. The warranty identification number tells management which work team assembled the car. Hence, management knows the quantity and quality of the output for each work team. With that knowledge, management is in a position to take corrective action if necessary.

The point is that management rarely has to take corrective action. The work teams can be viewed as small factories within a large factory or little companies within a large company. Since they have some say in what is going on and some control over their destiny, they have a much greater sense of job satisfaction and pride in their work. This increases their morale and productivity. These are the traditional "book" answers on why work teams have been so successful. There is another reason. The workers hate the old Taylor system so much that they will make sure that the new "Juran" system works. After all, Volvo is going to assemble cars, if not by work teams assembling the entire car, then by assembly line workers with its tedium and production quotas accompanied by a chorus of barking first line supervisors. The choice is theirs.

Management still manages at Volvo. The design of the car, organizing and scheduling production, choice of suppliers and technology, distribution, marketing, financing, and every other matter of importance are still in the hands of management. What management has lost is the first-line supervisory position. Years ago, books were written about the looming crisis in first-line supervisors: insufficient numbers, improper training, and few aspiring for the job. Work teams solved the crisis by assuming the responsibilities of first-line supervisors. Since few managers wanted to be first-line supervisors, what was lost? Absolutely nothing. What has been gained? Absolutely everything in the form of workers who take pride in their work, who are willing to accept responsibility and be held accountable for their performance.

TRADITIONAL CAR ASSEMBLY LINES STILL ABOUND

Volvo is an exception. Assembly lines still operate around the world. I visited a large automobile assembly plant in New Jersey and was impressed with its relative cleanliness and quiet. The company had a large employee involvement center at the main entrance. The walking tour took hours. The first portion of the walk went through a huge area of the plant devoid of people but populated with robots. It was an eerie feeling to be in a line of people snaking past robots putting together the shell of an automobile body. Robots mimic the arm, elbow, wrist, and hand motions of humans. The most sophisticated robots can do only the simplest human motions, but this is more than adequate to spot-weld bits and pieces of an automobile body.

Japanese workers welcomed robots because the workers knew they would be retrained and reassigned to more interesting and challenging work. U.S. workers opposed robots because the workers viewed robots as their replacements. Robots certainly have had an impact on job opportunities for those who either limit themselves or are limited to simple tasks such as spot welding, nut tightening, or spray painting. Robots are actually a source of employment for those who design, manufacture, operate, and maintain them, but this demands a higher level of worker skills.

The efficiency of robots was witnessed when, at one point, 140 spot-welds were completed in a single operation in seconds. The automobile body moved a few feet, and a laser light extravaganza made hundreds of measurements to ensure that body dimensions were within specifications. Then on to another large area where the automobile body disappeared for about two weeks for spray painting and drying. The spray room was isolated for environmental reasons and also void of people. Robots do the spray painting. Anyone who bemoans the social consequence of workers being displaced by robots should also consider the health consequences of breathing paint fumes for eight hours.

Finally car bodies emerged into the final large area of the plant, where a conventional assembly line was in operation. The workers rode along with the car body for a short distance, performing a specific task. The speed of the line was not rushed and a worker had adequate time to perform his or her assigned task and take a few steps back to the next car to repeat the task. Although the workers seemed satisfied and were able to carry on conversations, students who worked there informed me that work design is strictly Taylor-inspired. The employee involvement center is more show than substance. First line supervisors, while not visible, were present. The workforce is basically disassociated from the process, who dislike their supervisors, hate their work, and count the days to retirement—what a way to waste a life.

There was a major impetus to move toward just-in-time manufacturing at this plant. Success in achieving JIT manufacturing is measured by inventory turnover. If the plant received a supply of seats that would last six months, then the inventory turnover is two; that is, two shipments can supply the plant for a year. On the other hand, if the plant received a supply of seats daily, then the turnover rate would be 250, assuming 250 working days per year. The actual turnover rate for most parts was over 100 and climbing, meaning that shipments were large enough to supply about two days' of operation. Even the railroads were increasing their reliability to deliver smaller shipments on a more frequent schedule to combat competition from trucking firms. Turnover rate is constrained, to some degree, by the location of suppliers who may be hundreds of miles away, although Japanese transplant factories in the United States receive daily shipments from Japan.

The one item that best illustrated JIT manufacturing was the automobile seats. The seat manufacturing plant was 48 minutes away from the assembly. Trucks picking up seats do not pull up to a warehouse to be loaded. There is no warehouse with completed seats. The trucks are loaded at the production line. Seats are made in accordance with the schedule of assembly, but in reverse order since the first seats loaded on a truck trailer are the last ones removed. A truckload of seats arrives at the assembly plant about three hours before installation. This is the extent of the inventory. Shortly before the seats are needed, the trailer is backed up to the assembly line. If the first seat removed is green leather with fuzzy white bunnies, then the car passing by requires a green leather seat with fuzzy white bunnies.

THEIR DAYS MAY BE NUMBERED: THE NUMMI STORY

The General Motors assembly plant in Fremont, California, was known as the "worst plant in the world." Between 1963 and 1982, this plant had:

- the lowest productivity of any GM plant,
- abysmal product quality,
- rampant drug and alcohol abuse,
- high absenteeism requiring hiring 20 percent extra employees to man the assembly lines,
- highly militant union staging frequent wildcat strikes and sick-outs that closed the plant, and
- over 5,000 unresolved grievances.

GM closed the plant in 1982 and subsequently entered into a joint venture with Toyota. Toyota contributed its lean production system and assumed responsibility for product design, engineering, and management of daily operations. GM contributed the physical plant and was responsible for marketing and sales. The joint venture can be looked upon as formal admittance by the world's largest automobile company that it could no longer assemble cars or manage workers! GM management could at least be credited with the personal courage to admit its faults by entering into the New United Motor Manufacturing, Inc., or NUMMI joint venture.

Toyota was contractually obligated to deal with the same workforce. Rehiring of previously laid-off workers was a three-day process including written examinations, discussions, and interviews. Applicants were divided into either prospective team leaders or team members. Teams were generally 5 to 7 members. Division leaders, who oversaw the activities of four teams, denoted the first level of management. It is important to realize that 85 percent of new hires were old employees who had made life so difficult for GM, and vice versa.

The entire NUMMI management team and 450 work team leaders attended a three-week training program at a Toyota plant in Japan. This group was ultimately given the responsibility to set up the NUMMI plant and train team members. The eventual outcome was:

- productivity at NUMMI was higher than at any other GM plant and two times what it was at the Fremont plant,
- quality was highest among all GM plants and close to that of Toyota's Japanese plants,
- absenteeism fell from 20-25 percent to 3-4 percent, and substance abuse was virtually eliminated,
- suggestion program rose from nil at the Fremont plant to 26 percent participation in 1986 and to 92 percent in 1991 as the NUMMI plant,
- total number of grievances over 8 years fell to 700, and
- number of employees considering themselves to be satisfied or very satisfied with working at NUMMI rose to over 90 percent.

Some of the factors at work at NUMMI were:

- assembly line operations converted to just-in-time, eliminating WIP inventory,
- each workstation responsible for quality assurance,
- 18 skilled trades classifications reduced to 2,
- 80 hourly pay rates reduced to 1 with no extra pay for seniority, performance, or merit,
- worker cross-training and job rotation,
- designing jobs not done by management exercising its "divine right" or by engineers sitting in isolated offices,
- standardizing work done by work teams that ask for management and engineering help when needed,
- timing work done by team members, not engineers,
- cooperative and dynamic relationship of workers to production system, not adversarial or coercive,
- continuous improvement (*kaizen*) based on continual reiteration of a process of analysis, refinement, and standardization of work,
- commitment to communications within and among teams, and
- an active suggestion program initiated by work teams and handled by special *kaizen* work teams to study suggestions and carry out improvement projects.

In asking workers to contribute to the manufacturing process in a positive and active way, NUMMI instituted a Japanese-style no-layoff policy where management takes a pay cut first and where production is slowed before there are any layoffs. This is one prerequisite that management must be prepared to offer if active worker participation is desired. Since the quality of the product and the productivity of the workers improved to such a large extent, the NUMMI plant was about the last plant to suffer layoffs. As long as this is true, the cost of offering a no-layoff policy to the workers is nil. This is the same as promising lifetime employment to workers who will be needed for the rest of their working lives.

The following excerpts are of interest, particularly when one realizes that these comments are coming from a workforce that once held the worst performance record in the United States.[5]

EXCERPTS FROM INTERVIEWS WITH TEAM LEADERS

I'll never forget when I was first hired by GM many years ago. The personnel manager who hired us got the workers who were starting that day into a room and explained. "You new employees have been hired in the same way we requisition sandpaper. We'll put you back on the street whenever you aren't needed any more." How the hell can you expect to foster a loyal and productive work force when you start out hearing stuff like that? At NUMMI, the message when we came aboard was "Welcome to the family."

Once you start working as a real team, you're not just work acquaintances anymore. When you really have confidence in your co-workers, you trust them, you're proud of what you can do together, then you become loyal to them. That's what keeps the absenteeism rate so low here. When I wake up in the morning, I know there's no one out there to replace me if I'm feeling sick or hung over or whatever. At NUMMI, I know my team needs me.

We're the ones that make the standardized work and the kaizen suggestions. We run the plant—and if it's not running right, we stop it. We work harder at NUMMI, but I swear it, you go home at the end of the day feeling less tired—and feeling a hell of a lot better about yourself.

There are people here who will tell you they hate this place. All I can say is: actions speak louder than words. If people were disgruntled, there's no way that we'd be building the highest quality vehicle. You wouldn't have a plant that's this clean. You would still have the drug problems we had before. You would still have all the yelling and screaming. You can't force all that.

While Taylor-type standardization and time-motion studies still prevail at NUMMI, such standardization is voluntarily designed and entered into by the workers. What is missing from Taylor in the NUMMI plant can be found in the words of Taylor:[6]

It is only through the *enforced* standardization of methods, *enforced* adoption of the best implements and working conditions and *enforced* co-operation that this faster work can be assured. And the duty of enforcing the adoption of standards and of enforcing this cooperation rests with the *management* alone.

"Enforced cooperation" must qualify as an oxymoron. No wonder workers feel alienated from management and the company under the Taylor system. The psychological assumption underlying this quote is that workers are incapable of finding gratification in work. Consider this from a NUMMI team leader:

Before, when I saw a Chevy truck, I'd chuckle to myself and think, "You deserve that piece of crap if you were stupid enough to buy one." I was ashamed to say that I worked at the Fremont plant. A few weekends ago, I left my business card—the grunts even have business cards—on the windshield of a parked Nova with a note that said, "I helped build this one." I never felt pride in my job before.

STRATEGIC ALLIANCES

The NUMMI plant was a joint venture between GM and Toyota at the time it was organized. Today, it might better be described as a strategic alliance. A strategic alliance is a win-win collaborative effort between two competitors where they hope not only to profit but to learn. NUMMI gave GM the opportunity to observe and learn Japanese management and production techniques. GM incorporated the lessons learned from the NUMMI experience in the Saturn plant. The Saturn plant itself is a learning center to teach the rest of GM about Japanese style-production and management. Thus, the GM side of the win-win arrangement is clear, but what about the Japanese side? After all, Saturn is GM's competitive response to Toyota.

Toyota's aim in entering this arrangement was to learn how to manage a U.S. workforce. From this experience, Toyota opened up transplant factories in the United States. One aim of these transplant factories was to blunt criticism that Japanese automobile companies were robbing U.S. workers of their jobs. The real purpose was to counter an appreciating yen against the U.S. dollar. As the yen appreciated against the dollar, cars made in Japan for yen and sold in the United States for dollars earned less in terms of yen. Profit margins not only declined but could disappear unless the U.S. dollar price was increased, making Toyotas less competitive in the U.S. market. Building Toyotas in the United States would reduce Toyota's exposure to an adverse change in currency exchange rates by matching dollar revenue and dollar costs.

At first, 75 percent of a U.S.-assembled Toyota was built in Japan (primarily motors and transmissions). As Toyota gained experience in managing U.S. workers at its transplant factories, it embarked on a program to have more components manufactured in the United States. This further reduced its exposure to currency exchange risk and lessened the task of moving supplies halfway around the world. By the 1990s about 25 percent of the content of a U.S.-built Toyota was Japanese.

The GM-Toyota joint venture, whether or not called a strategic alliance, has to be considered extremely successful. Both made money, and, more importantly, both learned something that was to have an enormously positive impact on their respective operations. The success of NUMMI and Saturn should eventually spell the doom of the conventional Taylor-run assembly line.

ENDNOTES

1. Norman Bodek, *The Benchmarking Management Guide* (Portland, OR: Productivity Press, 1994).
2. As an example, see Web site: benchmarking.org.
3. Michael Hammer and James Champy, *Reengineering the Corporation: A Manifesto for Business Revolution* (New York: HarperBusiness, 1994).
4. Charles Singer, *History of Technology* (Oxford: Clarendon Press, 1958).
5. Paul S. Adler, "Time and Motion Regained," *Harvard Business Review* (January-February 1993).
6. Frederick W. Taylor, *The Principles of Scientific Management* (Norcross, GA: Institute of Industrial Engineers 1998).

Chapter 4

The World of Quantitative Models

Not all decisions lend themselves to quantitative analysis. Solving an ethical dilemma, selecting an individual for advancement, developing business relationships with clients, and many other facets of business are not quantitative exercises. Nevertheless, many aspects of operations do lend themselves to quantitative models.

The objective of quantitative models is not to make decisions but to improve the quality of decisions. Models are necessary to simplify reality in order to analyze a situation and arrive at a conclusion. In approximating reality, models cannot contain all the elements of reality. Left out are the qualitative or subjective elements. For instance, consider the quantitative model for deciding whether mover A or B should move your household goods. The quantitative model is to compare two bids and select the lesser. Mover A bids $1,200 and mover B bids $1,800—the quantitative solution is to select mover A. How else does one begin the process of selecting a mover without this model?

Having said that, the quantitative solution is not necessarily the final decision. An important element that cannot be quantified has been omitted: the level of service. In investigating both movers, you learn that mover B has a good reputation for service and reliability, whereas mover A is known for breaking everything that hasn't been stolen. Now what is your decision?

The quantitative solution presumed that both movers had comparable levels of performance. On that basis, choosing the lesser-cost mover would be correct. However, a qualitative or subjective evaluation led to the decision in favor of the higher-cost mover. This should demonstrate that a model is only an aid in making decisions. A model can only approximate reality and, therefore, by definition, leaves out important elements, particularly those not amenable to mathematical treatment or quantification.

MANAGEMENT SCIENCE

Management science, sometimes called operations research, is an approach to problem solving beginning with the recognition that there may be a model that can help in arriving at a decision. Model recognition implies that an individual knows about the existence of models for handling a type of problem. Often managers are not aware that a quantitative model exists that can assist them in making decisions; or if aware, they are not prepared to dedicate the time and effort to develop a model. Under these conditions, a decision-maker relies on an intuitive or heuristic approach to problem solving. The human mind can intuitively make good decisions based on past experience. A good dispatcher can ensure that goods and trucks are matched and assigned to routes using experience and rules of thumb to guide decisions. The decisions are probably close to being theoretically optimal. Many companies have been quite successful with limited assistance from models.

Once a model is selected to aid in decision making, it must be constructed in order to generate a solution. The solution should be evaluated as to reasonableness and applicability before being implemented, a somewhat subjective exercise. The final step of this process is rarely accomplished: evaluating the effectiveness of a model. A sufficient passage of time must pass after a decision has been made in order to judge the outcome of the decision. Then the efficacy of the model can be evaluated.

I know of only one occurrence of a model being evaluated after a decision has been made. A major oil company was supposed to make millions of dollars in a new investment but instead lost millions. This spurred an investigation to find out why the outcome was so different from that predicted by the model. The model, in this instance, was a multimedia presentation of charts complete with lights, bells, and whistles. Those watching the media event were so mesmerized by what they saw and heard that they did not realize that an important cost factor had been inadvertently omitted in preparing the charts. The omission in the model transformed a huge loss into a huge profit. Reality transformed the model's huge profit back into a huge loss. Those responsible for creating the media event were summarily fired.

PRODUCTIVITY

Productivity is output divided by input. Output for a steel mill would be tons of steel with an input of capital, labor, and material. Productivity can fall with rising output when input climbs faster than output. Productivity can rise with declining output when input falls faster than output. U.S. productivity has been rising partly as a consequence of declining real wages for the last two or three decades. Thus, for constant output, productivity climbs as labor input falls from lower real wages, eliminating excess layers of managers, removing deadwood from management and worker ranks, and increasing the workload for those remaining.

The U.S. steel industry has made noteworthy improvements in productivity. The most outmoded facilities were shut down, and those remaining were upgraded with the latest steel making technology. Minimills were built using scrap as a raw material rather than iron ore and metallurgical coal. Minimills are simpler in design and more efficient in operation than conventional steel mills, requiring far fewer workers and less energy. Continuous casting was introduced whereby molten steel is poured into molds to manufacture finished steel products without cooling and subsequent reheating–something Ford was doing at the River Rouge plant in the 1920s. Self-managing work teams handle operations inside a steel mill without first-line supervisors. Management layers were trimmed as organizational structures became mean and lean. As a consequence, the labor input for making a ton of steel fell from 12-15 man-hours in the 1970s to 3 man-hours in the 1990s, a tremendous reduction in man-power. U.S. steel prices and quality were competitive in the world market. However, in 1998, as a result of the Asian Contagion and devaluation of currencies, U.S. steel imports surged as affected nations attempted to export their way to recovery by cutting steel prices to boost exports. Nevertheless, the reformation of the U.S. steel industry can be contrasted to the European nationalized steel industry, which remains technologically obsolete, overmanned, and sustained by huge government subsidies–it is ripe for privatization.

Another way to enhance productivity is reducing waste. If the defect rate is 10 percent, and the input is 1,000 units per day, then the output will be 900 units per day. Cutting the defect rate to 1 percent increases the output to 990 units per day with no increase in input.

Productivity Model

A fast-food restaurant has a drive-through window, and during peak lunchtimes, a single employee can handle a maximum of 80 cars per hour in taking and assembling orders, and acting as cashier. The average gross margin is $2.50 per order (revenue less labor and material for preparing the food). Labor costs for handling orders are $5 per hour. A recommendation has been made to add two additional workers, dividing the tasks among them. With the additional workers, 120 cars per hour can be served. From the point of view of productivity, should this recommendation be approved?

The original productivity in serving customers is 80 units of output for 1 unit of labor input or a productivity ratio of 80/1 or 80. After the change, the output is 120 for 3 units of labor or 120/3 or 40. Productivity has fallen in half. The reason for this is that output has expanded 50 percent with a 300 percent increase in labor input. On the basis of the productivity model, the recommendation should be rejected.

Profit Model

The profit model is revenue less costs. Alternatives are weighed in terms of profits, and the one with the highest profit is selected. Referring to the previous problem, 80 cars per hour with a $2.50 gross margin per car generate $200 per hour in gross margin, less $5 per hour in labor to serve the customers or $195 in profits per hour. After adding two more workers, hourly gross margin is 120 cars per hour times $2.50 gross margin or $300 per hour less $15 per hour in customer service labor or $285 in profits per hour. On the basis of the profit model, the recommendation should be accepted.

Lesson

Use the right model! This may sound trite, but it is possible to address a problem with the wrong model and arrive at a wrong decision. Economists use productivity models to compare the respective productivity of, say, steel production in Japan, Europe, and North America. It is not clear to me why the productivity model failed; I do know that the right model for this situation is the profit model, and the correct decision is to add two more workers.

BREAKEVEN MODEL

The breakeven model has many uses in business. Revenue is price times volume or P X V. Total cost is fixed cost, F, plus variable cost, C, times volume, or F + C X V, shown in Fig. 4.1. Variable costs are mostly material and direct (factory) labor costs, expressed in terms of $/unit. Any cost can be treated as a variable cost such as utility and shipping as long as it is expressed as $/unit. If a cost is not variable, then it must be fixed such as financing costs of plant and equipment, insurance, property taxes, office expenses, salaries of executives and those in operations, marketing, accounting, finance, and research and development.

The revenue line is less than the cost line below the breakeven volume, resulting in a loss. Above the breakeven volume, the revenue line is greater than the cost line, resulting in a profit. The breakeven point is the transition from losses to profits. The volume to breakeven (Vbe) can be derived by equating the revenue and total cost lines. The Vbe is the fixed cost divided by the price to sell less the variable cost to make, or F/(P-C). The quantity P-C is called the contribution. Selling a single unit earns P dollars but costs C dollars to make. Thus, selling a single unit nets P-C dollars, which contribute to meeting fixed costs and, after that, contribute to profit.

The breakeven model is handy for determining whether to enter into a new investment. The new investment does not necessarily mean a start-up company. For instance, a book publisher can apply the breakeven model in deciding whether to proceed with a new book. Suppose that the fixed cost of transforming an author's manuscript into something ready for printing is $25,000. The publisher hopes to net $30 per book after author's royalties, unit shipping costs, and retail markups. The cost of printing a single volume in the form of paper, binding, ink, machine time, and labor is $5. The contribution of selling a single volume is $30 in revenue less $5 in variable (printing) costs, or $25. The breakeven volume is 1,000 books. Market research believes that a minimum of 1,500 books can be sold. On the basis of breakeven analysis, the decision is to proceed with the publication of the book since sales are above the breakeven volume.

Figure 4.1
Breakeven Volume

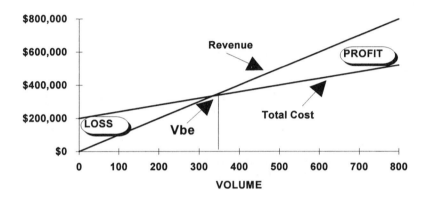

The breakeven model also provides a handy way to estimate profit and loss. All that has to be done is to take the difference between breakeven volume and sales and multiply by the contribution. For sales of 1,500, profits result because sales are above breakeven. The difference between sales and the breakeven volume of 500 books, when multiplied by the contribution of $25, yields a profit of $12,500. If sales were actually 500, then sales are 500 books below breakeven, and the loss would be $12,500.

Suppose that the breakeven model shows a promising outcome. Does that alone finalize a decision to proceed with the publishing of a book? Of course not. On the quantitative side, a publisher may consider the profit too small for the degree of effort. On the qualitative side, a publisher may feel that the book's content does not fit the company's public image. If so, there was no point in performing a breakeven analysis.

BREAKEVEN PROBLEM FOR CAPACITY PLANNING

Fly-High Airways is considering establishing a route between two cities where permission has been obtained for a maximum of five flights per week. Each plane holds 60 passengers. The price of a ticket is anticipated to be $42, and variable costs are $28 per ticket. Variable costs include the operating costs of the aircraft such as crew, fuel, maintenance, landing fees, and so forth. Fixed costs per month of $20,000 include the terminal fees that must be paid regardless of the number of flights and the financing cost of the aircraft. How many passengers are necessary to breakeven?

Fly-High Airways must sell 1,428 tickets per month, $20,000/($42-$28), to cover fixed costs. This is a weekly breakeven volume of 357 tickets. The service is limited to five flights per week, or 71 passengers per flight. Unless Fly-High Airways plans to install seats on the wings or in the baggage compartment, the service should not be inaugurated with a ticket price of $42. This demonstrates the ease and usefulness of the breakeven model to evaluate the feasibility of a new business venture.

In the 1980s People Express Airline was the rage of the business press. It had a unique form of management where everyone was a shareholder and a manager. Stewards and stewardesses, who had no one to manage, were known as service managers. Employees exchanged jobs serving passengers, selling tickets, handling baggage, and performing accounting duties. The airline operated out of North Terminal at Newark Airport. I enjoyed taking my daughter there when she was traveling to and from college. I'd join a massive throng of people slowly circling the terminal listening to endless renditions of "I'll never fly this airline again." Yet every time I went there, the terminal was packed with people moaning and groaning that they'll never fly this airline again.

People Express was a low price, no-frills airline flying in and out of Newark, one of the first, if not the first, to operate a hub system. To breakeven with a low-priced ticket, the airline had to have high load factors, and to do this, it habitually overbooked. Burly men stood by the gate counting those going on board. When the plane was full, they slammed the boarding gate shut, perhaps separating a mother from her screaming kids. Yet despite this abysmal level of service, the flying public flocked to North Terminal. People's fares were so low that the airline bankrupted two bus lines serving the same cities. In fact, People's fares were the same as the bus fares. Why would my daughter want to take a six-hour bus ride when People's would get her there in less than an hour at the same fare?

People Express Airline also had automated ticket sales where a customer talked directly with a computer. The computer did not ask for a particular flight but for an approximate time of departure to a desired city. The computer would respond with a choice of flights close to the desired departure time. Tickets were picked up at North Terminal using the passenger's telephone number for identification. This is how I booked my daughter's flights. I never had to wait for the computer to answer my call.

Yet, despite these innovations, People Express went bankrupt for two principal reasons. One was the decision by the president that there would be no staff positions. Hence, there was no one to do a simple breakeven analysis when starting up a new route. Rather than spend $30,000 for a person to analyze the breakeven volume on new airline routes, People Express lost millions starting up services that could not possibly break even. The second mistake was the acquisition of Frontier Airlines, which flew primarily in and out of Denver. People's idea was to convert Frontier Airlines to a Denver hub system and combine the two airline hubs with interconnecting flights to be able to serve many smaller-sized city combinations such as Richmond, Virginia, to Tacoma, Washington. Here, a passenger would fly from Richmond to Newark, then Newark to Denver, and finally Denver to Tacoma. Flights were frequent and schedules were arranged to minimize layover times. After acquiring Frontier, People' shut it down, stripped away all amenities, slashed fares, and reopened for business. Much to People's surprise and dismay, no passengers showed up at the ticket counters. Had People Express performed a simple market survey of any ten regular Frontier passengers, it would have learned that nine did not like the change in service. They preferred to pay more for a higher level of service. Apparently, Denver passengers were quite unlike Newark passengers. This survey was performed, unfortunately, after the fact, not before. The two mistakes, not using the breakeven model and not doing a simple market survey, in tandem, contributed to the fall of People Express.

LESSON

If a model exists, use it. No matter what its flaws, a model is better than nothing. The breakeven model, in common with all models, does not encompass all of reality. The breakeven model assumes both infinite production capacity and an infinite market. Reality is that both are finite. As a market gets close to saturation, price declines, also not incorporated in the breakeven model. The model presumes that whatever is made is sold (no inventory) and that a company can keep all its profits, which is a sharp departure from reality when one thinks of corporate income taxes. The model presumes that fixed costs remain fixed no matter the level of production. That is not true. As production increases, more marketing and accounting people have to be hired, utility costs of running more machines are higher, and executives may be more generous in giving themselves bonuses. Variable costs also change with production. As production approaches maximum capacity, overtime may be necessary, changing the labor unit cost. Discounts may be available for larger-quantity purchases of materials, changing material unit cost. If production declines, and management is slow in laying off production workers, the total cost line shifts as a supposedly variable cost is partly transformed into a fixed cost. Moreover, the model is severely limited if a company makes more than one product. Yet despite all these weaknesses, the breakeven model is extremely useful. It, along with a simple marketing survey, might have saved People Express.

ANOTHER LESSON

Models are manageable. In the previous example with Fly-High Airlines, the breakeven model showed that $42 was not an adequate fare for the airline to break even. Suppose that management decides to charge $48 per ticket. Now the contribution is $48 less $28 or $20. The $20,000 in fixed costs can be covered with 1,000 tickets per month, 250 per week, 50 tickets per flight. As noted, fixed costs covered the financing costs of the airline. Suppose that an analyst decides to treat financing costs as a variable cost just as crew costs had been treated as a variable cost. The analyst takes the annual financing costs of the aircraft and divides by the number of hours that the aircraft is expected to fly per year to obtain an hourly financing cost. The analyst then multiplies this by the flight time and obtains, for argument's sake, a new variable cost of $34 per passenger. The new contribution is $48 less $34 or $14 per passenger. Just suppose that the monthly fixed cost declines to $15,000 per month after removing the financing cost. The monthly breakeven volume is now $15,000 divided by the contribution of $14, or 1,071 tickets per month, 268 per week, or 54 passengers per flight. The analyst has created two breakeven volumes, 50 or 54 per flight, by treating the financing cost as fixed or variable. Both can be justified. Which one should the analyst use?

The answer may lie in what the analyst has been told. If the manager assigning the analyst this task has verbally, or by body language expressed a desire to "sink this bloody idea," the analyst will be tempted to use the higher breakeven volume. If the manager has expressed a desire to transform Fly-High to the largest airline "west of the Pecos," then the analyst will be tempted to use the lower breakeven volume.

To some extent, the results of any model are manageable. Suppose that a model is being employed to see whether a new factory should be built. Who's to say whether a sales forecast of 3 percent or 4 percent is right or wrong? Yet this assumption may affect a decision whether to build a new plant. Thus, an analyst may be tempted to use the higher growth rate if he or she feels that this is the desired outcome indicated by his or her manager. If an analyst is managing the outcome of a model to tell a manager exactly what he or she wants to hear, then the best thing may be to forgo the cost of having an analyst.

The best way to handle an analyst is not to communicate anything other than the assignment. Then the manager is more assured of getting an unbiased analysis. If the manager does not like the result, the report can always be tossed into the circular file or reworked until it does support a manager's position. However, if this is the manager's response to an unbiased analysis that goes against his or her preconceived notions, then, again, the best thing may be to forgo the cost of having an analyst.

BREAKEVEN PROBLEM FOR PRODUCTION PLANNING

A company makes a single product that is sold for $1,000. You have been hired as a consultant to help management select which alternative course of action the company should take:

1. Reduce fixed costs by $50,000 per month by eliminating certain staff positions in product development.
2. Purchase equipment that will reduce variable costs by 25 percent, but will increase fixed costs, in the form of financing costs, by $60,000 per month.
3. Purchase equipment that will reduce variable costs by 50 percent, but will increase fixed costs, in the form of financing costs, by $120,000 per month.

The chief financial officer provided the data in Table 4.1 for particular months where there was variation in the units produced at the factory. The method about to be presented does not work if production volume remains constant at all times.

Table 4.1
Production Cost Versus Production Volume

MONTH	TOTAL COST	UNITS PRODUCED
2	$375,000	400
7	$300,000	300
10	$400,000	500
12	$450,000	650

What is your recommended course of action if expected production averages 500 units per month? Marketing may land a substantial contract that will increase average monthly production to 800 units. How does this affect your recommended course of action?

ROLE OF THE CONSULTANT

Before attacking this problem, one has to wonder why the company has hired a consultant to perform an analysis that management can just as easily do itself. The reasons for hiring a consultant, who can be viewed as an external analyst, are to:

- obtain an unbiased view of a situation
- present an external view oriented to the outside world rather than an internal view oriented to the inside world of a corporation

- catch errors in the analysis (the aforementioned major oil company's presentation is a case in point)
- provide specific expertise on a temporary basis
- prepare presentations for financial institutions or the board of directors on behalf of management
- conduct due diligence to affirm that a management decision is reasonable and prudent on behalf of lenders or the board of directors
- conduct due diligence to ward off possible future litigation from lenders, shareholders, and other interested parties if the decision turns out to be wrong
- pin the blame on someone else if the decision does turn out wrong (rarely effective; managers normally bear the responsibility for their mistakes, not their consultants)

To do this assignment, a consultant would first have to determine the fixed and variable costs of the company. One way is to examine thousands of individual expenses and determine whether they are fixed or variable. This may take months. An easier way is to plot total cost versus volume and draw the "best-fitting line" through the data. The point where the line crosses the y-axis for zero production is the fixed cost. The slope of the line is the variable cost. The "best-fitting" line is, by definition, the regression equation.

Although "drawing the best-fitting line through the data" is a cumbersome way to describe regression analysis, that is exactly what it is. "Regression analysis" has no inherent meaning. Sir Francis Dalton, cousin to Charles Darwin and originator of regression analysis, was describing how tall parents tend to have shorter children and short parents tend to have taller children. Dalton noted that the height of the children tends to "regress" to the population mean. The use of this term gave birth to "regression analysis" to describe his mathematical approach to determine the best-fitting line through the data.

Regression analysis can be performed on a Microsoft Excel spreadsheet by invoking *TOOLS/DATA ANALYSIS/REGRESSION*. The y-values are what you want to know, and the x-values are what you do know. The objective is to predict total costs knowing production volume. Hence, the y-values are total cost, and the x-values are production volume. The regression equation allows one to substitute in production volume to obtain an estimate of total production costs. Table 4.2 shows the spreadsheet results after entering the appropriate y and x ranges and the cell for printing the output. The y-intercept value is 193224.3 and the coefficient for the x variable is 406.5421. Hence, the fixed cost of the factory is $193,224 and the variable cost to produce a single item is $406.54. The regression equation is Total Cost equals Fixed Cost + Variable Cost X Volume or $193,224 + $406.54 X Volume. If the R square was 1, or 100 percent, then all the data points fall on the regression line. The adjusted R square of 91 percent means that the data points lie close to rather than on the line as illustrated in Fig. 4.2.

Table 4.2
Regression Analysis Spreadsheet Results

Regression Statistics	
Multiple R	0.971173296
R Square	0.94317757
Adjusted R Square	0.914766355
Standard Error	18246.75109
Observations	4
	Coefficients
Intercept	193224.2991
X Variable 1	406.5420561

A high R square does not infer causality. This is a common mistake in employing regression analysis. In this example, the high R square can be expressed as a "high degree of correlation between total production cost and the volume of production." "High degree of correlation" suggests causality, which one expects to exist between production cost and volume. However, high R square can exist between two factors with no causality. Years ago, there was a high degree of correlation between stock market averages and the population of whales. When stock market averages and the population of whales were plotted over a period of time, the data points fell close to a straight line. Does that mean that there was a causal relationship between the two even though one could say, by virtue of there being a high R square, that the two were highly correlated? Of course not. It was just a coincidence that the whale population rose and fell with the Dow Jones average, not causality.

Figure 4.2
Data Points Versus Regression Equation

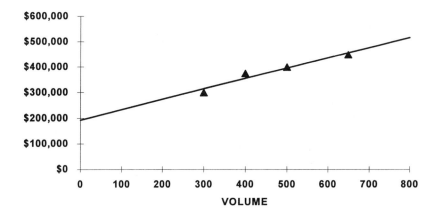

Referring to Table 4.2, the adjusted R square takes into account the amount of data. The greater the amount of data, the closer the adjusted R square is to the R square. The standard error means that one can be 95 percent confident that the actual production cost will lie in the range of the predicted cost plus or minus two standard errors. For a production volume of 500, the predicted production cost is $396,495, obtained by substituting 500 into the regression equation. With a standard error of $18,246 and a predicted value of $396,495, the 95 percent confidence interval for the actual cost is the predicted cost plus or minus 2 X $18,246 or $36,492. Thus one can be 95 percent confident that the actual production cost will fall in the range $360,000 to $433,000.

The higher the R square, the smaller the standard error and the narrower the range of possibilities. Conversely, the lower the R square, the larger the standard error and the wider the range of possibilities. The danger of using regression equations with low R squares is that the barn door of possibilities can open awfully wide. That is why a prediction using the regression equation should be accompanied by the 95 percent confidence interval. A wide range of possibilities should alert the reader not to be too confident in the prediction.

Now that the fixed and variable costs for the existing system (as is) have been assessed through regression analysis, the others are derived in Table 4.3. Alternative 1 has a negative fixed cost increment of $50,000 and the same variable cost. Alternative 2 has a positive fixed cost increment of $60,000 accompanied by a 25 percent reduction in variable cost while alternative 3 has a higher fixed cost increment of $120,000 accompanied by a 50 percent reduction in variable cost.

Table 4.3
Alternative Cost Factors

	As Is	Alternative 1	Alternative 2	Alternative 3
Fixed	$193,224	$143,224	$253,224	$313,224
Variable	$406	$406	$305	$203

Cost curves for each of these alternatives are in Fig. 4.3 along with the revenue line. The respective breakeven points for each alternative are where the revenue line crosses the applicable cost lines. For a factory output of 500 and 800, alternative 1 provides the lowest cost and, hence, the highest profit. However, a consultant in reviewing the quantitative results should query why product development is being cut. Cutting product development is not like cutting the number of newspaper and magazine subscriptions. In a competitive environment, it could be outright disastrous. The breakeven model does not contain that aspect of reality pertaining to the long-term implications of reducing product development. There may be a good reason for cutting product development. On the other hand, it may reflect an internal power struggle where a budget cut signifies the loser. Hidden agendas of managers should play no part in an unbiased consultant's report.

Figure 4.3
Cost Curves

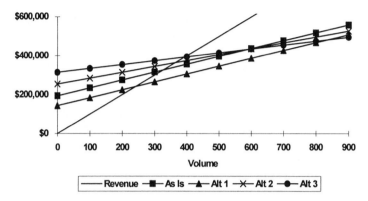

Suppose that alternative 1 is eliminated by the consultant on a purely subjective basis. For a volume of 500, the best recommendation is to do nothing, the clarion call for many managers. For a volume of 800, alternative 3 is best. Alternative 2, a halfway measure, is not the best choice at any production volume. If the company proceeds with alternative 3, and the contract generating sales of 800 units is subsequently lost, and sales revert to 500 units, the company's profit would be about the same as if the company did nothing. However there is greater financial risk with alternative 3 if volume falls below 500 because of its higher breakeven point.

BREAKEVEN MODEL FOR MAKE-OR-BUY DECISIONS

The River Rouge plant symbolized the latest thinking for organizing companies in the 1920s. Vertical integration absorbed a company's suppliers. Today, it is quite the reverse. Companies are identifying what they do best and buying the rest. Core competencies are those activities in a company's operations most responsible for creating profits. Modern thinking is for companies to concentrate scarce managerial, capital, and technical expertise on core competencies. Toyota, for instance, has identified its core competencies as the design, assembly, and marketing of automobiles. Toyota sees no inherent advantage in manufacturing automobile parts. Suppliers can do this as well as Toyota. A comparison of Toyota and GM shows that GM manufactures automobile parts to a much greater extent than Toyota.

Suppose that GM manufactures a certain component and asks a supplier to quote a price. Almost invariably, the quote will be less than GM's cost of manufacture even if the material costs are the same. A supplier can open a factory in a nonunion environment within the United States and have substantially less labor costs than GM who must pay United Automobile

Workers (UAW) pay scales. Labor benefits for the supplier are less than for GM, which is bound by UAW agreements on a benefit package covering medical, vacation, and pension, plus payments to the workers when they strike against GM. GM, like any large company, has a high overhead expense. A supplier focusing on a narrow product line is apt to have a mean and lean organization and, hence, a lower overhead expense. Perhaps, most important of all, the supplier's profit margin will be less than GM's. The combination of lower labor and benefit costs, lower overhead, and a lower profit margin means a substantial savings for GM to contract for automobile parts from external suppliers rather than rely on internal suppliers.

Other benefits accrue from outsourcing. When GM automobile parts plants strike, which they do, they can threaten to shut down GM's assembly plants in about two weeks' time–a good measure of the size of GM's parts inventory. In 1998 a strike by GM plants making automotive components lasted longer than two weeks, shutting down nearly all of GM's assembly lines and costing GM $50 million per day. This gives striking workers a strong bargaining card.

Consider a strike by the workers of a supplier to GM. The workers are not in a position to shut down GM. A supplier's contract is based on performance, and noncompliance can rescind a contract. While it is true that GM must find an alternative supplier once a supplier's contract is rescinded, there is no shortage of suppliers eager to come to GM's aid. Thus, workers for suppliers risk their jobs when they strike. Rarely, if ever, does one hear about strikes at suppliers' plants.

If a manufacturer makes a marginally acceptable batch of parts, the chances are that they will end up in the product. However, if a supplier attempts to foist a marginally acceptable batch of parts on the buyer, the chances are that the parts will be rejected. Hence, a supplier has a greater incentive to ensure high quality because a buyer has a proclivity to apply a higher standard of quality to outside suppliers than to its internal manufacturing organization. The same can be said for product development. An automobile company does invest a great deal of effort in product development for the automobile itself, but perhaps not for a particular part. An outside supplier, where a particular part is most of its business, has a greater incentive to spend money on product development than the buyer. Investing in product development is not done to keep the buyer satisfied as much as to ward off a potential competitor from improving the product and taking over the contract.

MAKE-OR-BUY BREAKEVEN PROBLEM

ABC Electronics is a successful small firm that has carved out a profitable niche in the electronic office products market. The production of a new line of calculators is being planned. As the firm's purchasing director, you have been asked to investigate the possibility of subcontracting a plug-in recharging unit for the new line of calculators or building the units within the firm. While the president was very enthusiastic about the prospects for this product, the marketing manager was rather uncommitted, "guestimating" that sales would be about 100,000 per year for three years if the product was well received.

The shop manager estimated that the new equipment to be purchased for the recharging units would cost $72,000 and have a 12-year physical life. However, the equipment can make only 80,000 recharging units per year. The space being set aside for production of the recharging units will require $12,000 in setup costs for running new electrical cables and installing the equipment. The controller mentioned in passing that the equipment could be written off in 7 years for tax purposes. The production manager and the controller provided the variable costs in Table 4.4.

Table 4.4
$/Unit Costs

	$/Unit
Direct labor	$1.70
Direct materials	2.80
Factory overhead	1.87
General & Administrative (G&A)	0.64
Total	$7.01

The controller told you that she estimated that factory overhead was 30 percent variable and 70 percent fixed. You asked about G&A being treated as a variable cost, and she stared at you. Meanwhile, you submitted the specifications for the recharging units to three suppliers. The best response was from Dover Manufacturing, eager to become a single-source supplier. Dover Manufacturing quoted $7.45 for order quantities up to 50,000, $7.12 for order quantities between 50,000 and 100,000, and $7.05 for order quantities of 100,000 or more. Subsequent orders for each 100,000 units would include the benefits of a 95 percent learning curve.

A number of approaches would result in somewhat different results, and possibly, conclusions. For instance, the cost factors could be treated as variable as presented, or $7.01 per unit. The decision based on simply using the cost figures would be to make the recharging units, as this is lower than the $7.05 offered by Dover Manufacturing.

This would be an incomplete analysis as it does not contain the investment in equipment and the benefit of the learning curve. The investment in equipment is a fixed expense. G&A expenses are also fixed in that they represent corporate overhead in the form of salaries for executives, operations, marketing and finance personnel, product research and development, home office expenses, interest, and others. This can be transformed into a fixed cost for a production level of 80,000 recharging units by multiplying 80,000 units by $0.64/unit, or $51,200.

In the same light, factory overhead is largely fixed, consisting of the cost of the factory in terms of depreciation or financing costs, property taxes, insurance, supervisory personnel, and the fixed portion of utilities, maintenance and repair, and others. Variable costs would be the variable portion of utilities and maintenance and repair plus other expenses that vary with production. Thus, 70 percent of factory overhead can be converted to fixed by 0.7 multiplied by $1.87/unit and 80,000 units, or $104,700. Another component is the write-off of the equipment. The write-off period could be the physical (12 years) or tax life (7 years), which for $72,000 in equipment cost, could be either $6,000 or $10,300 per year.

The selection of the write-off period for the equipment is an opportunity to manage the outcome of a quantitative analysis. If you are eager to manufacture the recharging unit, the analyst will be tempted to write-off the equipment over its physical life and provide you with a lower breakeven volume. If you prefer to outsource, the analyst will be tempted to write-off the equipment over its tax life and provide you with a higher breakeven volume. A sharp analyst can make a convincing argument for either case for writing-off the equipment, giving you a solution that nicely fits your preconceived notions.

While selecting the write-off period on the basis of tax considerations is common, one can argue that the U.S. tax code is the last thing that should be used in making a business decision. The purpose of the tax code is to prepare a tax bill, not to make a business decision. Neither should the physical life be used if there is a good chance that the equipment will become obsolete over its physical lifetime. Thus, the most appropriate write-off period is the economic life of an asset. It is possible for the economic and physical life to be the same, but not often in this modern age of technological change. Changes in the market or technology can make a piece of equipment obsolete long before age has taken its toll. How many personal computers are replaced because they are physically worn out versus becoming technologically obsolete?

While Dover Manufacturing could write off the equipment over its anticipated physical life since it is in the business of making recharging units, ABC Electronics should write off the asset over the anticipated economic life of the new calculators, which is only three years. Besides the cost of setting up the equipment, setup costs may also include running electrical cables, installing air-conditioning, moving walls, if necessary, plus the costs of hiring and training personnel. Setup costs are normally written off over the same period as the equipment. Thus, the annual fixed cost of writing off the equipment ($72,000) and setup costs ($12,000) over the three-year economic life is $28,000 per year. Hence the total fixed cost for making the recharging units is $183,900.

Variable costs are labor and material and the remaining 30 percent of factory overhead, or $5.06. This holds up to 80,000 units, the maximum capacity of the equipment for manufacturing recharging units. Between 80,000 units and 130,000 units, the variable cost is $7.45 per unit, as these must be purchased from Dover Manufacturing. From 130,000 to 180,000, the variable cost is $7.12 to reflect the volume purchase discount offered by Dover Manufacturing. Above 180,000, the variable cost is $7.05. The make curve is the sum of the fixed cost of $183,900 and the applicable variable cost for a given volume.

The buy curve is simply purchasing all the recharging units from Dover Manufacturing. Dover Manufacturing is willing to pass on to ABC Electronics the benefit of a 95 percent learning curve if Dover becomes the sole supplier for the recharging units. The learning curve can be explained by examining the cost of building a house. Suppose that a house is built for $100,000, and another buyer asks the builder to construct a second house with the same design. How much would the second house cost in relation to the first? Unless the builder faithfully replicated all errors made in building the first house, the cost should be less. For a 95 percent learning curve, the cost would be $95,000 as the builder eliminates the most costly errors made in building the first house. If the builder received a contract for a third house of the same design, the elimination of the next-tier of errors should reduce the cost of the house to 95 percent of $95,000 or $90,250. The degree of savings declines as succeeding houses are built; from $5,000 between the first and second houses to $4,750 between the second and third houses, and so forth, as the more costly errors are eliminated, and the building of each succeeding house becomes more routine. Some feel that the learning curve continues indefinitely; others feel that there is a practical limit to the life of a learning curve. For example, after building five or six houses, the process may become so routine that further savings are minuscule.

For purchasing recharging units in multiples of 100,000, the first 100,000 is $7.05, the second is 95 percent of $7.05 or $6.70, and the third is 95 percent of $6.70 or $6.36. The lowering of price from the benefits of the learning curve appears like a price discount for volume purchases. This is not true because a price discount for greater-volume purchases may not impact production costs. If so, then a price discount reduces profit margins. Passing on the benefits of the learning curve may not affect profitability. If the manufacturer actually experiences a 90 percent learning curve, profitability climbs as the savings from a presumed 95 percent learning curve are passed to the buyer.

The make-and-buy lines in Fig. 4.4 do not have a breakeven point. There is a near point of equivalence around 80,000 to 90,000 units. The make line does not become less costly than the buy line because of the maximum limit of 80,000 units in making recharging units internally. After 80,000 units, higher-priced Dover Manufacturing recharging units have to be purchased. At some point, a second system could be set up to make another 80,000 units, but this has been excluded from the model since it is anticipated that sales will be around 100,000 units.

The make curve can be managed to some extent by the selection of the appropriate write-off period for the equipment and in the nature of the calculations for the fixed and variable costs. Even so, three costs have been neglected in analyzing the make curve. One is the cost of quality. If Dover Manufacturing shipped a below-quality shipment of recharging units, it would be returned by ABC Electronics at no cost to itself. If ABC Electronics were to make the same below-quality batch, the cost of disposing of the bad recharging units and manufacturing replacement units would have to be borne by ABC Electronics.

Figure 4.4
Make-and-Buy Curves

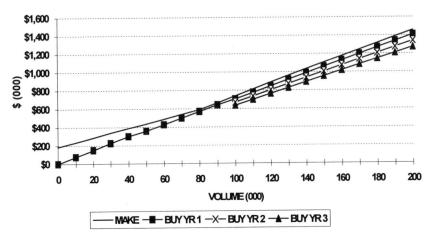

The second cost that has been left out is product development for the recharging units. Dover Manufacturing has an incentive to invest in product development to thwart competitors from taking away its contract with ABC Electronics. ABC Electronics, on the other hand, may be tempted to emphasize product development for the calculator, not necessarily the recharging unit. If so, then ABC Electronics risks building calculators with technologically outmoded recharging units at some point in the future. The third omitted cost is the additional drain on management resources in manufacturing recharging units internally rather than monitoring incoming shipments and maintaining liaison with an external supplier. These costs are often left out because they are difficult to quantify. One way to handle difficult-to-quantify costs is to ignore them. Cost accountants have a habit of doing this. Another important nonquantifiable aspect of the make-or-buy decision is judging Dover Manufacturing's reliability to honor its commitment.

Even if the economic analysis strongly supports making the recharging units, there is a strong counterargument not to make recharging units at this time. That argument is not quantitative but subjective–the management of financial risk. At this point, prospects for the new calculator are problematic, with the marketing manager displaying a distinct lack of enthusiasm. If the market does not develop for the new calculators, then all one has accomplished in setting up a manufacturing facility for the recharging units is to increase the loss by $84,000. From the point of view of managing financial risk, the analysis for internally manufacturing the recharging units is premature. It should be deferred until the new calculators have been successfully marketed. Then it would be appropriate to analyze whether it is better to make, or continue to buy, the recharging units.

LOCATION PLANNING

In the 1920s the Model T was assembled in the River Rouge plant, where most of the parts and components were manufactured. In the 1980s the Ford Escort was assembled with parts from thousands of suppliers located in 40 different nations. Clearly, production has been globalized, stemming from the:

- acceptance of common political (multiparty democracy) and economic (variations of Adam Smith) systems throughout the industrialized world,
- economic integration of entire regions in Europe, North America, South America, and Asia where national borders are increasingly transparent to the movement of goods,
- acceptance of English as a global language of business,
- acceptance of the dollar and possibly the European common currency, the euro, as a global currency,
- development of global banking by setting up bank branches and merging banks across national borders to ease handling the financial aspects of international trade,
- development of global communications for voice and global telecommunications for data, and
- development of a global logistics system.

Newly emerging nations, nations shaking off military dictatorships, and ex-communist nations commonly use the U.S. Constitution as a starting point for organizing a new political system. The U.S. Constitution comes from the British parliamentary system, whose roots can be traced back to the Roman Republic. Acceptance of a common political system fosters economic integration. Borders are increasingly transparent for the movement of goods, not necessarily people. North America is being integrated into a single trade bloc. Central America is a single trade bloc, and South America is divided into two trade blocs. Efforts are under way to unite these four trade blocs creating a single trade bloc for the entire Western Hemisphere.

Europe has made enormous progress in becoming a single trade bloc, nearly achieving the "United States of Europe." Several East European nations (Poland, Czech Republic, Hungary) want to become full members of the European Union, which could, conceivably, lead to Russia's application for membership. There is talk of the European Union and North America (NAFTA) joining together. Were all these to happen, most nations of the Northern and Western Hemispheres would have transparent borders for the movement of goods. Asia and Africa are developing their trade blocs. One only has to scan the newspapers to sense the general trend to a single global trade bloc.

Globalization of production is aided by the acceptance of English as the language of business and the existence of readily convertible hard currencies led by the U.S. dollar and others. Global banks are created by merging banks from different nations and by opening branch offices throughout the world. Global banks make it easier for clients to conduct international business by being connected to a common global telecommunication system for currency conversion and monetary transfers. A global communication system allows businesspeople to conduct business between any two locations on earth.

GLOBAL LOGISTICS

The movie *On the Waterfront*, starring Marlon Brando, depicted the old way of handling international trade. One hundred tons of cargo were moved between ship and shore a day by a gang of 30 stevedores in the ship and a gang of 30 longshoremen on the dock. The labor content of moving cargo from a factory to a ship entailed:

- loading a truck at a factory to move the cargo to a terminal warehouse,
- unloading the truck at the terminal warehouse and stacking the cargo until the ship arrived,
- when the ship arrived, loading the cargo on a small truck to take alongside the ship,
- unloading the cargo and stacking it on the wharf,
- loading the cargo into a cargo net and swinging it into the ship's cargo spaces,
- unloading the cargo net and stacking the cargo securely within the ship, and
- repeating the preceding process at the destination port.

On the Waterfront captures the essence of this labor-intensive, multistep process to move goods between two points on this earth. At each step, there is a chance of damage from physical handling and pilferage, vividly depicted in the movie. The cost of moving goods around the world was expensive and, therefore, an impediment to the growth of international trade and the globalization of production. Malcolm McLean, owner of a trucking firm, inaugurated the age of containerization, where goods are packed in a container, normally 8' by 8' by 40', and then the container is shipped as a unit. A container can be moved from one mode of transport to another in about 30 seconds of a crane operator's time. A container can hold up to 30 tons of goods. For fully loaded containers in terms of weight, one crane operator can do in 90 seconds what 60 men could do in a day. Before containerization, dockside labor manually handled cargo a dozen or more times. After containerization, the contents of a container are handled only twice: once to load at the source and once to unload at the final destination. Thus containerization reduced labor requirements by over 90 percent by virtually eliminating the need for dockside labor. Since the container itself protects cargo from damage and pilferage, these costs were also drastically reduced.

The ease and low cost of moving containers between modes of transport (truck, rail, vessel and to a lesser extent, barge and aircraft) have brought about the age of intermodalism. Intermodalism is basically the worldwide integration of various modes of transport to provide a relatively seamless movement of containers between sellers and buyers. Moreover, the ease of switching from one mode of transport to another opens up a plethora of alternatives for shippers. For instance, consider the choice of routes for moving a container from Japan to Cleveland. The container is first loaded at a factory and moved by truck or rail to a Japanese port and loaded on a container vessel. From there, the container vessel may unload the container at three different North American West Coast ports for unit train service across the continent. Unit trains are dedicated to perform a single service, in this case, providing transcontinental transportation for containers. At any point near Cleveland, the container can be switched to a truck to complete the movement. The container vessel may transit the Panama Canal and the container transferred to a barge at New Orleans and be towed up the Mississippi and Ohio Rivers to Cleveland. More commonly, the container vessel unloads the container at any East Coast port from Savannah to New York for completing the final leg by either truck or train or a combination of both.

Consider the choices for shippers in moving a container from Japan to Europe. The container vessel may unload the container at Vladivostok, the eastern terminus of the TransSiberian Railroad for direct service to Vienna. This is known as the Russian land bridge connecting Asia and Europe. From Vienna, the container is shipped to its final destination by barge on the Danube or by rail or truck or a combination of both. Alternatively, the container vessel may pass through the Suez Canal and unload the container at a Mediterranean or Northern European port for barge or truck or rail transport to its final destination. Lastly, the container may be shipped from Japan across the Pacific to a West Coast port in North America, then across the American land bridge by rail, and then by vessel across the Atlantic to Europe.

This profusion of routes connecting the principal trading areas, made possible through containerization and intermodalism, provides a shipper with many choices of carriers as different routes are served by different carriers. Competition among carriers for a shipper's business is fierce and has lowered the cost of moving containers considerably. In addition, the development of ever-larger-sized container vessels, now approaching 8,000 containers per vessel, has reduced the seaborne cost of moving containers. Inaugurating around the world service along with container lines entering into strategic alliances provide a better performing and more economical service for shippers. A global telecommunication system keeps track of millions of containers scattered throughout the earth as they are picked up from shippers, shift among carriers and modes of transport, cross national borders, and are finally delivered to their destinations.

All this has significantly lowered the cost of moving goods. Semifinished or finished goods can move halfway around the world for 2 percent to 5 percent of their value. Thus, any place in the world that offers cost savings of just a few percentage points of the manufactured value of goods to cover the extra shipping costs can be considered as a potential site for a new factory. Thus, one can build a factory just about anywhere. That's why the Ford Escort is assembled from parts made in 40 different nations.

LOCATION PLANNING IN THE UNITED STATES

A common operations problem is the decision whether to locate a factory in, say, New Jersey or Arkansas. On the surface, this appears to be primarily a quantitative exercise. Costs are first obtained, aggregated, then compared between the two locations. The site with the lesser aggregate cost wins.

In actuality, qualitative factors have to be taken into account. While labor cost is certainly a consideration, what about labor availability and skills? Would one locate a factory in a location just because labor is cheap but where there are no available workers with the requisite skills? This is a primarily qualitative or subjective judgment. Even if both locations had the requisite skills, the location with the lower cost labor may not be the best. One firm I visited bemoaned building a new plant in the South rather than expanding their plant in the North. True, labor rates were lower in the South, but so was worker productivity. The high labor-cost plant in the North turned out to be more profitable.

Table 4.5 is a listing of factors to be considered in siting a new factory in the United States. The table illustrates the relative number of qualitative to quantitative factors.

Table 4.5
Listing of Factors

ITEM	QUANTITATIVE	QUALITATIVE
Labor		
Cost	X	
Availability		X
Skills		X
Material		
Cost	X	
Availability		X
Shipping In & Out		
Cost	X	
Availability of transport		X
Utilities & Communication		
Cost	X	
Availability		X
Factory cost	X	
Permitting process		X
Environmental regulations		X
Desirability for living		X
Local acceptance		X
Property taxes	X	X
Grants and aid	X	X

Property taxes might be considered purely quantitative in the sense of comparing taxes in two locations. But property taxes are actually agreed to before a factory is built. A company can negotiate property taxes with several towns prior to selecting the final site for a new factory. Negotiations are essentially a qualitative exercise. The same is true for state grants and aid. The quantitative aspect is comparing grants and aid packages from different states; the qualitative aspect is negotiating the final terms.

Saturn Corporation Selection of Tennessee

The reasons given for Saturn's selecting Tennessee, taken from company literature, illustrate the importance of qualitative over quantification considerations. Outside of the first item, the remaining are primary subjective in nature.

- Tennessee is within 600 miles of 65 percent of nation's population.
- Good connections to interstate highway system and an existing railroad connection for transport of materials and supplies into the plant and shipment of cars out of plant.
- Adequate water, sewer, electricity, and natural gas utility services at site.
- Able to purchase the necessary land at reasonable prices.
- The topography of the site was conducive for building a large plant. The rolling hills served to "hide" the plant to fulfill Saturn's promise to the local community to maintain rural aesthetics.
- Local weather was comfortable for workers and conducive to just-in-time delivery.
- Local people were supportive of the new plant, and there were an adequate number of potential workers.
- Good social services with respect to schools, medical care, and general services such as shopping malls were available nearby.
- A variety of lifestyles were available for the workers from rural living to city living (Nashville).
- A favorable business climate was created by state and county governments eager to expand their industrial base.

Expanding on the latter point, state, county and local governments worked with Saturn to induce the company to build in their area. This included $30 million of state funding for connector roads into the interstate highways, $22 million for training Saturn employees, and a county agreement not to tax Saturn for 40 years. In return, Saturn provided funds for community growth including $1.25 million for a new city hall and a donation of 50 acres of land for a new high school—not a bad bargain. This is not to say that there was no role quantitative analysis. A great deal of number-pushing entered into the decision. Yet when the principal reasons for the decision are revealed by the company, the qualitative factors seem to overwhelm the quantitative factors. The following exercise on location breakeven shows that making a decision purely on quantitative factors leaves much to be desired.

BREAKEVEN METHOD FOR SITE SELECTION

You have been assigned to make a recommendation about whether the new factory should be located in New Jersey or Arkansas. Average production is estimated to be 60,000 units per year. Estimations for various cost factors were obtained for full production at 100,000 units per year as a result of a yearlong study conducted by someone else. The controller divided these estimates into fixed and variable costs shown in Table 4.6.

Table 4.6
Cost Factors for New Jersey and Arkansas

	FIXED	VARIABLE	COST (NJ)	COST (ARK)
Financing of Building and Equipment	100%	0%	$1,610,000	$730,000
Property taxes	100%	0%	$850,000	$150,000
Insurance	100%	0%	$100,000	$100,000
Overhead staff	90%	10%	$650,000	$700,000
Utilities	30%	70%	$340,000	$250,000
Maintenance staff	50%	50%	$215,000	$300,000
Repair	20%	80%	$300,000	$300,000
Product Development	80%	20%	$150,000	$170,000
Material	0%	100%	$2,090,000	$3,500,000
Direct Labor	10%	90%	$2,180,000	$1,900,000
Shipping in and out	0%	100%	$540,000	$1,620,000

As an aside, the 90 percent allocation of direct labor as variable implies a hire-and-fire policy as production volume changes, the traditional U.S. approach to factory labor. Many firms in the United States and certainly nearly all firms in Japan would switch these values to 90 percent fixed and 10 percent variable. Promising steady employment is a sine non qua for gaining worker cooperation.

Anyway, the fixed and variable costs can be calculated by totaling the respective portions of fixed and variable costs at full production and dividing total variable costs by 100,000 as contained in Table 4.7.

Table 4.7
Fixed and Variable Costs

Costs	New Jersey	Arkansas
Fixed	$3,753,000	$2,221,000
Variable	$52.73	$74.99

The chart of these two locations in Fig. 4.5 shows that below the breakeven volume of about 68,000 units per year, the preferred location is Arkansas.

Figure 4.5
Location Breakeven

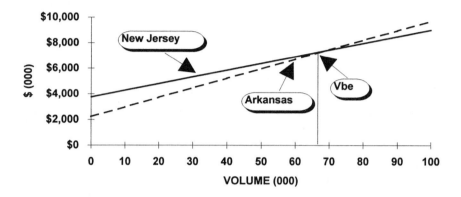

For a planned production level of 60,000 units per year, the best site is Arkansas. However, would this be the final recommendation? The quantitative solution does not contain a single qualitative factor listed in Table 4.5. For instance, in New Jersey the permitting process is highly time-consuming compared to states in the South. There, one permit satisfies all levels of government (local, county, state), quite unlike New Jersey, where each level of government has a separate permitting process. How does one deal with the impact of three years to overcome legal permitting hurdles in New Jersey versus six months in the South? Or does one simply dismiss New Jersey as a place to build a new factory regardless of the quantitative results?

There is something else that should be questioned and that is the conclusion of the quantitative analysis itself. Despite the results of the location breakeven model, no practical-minded businessperson would build a factory in Arkansas where variable costs are nearly 50 percent higher than in New Jersey. Why build a factory where the variable cost is $75 per unit when a factory could be built elsewhere for a variable cost of $53? The material and shipping costs are significantly higher in Arkansas than in New Jersey. This suggests that the material consumed in the finished product is not as available in Arkansas as in New Jersey and that the market for the product is in the Northeast. If this is so, why build a plant in Arkansas?

Yet, the results of the quantitative analysis point to Arkansas. The reason is the significant difference in fixed costs. In examining the figures in Table 4.6, most of the difference is in annual financing costs and property taxes. The value of a factory is mainly its machinery and equipment, not the building. While a building can be more cheaply built in the South, the machinery and equipment cost would be essentially the same at both locations. The difference in factory costs between the two locations would hardly amount to 10 to 20 percent. Obviously, there is a major difference in the way the factory is being financed. Perhaps, Arkansas is offering long-term financing at a low interest rate to attract business, whereas the factory in New Jersey is financed on a short-term basis at a higher interest rate. In addition, the respective property taxes are out of line. The higher New Jersey property tax presumes a particular town. Perhaps it is appropriate to visit other towns in New Jersey and negotiate a lower property tax with the local tax authorities. There are several depressed urban areas in New Jersey where local property taxes are virtually nil to attract industrial development.

In examining this situation, it's not the qualitative factors that are of concern, but the quantitative analysis itself. An analyst has to learn to critically view data. Blind acceptance of data, even with an appropriate model, can lead to an erroneous or misleading conclusion. In this example the variable costs point to New Jersey, and the fixed costs suggest that an analyst's time would be better spent revisiting the cost estimates on financing the factory and property taxes than in conducting a breakeven analysis.

So far, the location breakeven model has been confined to the United States. The following is a listing of other factors that have to be considered for an overseas site in addition to those already mentioned for a domestic site. There is no point in differentiating between quantitative and qualitative, as most are qualitative matters or issues.

- Different legal, accounting, and tax systems
- Different language and work culture
- Different market culture
- Currency exchange rate risk
- Restrictions on hard currency remittances
- Import/export restrictions on importing components and exporting finished goods
- State of the utility, communication, and logistics infrastructure
- Political risk
- Graft and corruption

If the factory is built in a hard-currency nation, the financial risk of an adverse change in currency exchange rates can transform a profit in the domestic currency into a loss in the home currency. If the factory is built in a soft-currency nation, careful planning has to be conducted to ensure that a company's return on its investment is something other than a truckload of nonconvertible soft currency of dubious value. There would be no currency exchange risk or a risk of accumulating a soft currency if the factory were built in Ohio.

Political risk can be envisioned in building a factory in Iran during the shah's reign. Further suppose that the plant requires the import of a vital component from the United States. A contract has to be negotiated with a government agency stipulating the terms and conditions of the factory's operation in Iran before it can be built. After the factory is built and in operation, the shah fell from power. What is the value of the contract signed by his government? The factory cannot continue to operate if the contractual arrangements are no longer honored. The factory may become an easy target for anti-American sentiment. The workers may be too scared to come to work, or if they did, they may not be sympathetic to the company's objectives. Even if the factory continued to operate under the new Iranian government, the U.S. government, upset over Iranian foreign policy, eventually instituted a ban on all exports from the United States to Iran. Where would the vital component come from? None of these political risks would exist if the factory were built in Ohio.

Graft and corruption are universal, but in some nations, it is endemic. Graft and corruption are normally glibly dismissed as something that has to be done if a businessperson wants to conduct business. A U.S. citizen participating in acceptable and legal business practices in foreign nations can still be prosecuted under the U.S. Foreign Corrupt Practices Act if those actions violate the provisions of the act. Disregarding this, there are major practical issues arising when one engages in graft and corruption. For instance, how do you know the proper amount of a bribe? Isn't it foolish to offer $50,000 when the individual would have accepted $500? How do you know if you are bribing the right person? One company was declared persona non grata when a superior discovered that an underling was being bribed. The superior was extremely upset over the company's bribing his underling. It should have bribed him. Even if a company thinks that all is well with its investments because it has made the right bribe to the right person, there is still the risk of discovery and its consequences.

Taking these factors into consideration, starting an operation overseas must take many times the effort of simply staying within the United States. One may wonder why companies are so eager to expand overseas. The basic reasons are simple: the United States represents about 5 percent of the world's population and about one-third of the world's purchasing power. Expanding operations overseas multiplies the market in terms of potential consumers 20 times over, and in terms of purchasing power, 3 times over. Moreover, one defense against overseas competition in a company's home market is competing against a competitor in his or her home market. The annual reports of many major U.S. companies list over one hundred subsidiaries in different nations. Companies really have little choice as they must conduct business on a global scale to ensure their survival.

OTHER LOCATION MODELS

In addition to the location breakeven model, three others are to be examined. These models can be used to locate either a factory to serve warehouses, or warehouses to serve consuming centers. The first is the center-of-gravity method, the second utilizes What's Best linear programming, and the third Evolver optimization.

Center of Gravity

The center-of-gravity method takes into account both distance from the warehouse to consuming centers and the volume. The distance here is measured from an arbitrary origin where the locations of the warehouse and the consuming centers are expressed in miles east and north of the origin for positive values. The volume can be in tons, number of packages, number of truckloads or containers, or any other measure. The formulas for calculating the weighted average distance X volume location for a new warehouse are shown in Fig. 4.6.

Figure 4.6
Center of Gravity

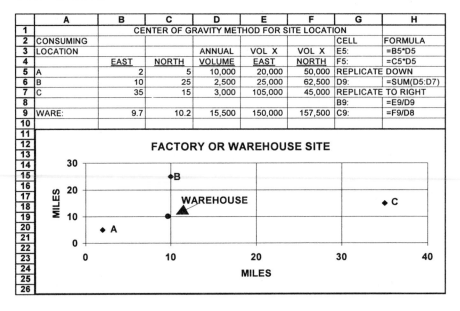

	A	B	C	D	E	F	G	H
1			CENTER OF GRAVITY METHOD FOR SITE LOCATION					
2	CONSUMING				ANNUAL	VOL X	VOL X	CELL	FORMULA
3	LOCATION							E5:	=B5*D5
4		EAST	NORTH	VOLUME	EAST	NORTH	F5:	=C5*D5
5	A	2	5	10,000	20,000	50,000	REPLICATE DOWN	
6	B	10	25	2,500	25,000	62,500	D9:	=SUM(D5:D7)
7	C	35	15	3,000	105,000	45,000	REPLICATE TO RIGHT	
8							B9:	=E9/D9
9	WARE:	9.7	10.2	15,500	150,000	157,500	C9:	=F9/D8

The site is not the geographic center of the consuming centers unless each consuming center is receiving the same volume of shipments. For instance, if the volume from the warehouse to consuming center A is 1,000 units and 10 units to consuming centers B and C, then, to minimize shipping costs, the location of the warehouse would be very close to consuming center A.

There are two qualitative factors to consider. The first is the volume of shipments from the warehouse to the consuming centers. Are these values historical, current, or projected? Since they are being used to build a warehouse that can last for 20 or more years, the figures should be the average future volume expected to be shipped from the warehouse to the consuming centers. The second consideration is the site itself. The calculations place the warehouse to the 15th decimal point of accuracy. But is that all there is? Some years ago, a company entered into a contract for a consulting firm to determine the best site of a centralized warehouse to serve its customers. The calculations were done in terms of latitude and longitude. Finally, a hefty report was sent to the client accompanied by an equally hefty invoice. The client was curious about the actual location depicted in latitude and longitude and got hold of a map. The location turned out to be the middle of Lake Superior. What would you do with the report and its invoice?

Linear Programming with What's Best

Linear programming uses the Simplex method for solving a system of linear equations. The Simplex method, which the author considers somewhat complex, was created during World War II to solve a problem for which there was no heuristic solution. How many destroyers should be assigned to a convoy crossing the Atlantic for best protection against Nazi submarines? The admirals at the time had no answer because they had no experience to draw upon. The Operations Research division of the U.S. Navy undertook this problem by creating a mathematical model of linear equations. The objective was to minimize damage by adjusting the number of destroyers with a constraint on the availability of destroyers. This is the origin of the term "operations research" commonly used interchangeably with "management science."

Linear programming requires three steps:

1. identification of an objective cell to be either maximized or minimized,
2. identification of adjustable cells whose values affect the objective cell, and
3. construction of constraints.

The classic linear programming problem is Redwood Furniture, which makes two products, tables and chairs. The tables generate eight dollars in gross margin (revenue less variable costs) and consume 30 board feet of lumber, and 5 hours of labor. The chairs generate six dollars in gross margin and consume 20 board feet of lumber and 10 hours of labor. How many tables and chairs should be made to maximize profits?

In Fig. 4.7, cells F4 and F5 are adjusted in order to generate the profit shown in cell F7. Thus the former are designated as adjustable cells and the latter as the objective cell to be maximized. The solution at this point is to make an infinite number of tables and chairs. But there are constraints in the form of available material and labor; machine availability is usually another common constraint.

Material and labor constrain the output of tables and chairs since resources consumed cannot exceed their availability. Constraints in What's Best linear programming software[1] can be placed directly on the spreadsheet as shown in cells F14 and F21. This is a major difference between What's Best and Microsoft Excel Solver. Moreover, formulas can be embedded in the constraint. For instance, the constraint in cell F14 that the amount of lumber consumed cannot exceed the amount available could have been written as =WB((C17*F4+C18*F5), "<",F20).

Figure 4.7
Redwood Furniture

	A	B	C	D	E	F
1	REDWOOD FURNITURE					
2			PROFIT			
3			MARGIN			
4			$ 8	# OF TABLES		4
5			$ 6	# OF CHAIRS		9
6						
7	CELL F7:	=C4*F4+C5*F5		PROFIT:		86
8						
9			LUMBER			
10			30	PER TABLE		
11			20	PER CHAIR		
12	CELL F12:	=C10*F4+C11*F5		USED:		300
13				AVAILABLE:		300
14	CELL F14:	=WB(F12,"<",F13)				=<=
15						
16			LABOR			
17			5	PER TABLE		
18			10	PER CHAIR		
19	CELL F19:	=C17*F4+C18*F5		USED:		110
20				AVAILABLE:		150
21	CELL F21:	=WB(F19,"<",F20)				<=

The solution in Figure 4.7 is to make 4 tables and 9 chairs. All the lumber, but not all the labor hours have been consumed. Thus there is value in having more lumber, but not in having more labor. The dual value for lumber (not shown) is the incremental change to profit of having one more unit of lumber. The dual value for labor is zero because there is no point in having another unit of a resource already in excess. The upper limit for the dual value for lumber occurs when enough lumber has been added to absorb the slack in labor.

Designing a Two Warehouse System with What's Best

Suppose that it is desired to site two warehouses amid a group of consuming centers. The spreadsheet in Fig. 4.8 contains the location of the consuming centers, and the yet unknown location of the two warehouses in adjustable cells B4:C5 referenced to an arbitrary origin. These cells will be adjusted to select a location that minimizes total shipping costs.

Figure 4.8
Warehouse Location Using What's Best Software (A)

	A	B	C	D	E	F	G
1	SELECTING TWO WAREHOUSES						
2							
3	W.H.	X	Y		SHIPPING IN:	$ -	
4	#1	0.0	0.0		SHIPPING OUT:	$ -	
5	#2	0.0	0.0		TOTAL:	$ -	
6							
7				CELL E11:	=C11*D11		
8	COORDINATES				VOLUME	DISTANCE	
9	CONSUMING CENTERS			YES/NO	TO	W.H.#1	
10	X	Y	VOLUME	W.H. #1	W.H.#1	E-W	N-S
11	1	3	100	1	100	0	0
12	2	4	200	1	200	0	0
13	3	7	500	1	500	0	0
14	4	13	200	1	200	0	0
15	5	12	300	1	300	0	0
16	6	10	400	1	400	0	0
17	7	6	1000	1	1000	0	0
18	8	12	500	1	500	0	0
19	9	9	200	1	200	0	0
20	10	10	100	1	100	0	0
21	11	13	300	1	300	0	0
22	12	14	400	1	400	0	0
23	13	20	200	1	200	0	0
24	14	22	200	1	200	0	0
25	15	24	100	1	100	0	0
26							
27				VOLUME X DIST:		-	-
28			CELL F27:	=SUMPRODUCT($E11:$E25,F11:F25)			
29			CELL G27:	=SUMPRODUCT($E11:$E25,G11:G25)			

The shipping-in cost is the cost of large truckload shipments from a factory that pass through a transportation choke point at the origin. The shipping-out cost is from the warehouses to the consuming centers in more expensive, small truckloads. Total shipping cost in cell G5 is to be minimized. Column D contains binary integer adjustable cells that can have values only of 0 or 1. With values of 1, the consuming centers are initially assigned to warehouse 1. The volume shipped to warehouse 1 is the sum of the product of columns D and E. The shipping cost for moving goods from warehouse 1 to the respective consuming centers is the sum of the E-W and the N-S volume X distance multiplied by the unit shipping rate. Cells in columns F and G are adjustable, as they depict the E-W and N-S distances between the consuming centers and the warehouse for calculating shipping costs. The shipping cost formulas are shown in Fig. 4.9. The rate for the shipping-in cost is $0.25 per unit volume X distance measured from the origin to the two warehouses. The rate for the shipping-out cost is four times higher, or $1 per unit volume X distance for the shipments from both warehouses to their assigned consuming centers. Column N contains the constraints that consuming centers must be assigned to either warehouse 1 or 2.

Figure 4.9
Warehouse Location Using What's Best Software (B)

	H	I	J	K	L	M	N
1							
2							
3	CELL G3:	=0.25*(SUM(E11:E25)*(B4+C4)+SUM(J11:J25)*(B5+C5))					
4	CELL G4:	=1*(F27+G27+K27+L27)					
5	CELL G5:	=G3+G4					
6							
7		CELL J11:	=C11*I11			CELL N11:	=WB(D11+I11,"=",1)
8			VOLUME	DISTANCE			ONE
9		YES/NO	TO	W.H.#2			CENTER
10		W.H. #2	W.H.#2	E-W	N-S		PER W.H.
11		0	0	0	0		=

Distances are measured as the sum of the E-W and N-S distances to preserve linearity. However, a problem arises in that distances to consuming centers to the south and west of a warehouse would have a minus sign depicting a negative distance to the warehouse. A negative distance introduces a negative cost. "Forcing" constraints ensure that all distances are positive. The "forcing" constraints for warehouse 1 are shown below; those for warehouse 2 are similarly constructed.

	P	Q	R	S
11	=WB(F11,">",A11-B$4)	=WB(F11,">",B$4-A11)	=WB(G11,">",B11-C$4)	=WB(G11,">",C$4-B11)

Fig. 4.10 shows the location of the two warehouses (designated as squares) and the line of demarcation for assigning consuming centers to the two warehouses. The methodology can be expanded to include a greater number of warehouses.[2]

Figure 4.10
Location of Two Warehouses

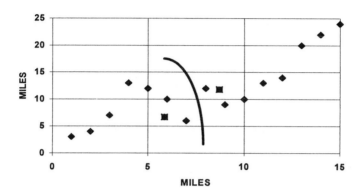

Evolver Optimization

Linear programming can be envisioned as a single mountain with sloping sides. Linear programming, in maximizing an objective cell, locates the highest peak of the mountain by proceeding in an upward direction. As long as linearity exists, then the initial values given to the variables, or adjustable cells, are no barrier in identifying the set of values marking the mountain peak, commonly, profit. Similarly, finding the low point in a valley to minimize costs is guaranteed to be globally optimal as long as linearity is preserved. This is the problem: linearity may not be preserved in modeling a business situation.

A nonlinear set of equations can be envisioned as a landscape where there are hills and valleys of various heights and depths. The application of linear programming to finding a mountain peak or valley floor depends on the initial settings. Starting from that point, a linear program climbs to the top of the nearest hill or the bottom of the nearest valley. However, there is no guarantee that the nearest hilltop or valley floor is globally optimal, although it is locally optimal. Dealing with hilltops, an analogy for maximizing the objective cell, one can start moving up a slope until one is standing on the top of the hill. From the top of the hill, one can view a mountain in the distance. The hill can be viewed as the local optimal solution, and the mountain as the global optimal solution. The problem of applying linear programming to a nonlinear system in maximizing an objective cell is that you can move only in an upward direction. You cannot proceed down into a valley in order to climb to the top of a higher mountain. Hence, the initial set of values becomes critical. If the initial set of values places you on the side of a hill rather than the mountain, the solution will be locally, not globally, optimal.

This can be observed when applying linear programming techniques to a nonlinear system. Change the initial values of the adjustable cells, and you may end up with a different solution, which may or may not be better than the previous one. Thus, the user is not assured that a solution is global. Evolver utilizes an entirely different methodology.[3] It is an optimization technique that can be likened to intelligent trial and error. Evolver assumes that there are mountains of different heights and valleys of different depths. Evolver experiments with different sets of values for the adjustable cells, or variables, and compares the output with other iterations. It "evolves" values for the next iteration, incorporating the results of previous iterations. There is no ascending to the top of a hill or descending to the bottom of a valley in the sense of linear programming. While Evolver makes its way up or down a mountainside, a few mutations are thrown in to make sure that it is on the mountain with the highest peak or deepest valley. Evolver may not necessarily generate the absolutely best solution. At some point, the optimization process is stopped, and it is always possible that running the optimization a bit longer might have resulted in a better solution.

Designing a Two Warehouse System with Evolver

Considering distances not as the sum of E-W and N-S distances but as the hypotenuse of a right triangle introduces sufficient nonlinearity for Evolver to take over from linear programming.[4] Figs 4.11 and 4.12 show the same problem with the new measure for distances for the warehouses.

Figure 4.11
Warehouse Location Using Evolver Software (A)

	A	B	C	D	E	F	G
1	SELECTING TWO WAREHOUSES						
2							
3	W.H.	X	Y		SHIPPING IN:		$ -
4	#1	0.0	0.0		SHIPPING OUT:		$ 61,995
5	#2	0.0	0.0		TOTAL:		$ 61,995
6		CELL E11:	=C11*D11				
7		CELL F11:	=SQRT(($B$4-A11)^2+($C$4-B11)^2)				
8	COORDINATES						
9	CONSUMING CENTERS			YES/NO	YES/NO		
10	X	Y	VOLUME	W.H. #1	W.H. #2		
11	1	3	100	1	0		

Similar to linear programming, cell G5 is the objective cell to be minimized. Cells B4:C5 are designated as adjustable cells. The "recipe" method of solution is used where the adjustable cells can have any value within prescribed limits, here set at 0 and 25. Cells D11 and E11 are designated as adjustable integer cells using the "budget" method of solution. This keeps the sum of D11 and E11 the same as originally set up in the spreadsheet removing the need for constraints. Here, their sum is 1, which stipulates that a consuming center must be served by only one warehouse. This has to be repeated for the remaining pairs of cells associated with each consuming center.

Figure 4.12
Warehouse Location Using Evolver Software (B)

	H	I	J	K	L	M	N	O
2								
3	CELL G3:	=0.25*(SUM(H11:H25)*SQRT(B4^2+C4^2)+SUM(K11:K25)*SQRT(B5^2+C5^2))						
4	CELL G4:	=1*(SUMPRODUCT(H11:H25,I11:I25)+SUMPRODUCT($K11:$K25,L11:L25))						
5	CELL G5:	=G3+G4						
6	CELL I11:	=C11*H11						
7	CELL J11:	=SQRT(($B$5-A11)^2+($C$5-B11)^2)						
8	VOLUME	DISTANCE		VOLUME	DISTANCE			
9	TO	TO		TO	TO			
10	W.H.#1	W.H.#1		W.H.#2	W.H.#2			
11	100	3.2		0	3.2			

The run time for an Evolver solution is longer than for What's Best. The two solutions are compared in Table 4.8.

Table 4.8
What's Best and Evolver Results

	What's Best	Evolver
Location Warehouse 1 (x,y)	(10,12)	(9.5,12.3)
Location Warehouse 2 (x,y)	(5,6)	(4.7,6.6)
Total cost	$39,925	$30,618

The two costs are not directly comparable as their means of measurement is different. What's Best should be greater, as its measure is the sum of the two sides of a triangle in dealing with E-W and N-S distances. Evolver's measure of distance is the hypotenuse of a triangle, which is shorter than adding the two sides. Nevertheless the locations of the two warehouses are quite similar with the same assignment of consuming centers. Running Evolver for a longer period of time may marginally improve its solution.

SUMMARY

Quantitative models are useful as an aid to making those decisions that have a quantifiable element. Quantitative models, being a proxy for reality, leave out important aspects of reality, particularly those elements not easily quantifiable. Nevertheless, for all their weaknesses, models can be very useful in helping to make decisions. If a model exists, it should be used. Employing What's Best and Evolver for locating warehouses to serve consuming centers provides a better solution than throwing a dart at a map.

It should be borne in mind that models are to some degree manageable to support preconceived notions. Moreover, analysts, whether internal or external (consultants), are sensitive to the desires of those who sign their checks. Thus, the best way to manage analysts is to let them act impartially by not communicating anything other than the assignment. This is a tall order because managers often have a hidden agenda that they are pursuing. If managers communicate their feelings, and an analyst arrives at a conclusion at variance with this preconceived notion, then an analyst faces an ethical issue on how to proceed. One way is to tell it as it is and hope not to be fired or shunted aside, if an internal analyst, or to be paid if a consultant. Another way is to communicate the likely outcome verbally and let the manager decide the next step.

ENDNOTES

1. See Web site: www.lindo.com.
2. Problem adapted from *What's Best Linear Programming (Fifteen Cases)*, available from Web sites www.palisade.com and www.nerses.com.
3. See Web site: www.palisade.com.
4. Problem adapted from *Evolver-Solutions for Business (Nineteen Cases)*, available from Web sites www.palisade.com and www.nerses.com.

Chapter 5

Work Design and Work Teams

Achieving a desired output from a plant depends on setting up the requisite number of machines. Line balancing and input/output analysis determine the number of machines for each step of the process and system performance, respectively. The workforce can be organized following the principles of Taylor or Juran. Once a plant is in operation, attention has to be paid to debottlenecking to improve productivity and improving the product itself, the first step in Deming's chain reaction. Making a better product involves both blue- and white-collar contributions. Cultural differences between Japan and the United States have made it easier for Japan, and more difficult for the United States, to adopt Deming's and Juran's management philosophies. Easy or not, survival in the global economy allows little choice in converting a do-what-you-are-told workforce to self-managing work teams. A work team driven to excel can achieve much more than isolated individuals bound by dislike of their work and distrust of their supervisors.

LINE BALANCING

Suppose that a machine can accomplish a task in 30 minutes. Its output is 2 items per hour or 14 per day (7-hour day with allowances for lunch and personal time). Now suppose that a process consists of two machines in series where the first accomplishes the initial part of a task in 20 minutes, and the second completes the task in another 30 minutes. While the first can complete 3 items per hour, the second limits system performance to 2 items per hour. Once the system is in operation, system output is determined by the slowest machine, in this case, 2 per hour or 14 per day, as shown in Fig. 5.1.

Figure 5.1
Line Balancing (A)

The operator of the 30-minute machine is limited to starting a new operation twice per hour. It doesn't matter how efficient the 20-minute machine is; its output cannot be removed faster than twice per hour. As long as system output is constrained by input to the second machine and ruling out work-in-process (WIP) inventory accumulation, the operator of the first machine effectively works 20 minutes and is idle 10 minutes.

Something always constrains system performance. What is the speed of a convoy of ships if the convoy is to remain together? The slowest ship determines the speed of the convoy. A leader wants a group of kids walking through the woods to stay together. What is the speed of the group? The slowest kid determines the speed of the group. To improve system performance, something has to be done to increase the speed of the slowest kid. Perhaps having someone else carrying his or her pack may speed up the group.

The two-machine system is constrained by the 30-minute machine. The only way to improve system performance is to add another 30-minute machine. Two 30-minute machines have a combined output of 4 items per hour, but the output of the first machine is still 3 items per hour. Hence, system output or performance shown in Figure 5.1 is constrained to 3 per hour or 21 per seven-hour day.

Suppose system performance has to be further improved. The constraint is now the 20-minute machine. Adding another 20-minute machine increases output to 6 items per hour, but the output of the two 30-minute machines is still 4 per hour. Hence, system performance is 4 per hour, or 28 per day, as seen in Fig. 5.2. The two 30-minute machines now constrain system performance. To further improve system performance, another 30-minute machine is added, enhancing output to 6 items per hour, or 42 per day, same as the two 20-minute machines, illustrated in Fig. 5.2.

Figure 5.2
Line Balancing (B)

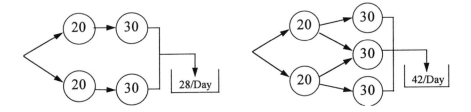

The system of two 20-minute machines and three 30-minute machines is perfectly balanced since both stages of production are producing the same number of items with no idle time. Part of Ford's genius was his being able to perfectly balance a multitude of subassembly and assembly lines within a single plant to produce mass numbers of the Model T with minimum WIP inventory.

Suppose that a subassembly line makes a component consisting of an upper half and lower half. The first workstation makes the two halves, a task that requires 10 minutes. The upper half passes through two workstations requiring 2 and 5 minutes, respectively, to complete their respective tasks. The lower half goes through one workstation where 7 minutes are consumed to complete its respective task. The last workstation takes 6 minutes to assemble the two halves and test the component, illustrated in Fig. 5.3. Design a subassembly line that can feed an assembly line at a rate of 20 parts per hour.

Figure 5.3
Subassembly Line

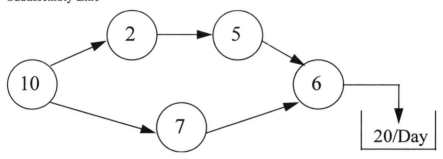

The first workstation completes 6 items per hour. As 20 are needed, four machines are necessary to have an output of at least 20 per hour. Three machines, with a combined output of 18 per hour, are not enough. Proceeding along the upper portion of the diagram, the next workstation completes its task in two minutes, or 30 per hour; therefore, one machine is adequate. The next can handle 12 per hour, so two machines are necessary. The workstation at the bottom for the lower half can handle 8.6 per hour; therefore, three machines are needed. The last workstation can handle 10 per hour. For a system output of 20 per hour, two machines are necessary. This workstation is also the system constraint, as the others have some degree of slack, or idle time, when producing 20 items per hour.

THEORY OF CONSTRAINTS

An effective manager, according to Eliyahu Goldratt, co-author of *The Goal*, must be able to evaluate business performance in order to be in a position to improve it. However, there are various ways to measure performance and the selected measure of performance establishes a goal. Anything a manager does that brings a company closer to achieving its goal is deemed productive.

If a manager does not understand a company's true goal, his or her actions may not actually benefit a company. Managers may be misled into thinking that a company's goal is a high-quality product, operational efficiency, excellent communications, customer service, or organizational effectiveness. These may be necessary conditions for a company to conduct business, but a company's true goal is to make money. A company can go out of business if it fails to generate a profit. However, common measures of making money, such as profit, return on investment, and cash flow, do not adequately evaluate the goal to make money. According to Goldratt, a better measure of making money is productivity in the form of throughput, operating expense, and inventory. Throughput is the rate money is generated through sales, not production. Operating expense is the money spent to transform inventory into throughput. Inventory is the money dedicated to manufacturing a product until it is sold. Traditional cost accounting practices cannot handle these measures of productivity, necessitating a new approach to cost accounting. Moreover, these measures of productivity are to be considered together, not in isolation. Productivity can be improved if a manager takes action to increase system throughput while simultaneously reducing operating expense and inventory.

The previous line balancing exercise has a constant output/input relationship. Actual plant productivity is affected by the changing relationship between input and output at each stage of manufacturing, known as statistical fluctuations. The output of each stage of manufacturing depends not only on its own performance but also on the performance of previous stages of manufacturing, known as dependent events. Managers are in a better position to optimize system performance if they are aware of statistical fluctuations and dependent events.

The flow of product is affected by bottlenecks that constrain system performance. Bottleneck capacity can be expanded by minimizing downtime and the number of defects. Downtime for maintenance restricts the effective output of a bottleneck, while defects wastefully consume bottleneck capacity. Outsourcing or subcontracting incremental capacity expands bottleneck capacity. Even if outsourcing is relatively expensive, its benefit must be evaluated in terms of increasing factory throughput.

Nonbottleneck stages of manufacturing are not to operate above bottleneck capacity to avoid accumulating excess inventory. A manager controls the flow between and among various stages of manufacturing to minimize inventory. Making parts and components in small batches better matches product flow to demand. Small batches reduce time for parts to be manufactured and assembled in the final product. While small batches do increase setup time, this is not a constraint for setups associated with nonbottleneck stages of manufacture. As long as setup times do not transform nonbottlenecks into bottlenecks, small batches not only better match product flow with market demand but also reduce inventory and operating expense.

Conventional business wisdom based on Taylor-inspired efficiency is to make sure that machines and labor are kept busy. Machines and labor can be kept fully utilized if a factory is sized for average demand. This also minimizes the capital investment. However, the factory sized to average demand cannot respond to fluctuating demand without having a great deal of inventory. When demand is slack, the factory builds to inventory. When demand peaks, inventory is liquidated. Over the course of the year, inventory accumulation and liquidation (hopefully) balance out with machines and labor always fully utilized.

Another approach is to balance the flow of product through the plant with actual rather than average demand. A factory is sized to something closer to peak rather than average demand. During peak demand, the factory operates at maximum capacity to satisfy demand with little inventory to draw upon. During periods of slack demand, the factory does not accumulate inventory. Partially employed production workers perform needed maintenance and repair on idle machines, research new ways to improve productivity, and carry out a program of continuous improvement. In a way, this is similar to the workings of a supermarket. When demand peaks, store clerks man the checkout counters and bag groceries. When demand is slack, clerks not needed at the checkout counters restock shelves and perform housekeeping duties.

A factory sized close to peak demand does have excess funds invested in capital equipment and has a higher labor cost. However, since production is essentially geared to demand, there is little finished goods inventory. The cost of higher capital and labor costs must be compared to lower inventory carrying costs to properly evaluate this alternative. Inventory carrying costs should contain a provision for the risk of a company ending up with unsold inventory when expectations of average demand and reality part company. The weighing of capital, labor, and inventory carrying costs for some companies favor gearing production to real demand with some excess capacity rather than to anticipated average demand with fully utilized capacity. Matching product flow to actual demand requires identifying the weak link or constraint in a production chain. Actions taken to debottleneck operations improves system performance making it possible to have a smaller plant with fewer workers to meet peak demand.

WORK DESIGN IN THE SERVICE INDUSTRY

Suppose that you are assigned to set up a system to process a three-page credit application. If Taylor is your guide, then the task is divided into its simplest elements and an individual assigned to each element. Table 5.1 describes the nature of the tasks along with their time elements.

System performance is determined by the tasks that take the longest time, or positions B and G. Once the system is in operation, individuals filling these positions are fully utilized with no associated idle time. Thus, completing applications cannot proceed faster than 30 seconds per application. The other positions have some degree of slack, or idle, time. For instance, the individual filling position A takes 15 seconds to open an envelope and split the application into three separate pages. Since the system is constrained to handle an application every 30 seconds, individual A works for 15 seconds and is idle for 15 seconds without adversely affecting system performance. Fig. 5.4 shows the set up of a credit application processing line following Taylor's principles along with the amount of idle time associated with each work station.

Table 5.1
Work Design by Taylor

Person	Task	Time Seconds	Job Content
A	Opens application, separates the three pages and places in boxes for B, C, and D	15	Boring and Tedious
B	Reviews first page for personal information to evaluate character of applicant	30	Interesting
C	Examines second page for income and annotates total income	25	Boring and Tedious
D	Examines third page for current debt load and annotates total debt	20	Boring and Tedious
E	Takes annotations from C and D and refers to a table for amount of incremental debt	15	Boring and Tedious
F	Supervisor oversees line, reviews three pages, and makes final decision	20	Challenging
G	Completes form letters to communicate to applicant	30	Boring and Tedious

Figure 5.4
Work Layout by Taylor

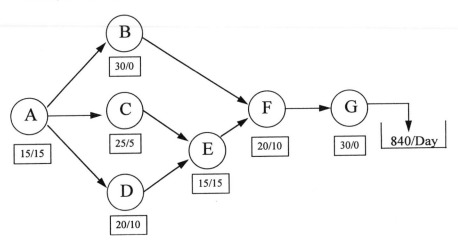

A completed application takes 30 seconds, therefore 120 can be completed per hour, or 840 per seven-hour day for each credit application processing line of 7 workers. For anticipated demand of 2,000 applications per day, 2.4 lines have to be set up. As there is no such thing as a fractional line, three lines are necessary. The total number of personnel required to handle 2,000 applications a day is shown in Table 5.2.

Table 5.2
Number of Personnel

Three lines at 7 people each	21
Manager	1
Assistant manager	1
Spares to cover absentees as the lines must be fully manned to be operable	2
Total	25

The job content of 5 of the 7 positions in a line, 15 in all, is boring and tedious. Unless a worker is brain-dead, he or she will become dissatisfied with Taylor-inspired work design. Dissatisfied workers vent their frustration by not showing up at work or getting another job. A dissatisfied workforce can be easily identified by high turnover and absentee rates. This creates a job for the assistant manager to continually recruit spares and new personnel to fill vacancies. Can anything be done to make the system more productive?

Rather than split a task into its simplest elements and assigning a worker to each element, Juran espouses giving the entire job to a single person, as here, or a small group, as in the assembly of Volvo automobiles. Fig. 5.5 shows the work design for an individual along with the length of time to complete an application and daily output.

Figure 5.5
Work Layout by Juran

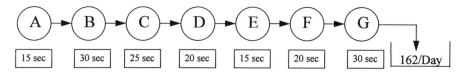

An individual takes 155 seconds to complete every step of an application and can complete 162 applications in a seven-hour day. The number of people needed to complete 2,000 applications a day is 12.3 or 13 people. In addition, there is need for a manager, plus two others to act as a resource for more difficult applications, train new personnel, and spot check the quality of work. This raises the number of people to 16 individuals, far below that needed by the Taylor system, whose hallmark is efficiency. This is another ironic situation where the paradigm for greatest efficiency turns out to be rather inefficient.

The inefficiency of the Taylor system stems from idle time such as individual A effectively being employed half the working day opening envelopes. In fact, five of the seven workers have idle time because the system is not perfectly balanced. Moreover, three lines were needed to cover 2.4 lines of work, introducing another 0.6 line of wasted resources.

In the Juran system, spares are not necessary because worker absence no longer shuts down a line. The assistant manager is not needed because turnover is low, reflecting a higher degree of job satisfaction. Higher morale enhances productivity, which may cause daily output to rise above 162 applications per individual. The new system permits flexible work hours and perhaps working at home. The fact that an individual is not at his or her desk does not mean loss of management control. No matter where and when the individual reviews credit applications, there is one sure measure of performance: output.

However, converting from the Taylor to the Juran system cannot be done by issuing a corporate directive. In the Taylor system, at least five of the individuals are totally unqualified to handle the complete task. Only position F knows the complete task, with position B next in line. Therefore, when switching from Taylor to Juran, a major investment in training and education is necessary. There is no way to avoid this expense because every individual must be as proficient as the individual in position F who makes the final decision.

The Taylor system does have one great advantage: it provides the best training mechanism imaginable. An individual can learn each individual step of a process in a Taylor system of work design. One Taylor line could remain in operation as a training aid. An individual starts out with the least demanding station, opening the letters. After a solid 15 minutes of learning this step of the process, the individual proceeds to the next least demanding position such as G, then C, and D, and E. A checklist records an individual's progress from the simpler to the more complex steps in a process. The most demanding positions are B and F, the last to be covered. An individual is deemed qualified when the checklist is completed. The most qualified individuals holding position F under the Taylor system should remain as instructors, a resource to aid in the more difficult credit applications, and a quality check on the output.

In this situation, the Juran system is more efficient than the Taylor system. Moreover, being given responsibility and held accountable for performance promotes job satisfaction, higher morale, and enhanced productivity. These are good reasons to support the management decision to switch work design from Taylor to Juran. Another reason for switching is that the workers themselves will ensure the success of the Juran system. They realize that the credit applications will be processed regardless of the choice of work design. If it is not by the Juran system, which they like, then it is by the Taylor system, which they hate.

WORK DESIGN IN MANUFACTURING

The Taylor method of work design in a manufacturing setting is to place all the cutters in one area of the plant, all the drillers in another area, all the grinders in still another, and all the polishers in their area, illustrated in Fig. 5.6. Work flows from one part of the plant to another where the needed workers are located. A worker associates no meaning to the work other than performing his or her specific task. In fact, a worker may not know or care what the final product is. All that a worker knows is that he or she is either cutting, drilling, grinding, or polishing something. The worker becomes disassociated from the process.

Figure 5.6
Work Design by Taylor

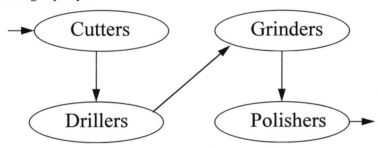

The Juran way is to identify a family of parts that can be manufactured using the same group technology. All the machines and people necessary to make a family of parts are placed on a U-shaped table, called cellular manufacturing, illustrated in Fig. 5.7.

Figure 5.7
Work Design by Juran

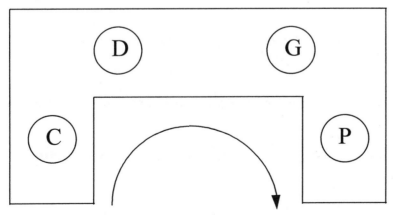

The benefit of cellular manufacturing is that everyone sees what is going on and develops a holistic view of the operation. They get to know one another, help one another as difficulties arise, and teach one another if a worker learns something new. Two-way communication among a group of individuals creates a team. The team is given responsibility for its output in terms of volume and quality and held accountable for its performance. It becomes a small, independent factory within a factory or a small, independent company within a large company. Following the teachings of Feigenbaum and Ishikawa, the team treats the next workstation as an internal customer with the same commitment to quality and service associated with an external customer.

U.S. managers initially liked Deming's idea of making workers responsible for quality. They had a change of heart when they realized that this meant giving workers control over output. How can workers improve quality if they have no control over output? Deming was rebuffed when managers insisted that the rheostat controlling the speed of an assembly line was to remain strictly in their hands. U.S. managers saw no inconsistency in giving workers responsibility for quality and speeding up the assembly line whenever they wished.

However, giving workers responsibility for quality does mean giving them control over output. When workers are asked to reduce the number of defects, output declines on day 1. However, improved worker satisfaction coupled with higher morale does eventually lead to greater output, but unfortunately, this is beyond the time horizon of traditional Taylor-inspired managers. U.S. managers rejected Deming's principles not only because they could not see beyond day 1, but also because they were not about to give up their most cherished prerogative, control over the rheostat. Interestingly, U.S. labor union leaders were not enamored with Deming. They thought that a workforce responsible for, and held accountable for, their output would become more sympathetic to the aims of management and, consequently, more reluctant to strike. They wanted to maintain the traditional adversarial relationship of hate and distrust between management and labor to hone their ultimate bargaining chip: the threat of a strike. The Deming show really bombed in America.

Another task assigned to work teams is job assignment and rotation. Isn't it better for a work team to decide whether Agatha or her sister Bertha is to spend her day on the lathe? Shouldn't a manager have more important things to worry about? Actually, work teams do their own hiring. Workers are better able to assess whether Bertha is as proficient a lathe operator as she says she is. Few managers have the necessary lathe experience to judge Bertha. It is also easier for the work team than a human resource manager to handle the situation where Bertha does not live up to her promises.

WORKER CONTRIBUTION TO MAKING A BETTER PRODUCT

Work teams are also given responsibility to perform simple maintenance and repairs and keep statistical control charts up-to-date. They are also responsible for the blue-collar contribution for making a better product, the first step in the

Deming chain reaction. The workers can make a contribution because they are closest to the process of making a product. Tapping the brains of the workers is done by:

1. detecting and keeping a record of defects,
2. creating a Pareto diagram,
3. generating suggestions with the Ishikawa or fishbone diagram,
4. testing suggestions using the Deming plan-do-check-act (PDCA) cycle,
5. repeating the preceding for never-ending improvement (*kaizen*).

Defect Detection

Defect detection and record keeping are simply keeping track of the nature of defects and their number. While this sounds simple enough, work teams must be taught elementary statistical principles. Basically, work teams must inspect their work, note the type of defect, and record their occurrence. A portion of this record keeping is shown in Table 5.3.

Table 5.3
Partial Listing of Defect Types and Number

DEFECT TYPE	NUMBER OF OCCURRENCES
X73	✓✓✓✓✓✓✓
X81	✓✓
X65	✓✓✓✓✓✓✓✓✓✓✓✓✓✓

Pareto Diagram

The data of number and type of defects can be graphed as a Pareto diagram, shown in Fig. 5.8.

Figure 5.8
Pareto Diagram

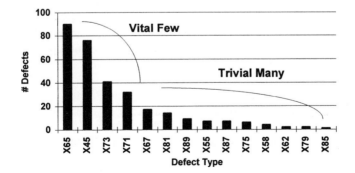

Pareto was an early twentieth-century economist who noted that 80 percent of a nation's wealth is owned by 20 percent of the people. This observation seems true regardless of the nature of the political system, including Marxism. The 80/20 rule applies to other phenomena such as defects where most defects (80 percent) can be attributed to relatively few types of defects (20 percent). Thus a "vital few" types of defects are responsible for most of the number of defects. The "trivial many" types of defects are responsible for only a small number of defects. The Pareto diagram identifies that defect type X65 is the most deserving of the finite resources of time and money to deal with defects.

Ishikawa or Fishbone Diagram

The most common type of defect is then exposed to a brainstorming session for workers to generate suggestions on how to deal with the defect, shown in Fig. 5.9.

Figure 5.9
Ishikawa or Fishbone Diagram

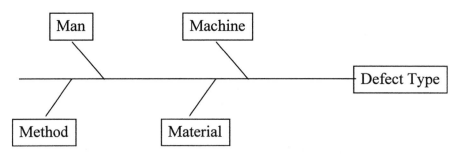

Workers assemble after or before work for a brainstorming session to generate suggestions on how to correct a defect. One of the principal responsibilities for a junior-level manager overseeing several work teams is to lead, not manage, a brainstorming session. Leadership means keeping the workers focused on the problem and maintaining a dialogue to ensure that all workers participate. This is done by creating an atmosphere where workers want to participate. This is quite unlike the situation of a traditional boss' sitting in his or her office issuing a directive to a work team to come up with a list of 10 written suggestions by Friday. Then the boss waits for the response, planning some form of retribution if the team doesn't respond.

Suppose that the most frequent defect from the Pareto diagram, defect type X65, is bubbles in the paint. Who is in a better position to make suggestions about the possible causes of bubbles in the paint than the workers associated with the process? There is no better way to tap the brains of the workers than orchestrating an effectively led brainstorming session generating, in relatively short order, the list of suggestions contained in Table 5.4. These brainstorming sessions are the ultimate source of the millions of suggestions made by Japanese workers for the benefit of their companies. Millions of suggestions do not come from suggestion boxes conveniently hung next to coffee machines or located next to toilets, but from a highly organized activity where leadership is exerted to encourage worker participation.

Table 5.4
Fishbone Suggestions

MATERIAL	Try another type of paint
	Try another supplier
	Paint too thick, needs thinner
METHOD	Surface not properly prepared
	Paint nozzle too close to surface
	Paint coming out with too much force
MAN	Improperly trained
	Too much paint fumes
	Room too dark
MACHINE	Needs adjustment
	Needs overhaul
	Needs replacement

DEMING PDCA CYCLE

The Deming PDCA cycle is a trial and error process of identifying which suggestion can remove the defect. Deming refers to this as the Shewhart cycle, which dates the concept to the 1920s. Since most suggestions don't work, it pays to start with suggestions that involve little cost and effort.

- Plan a course of action to improve the product or the process of making a product.
- Do a test.
- Check results.
- Act on results.

If the test results do not correct the defect, make no change and select another suggestion. If a suggestion partially corrects the defect, incorporate the suggestion in the system and select another. Continue until the defect is gone.

KAIZEN

Once the defect is gone, the next defect from the Pareto diagram (defect type X45) now has the greatest number of occurrences. Another brainstorming session is held using the Ishikawa diagram as an aid to come up with worker suggestions. Then the Deming PDCA cycle is repeated until that defect type is gone; then on to the next never stopping the cycle. This is Deming's never-ending improvement, which in Japanese is *kaizen*. "If it ain't being fixed, it is broke" means that if the Deming PDCA cycle is not in operation, then the system of continuous improvement is broken. If improvement is continuous, one may wonder why Japanese products aren't perfect–annual product changes and technological advances take care of that.

Reinforcement through a Bonus System

One-third or more of a Japanese worker's remuneration is in form of a bonus tied to the profitability of a company. Following World War II, workers were unemployed and factory owners could not afford to hire them. The factory owners asked the workers if they were willing to work for room and board only. The workers agreed because the alternative was even worse. They were housed in factory-provided barracks. For making this sacrifice, the factory owners promised to give the workers a share of a company's profits when earned. This arrangement inadvertently and serendipitously allied Japanese workers and their unions with management. Anything that added to profits increased workers' pay. Thus, Japanese workers and their unions adopted essentially a management outlook with regard to profits and the operations of a plant.

Unlike unions in the West, Japanese unions do not support restrictive work rules. They actively promote operating efficiencies on the production floor. They are just as interested in a corporation's being profitable as management. Unions are a conduit to ensure that workers and management clearly understood one another. Strikes, on the rare occasions when they do occur, last scarcely more than a day. Their purpose is to stress a point between labor and management, not to increase worker pay. Unions acknowledged that prolonged strikes hurt the long-term interests of the company. In the West, unions seem to take particular delight in bringing corporations to their knees. Strikes in the West focus fairly exclusively on worker pay, benefits, and working conditions often involving restrictive work rules. The ultimate reason why Japanese workers are so cooperative with management is that they are paid to be cooperative through a bonus system based on corporate profits.

Responsibilities of Work Units at the Saturn Plant

The list of responsibilities on the next page is drawn from Saturn literature. In reviewing this list, are not work teams behaving as though they are little, independent factories within a large factory or little, independent companies within a large company?

- reach decisions by consensus
- self-manage assigned work tasks and schedule work
- assign jobs, hire new members, and resolve work conflicts
- schedule relief and vacation time, and provide absentee replacements
- maintain a health and safety program
- plan work, design jobs, control scrap, material flow, and inventory
- produce quality products on schedule
- perform simple equipment maintenance, repairs, and housekeeping details
- maintain lines of communication within and without the work unit
- integrate activities with other work units
- constantly seek improvement in quality, cost, and work environment
- prepare work unit's budget, obtain supplies and resources, schedule and hold meetings
- assist in developing and delivering training
- initiate consultation with management and industrial engineers when needed

No wonder Saturn workers were primarily recruited from the local population, with partiality for those with no previous experience working in a union shop! Although the workers are represented by UAW in the Saturn plant, the UAW plays a key role in both operational and strategic planning activities. Ironically, the same union that plays a vital role in maintaining a constructive win-win working relationship between labor and management at the Saturn plant also maintains a lose-lose adversarial relationship in other GM plants. However, the Saturn plant is an agent for change in labor management relations in GM.

Responsibilities of Work Unit Team Leader

The team leader ensures that the individual members of a work unit function as a team.

- promote partnership among team members and manage daily production
- lead team in completing job certifications and implementing job rotation
- lead team in establishing priorities and setting goals
- resolve conflicts among members
- communicate team's needs to work unit's adviser
- monitor training, budget, quality, housekeeping, and safety issues
- use Saturn's tools, processes, and resources to promote growth and development of teams into self-managed work units

Responsibilities of Work Unit Adviser

The adviser ensures proper coordination and cooperation among the work units. The advisers may have 20 or more years of experience and are mature individuals who can fulfill what really is a managerial position.

- promote partnership among teams
- participate in operational and tactical planning
- participate in setting and monitoring work units' goals
- provide leadership and guidance, and act as a resource to the work units
- facilitate communication, coordination, prioritizing, and conflict resolution within and between work units
- integrate and consolidate work units' requirements and communicate them to higher organizational levels
- represent work units at the business unit level

The investment in training and education for the Juran system of work design is costly and time-consuming. It must be viewed as a disadvantage not present in the Taylor system. Members in work units at the Saturn plant are given 350 hours of training and educational programs to become job-ready plus over 90 hours per year on management and technical training. Emphasis is on behavioral subjects, emphasizing leadership and team development. Worker pay consists of base pay, which is lower than the market rate, plus risk and reward pay for achieving quality and productivity goals, which has increased pay to above the market rate. Sound familiar?

IS MANAGEMENT WITHOUT A MISSION?

Management has lost the first-line supervisory position, a position that few wanted. But management is still responsible for the nature of the product, production volume, price, distribution and marketing, plant location, and finance. Management is well aware of what is going on among the work teams. Management knows the output from observation and quality from exercising of warranties plus market surveys and other means to measure customer satisfaction. It is also management's responsibility to exercise leadership in originating workers' suggestions for improving the product or the process for making the product. Managers are asked to intercede when problems arise within work teams that cannot be resolved or corrected internally. This means that managers are involved with the more difficult personnel and operational problems, which is a better use of their time than micromanaging Agatha and Bertha. Managers, not the workers, deal with outside suppliers and new technology. Managers run the show except for what is happening on the production floor that falls within the purview and capabilities of the workers. Even here, managers know exactly what is happening on the production floor and are always in a position to act if necessary.

CONCURRENT OR SIMULTANEOUS ENGINEERING

Worker suggestions are focused on improving an existing production system and product. But this is not sufficient. Companies cannot survive on improving yesterday's products. To remain globally competitive, companies must bring out new products or new models of existing products. For the most part, this is beyond the capabilities of the workers. The white-collar contribution in making a better product is primarily associated with new products or new models of an existing product. This is carried out through four separate activities: research and development (R&D), product development, process development, and manufacturing. The traditional organization of these activities is in Fig. 5.10.

Figure 5.10
Traditional Organization for Creating New Products

The traditional approach to introducing new products and new models of existing products is to house these four activities in separate organizations, often located in different cities. Research thinks of a new idea and "passes it over the wall" to product development. Initial resistance by product development to starting a new assignment may well take the form of "you've thought up dumb ideas before, but this has got to be the dumbest!" A round-robin discussion ensues between research and product development until product development is convinced that maybe the idea "from the dreamers" in research does have merit.

Then product development builds a model and "passes it over the wall" to process development. Again, there is resistance to starting a new assignment, with another round-robin discussion on the relative merits of the new product, replete with mutual recriminations. After being convinced of the merit of the idea, process development creates a small-scale version for manufacturing the new product. When completed, they "pass it over the wall" to manufacturing, those responsible for setting up large-scale production for the new product. Again resistance, again time lost. Each of these organizations thinks only of its narrow function and considers its role completed when the work is packaged up and "passed over the wall."

Concurrent or simultaneous engineering has little to do with engineering but a great deal to do with managing engineers. The research people no longer sit in isolation thinking of new ideas. They establish a collaborative relationship with customers and marketing personnel to aid in their coming up with new ideas on what should be incorporated in a new product or a modification to an existing product. Research, product and process development, and manufacturing no longer remain in separate organizations but a single organization located in the same building and, if at all possible, on the same floor, illustrated in Fig. 5.11.

Individuals eat in the same dining room, park in the same lot, and are encouraged to socialize with one another. There are no private offices where one can remain in isolation with a secretary acting as a barrier and shield to what is going on. The open area seating arrangement is not segregated by group but integrated with individuals from all groups mixed together. Most importantly, no single group can meet without representatives from the others.

Figure 5.11
New Organization for Creating New Products

All this encourages individuals to become aware of the various disciplines associated with bringing out a new product. They learn the entire process of developing a new product and take an interest in the status of new products. This leads to a holistic appreciation of what it takes for an idea to be transformed into something sitting on the shelf available for purchase. The results of simultaneous or concurrent engineering are:

- cycle time, the time from a new idea being conceived until the product is on a shelf, cut from an average of 7 years to 3.5 years,
- new products have fewer moving parts, which means fewer parts to break and therefore higher quality, and
- remaining parts are easier to manufacture and assemble, lowering manufacturing costs.

Companies switching to simultaneous or concurrent engineering have reported major cuts in cycle time and manufacturing costs from fewer parts that are easier to manufacture and assemble, and higher-quality products. One reason for this is the presence of manufacturing at early stages of product and process design. They can interact to reduce the number of parts and to ensure that those remaining are easier to manufacture and assemble. In the old system, manufacturing could not interact until process development had passed its work over the wall. By then it was too late: the product and its production process were cast in concrete.

CULTURAL DIFFERENCES

Why was Japan able to take the teachings of two Americans, Juran and Deming, and literally backed us up against the wall? One reason why American managers find it difficult to accept Juran's and Deming's management philosophy is because it is at odds with our culture. Unfortunately for us, what Juran and Deming did was to give the Japanese a management philosophy more compatible with their culture than Taylor's. That's what made it so much easier for Japanese managers to accept Juran and Deming than U.S. managers.

The Japanese take a more collaborative approach to business whereas our approach is more competitive. A tendency to collaborate rather than compete stems from cultural values deeply embedded in Japanese society. When Japan was primarily agrarian, families had to collaborate to grow rice. In the United States the land was farmed by individual families. The pioneering family settled the wilderness as a single unit, not as part of a village collective. For the most part, families did not cooperate, not even to defend themselves against the Indians. For many, seeing smoke from a neighbor's chimney was the signal to move deeper into the American wilderness. U.S. industry was developed by the efforts of strong-willed individuals such as Vanderbilt, Carnegie, and Rockefeller, who brooked no opposition. Japanese industry, particularly after World War II, was rebuilt by a cooperative and concerted effort between government, industry, and labor where the latter was willing to work for room and board until industry was in a position to pay. The collaborative spirit is seen in labor unions' pursuing fundamentally different goals from those in the West, and in their interpretation of the role of strikes. While Japanese firms certainly compete among themselves for market share; within a *keiretsu*, the key to success is collaboration. The collaborative approach to conducting business is more congruent with Deming's and Juran's management philosophy than the American spirit of individualism and competition.

Attitude to Employees

The primary difference between Japanese and American management philosophies lies in the dramatically different attitude to employees. No other characteristic stands out as much as this. U.S. companies have traditionally followed what Douglas McGregor calls theory X type of human behavior. A theory X employee inherently dislikes work; needs to be controlled, if not threatened, to perform, and avoids responsibility. Taylor thought of no good reason for a worker to spend a major portion of his or her life in a factory other than the need to support hearth and home. His piecework rates were directed at enhancing a worker's productivity by providing enough pay to adequately support a family. These were eventually degraded to performance quotas to enforce minimum levels of output. Theory X workers are "motivated" primarily through fear of losing their jobs.

Obviously, not everyone is a theory X person who must be driven to perform well. A theory Y individual, according to McGregor, is driven to perform well. A theory Y person wants to perform well from a sense of self-satisfaction and self-worth. Theory Y applies when managers recognize the intellectual and creative potential of workers. A corporation shows that it believes that its employees can make meaningful contributions by providing training, setting aside time for meetings, and giving recognition for employee achievements. Theory Y workers are given responsibility and held accountable for their performance. Theory X workers report to work and do what they are told to do. The irony is that the same workers can be either theory X or theory Y depending on how they are treated. It is a matter of management attitudes and work design. The story of the NUMMI plant vividly demonstrates that theory X workers can be transformed into theory Y workers through a change in management attitudes and work design.

Theory Z

William Ouchi in his book *Theory Z* proposed a new category. A Theory Z individual wants some control over his or her destiny, embodied in self-managing work teams. Workers want to be involved in the decision-making process that effects the quality of their work life. In Japan, productivity gains do not rely as much on technological advances as on trust between labor and management. This is difficult to understand in the United States, where the relationship between labor and management and, for that matter, between government and corporations is adversarial. Japanese management instinctively trusts work teams to check and monitor their own performance. Traditional American management relies on supervisors to review employee performance.

Non-Western Values

Trust, subtlety, and intimacy are the management techniques most commonly employed in Japan, which, for the most part, are absent in the West. In fact, "subtlety" and "intimacy" are not expressions found in a Western manager's lexicon. The Japanese commitment to trust has a positive impact on the personal life of employees. They are willing to fully commit themselves to their companies. Many blue-collar workers in the United States do not trust management. This is the lesson learned from a long history of antagonism between management and labor and decades of downsizing still ongoing in the wake of megamergers. In Japan corporations are similar to social organizations in providing intimacy to workers. In the West intimacy is associated with the family, church, and clubs, not corporations.

While not universal, most full-time employees of large Japanese companies are employed for life, retiring at age 55. Interestingly, there are no pension or social security benefits other than a significant departing bonus. A large company may provide part-time employment for retirees within a satellite company in the same *keiretsu*, usually a supplier. Since Japanese salaries are base pay plus a bonus tied to a company's profitability, labor costs decline along with a company's profit. In effect, workers are taking a pay cut that preserves job security for all. This is quite unlike the situation in the West where pay remains unchanged when a company is experiencing financial difficulties. Rather than all the workers taking a 10 percent pay cut, 10 percent of the workers lose their jobs. Japanese companies can maintain their workforce during economic downturns, whereas a U.S. company is forced to downsize. Not only do layoffs cause distress among those directly affected, but spreads fear among those remaining that they may be next. Fear prevents developing a sense of loyalty to a company. Without a sense of loyalty, a worker is hardly willing to contribute beyond the narrow confines of his or her job assignment.

Japanese companies do rely on temporary workers in order to preserve the security of the full-time workers. They are called women. Women rarely obtain the status of full-time workers and even more rarely achieve management positions. They are employed on a part-time basis, accepting the risk of being laid off. The primary role of a woman in Japan is mother and wife. Western women have a much greater opportunity to participate in business and the professions, but, as the Japanese are quick to point out, at the cost of family stability.

Employee turnover, by definition, is much higher in the United States, necessitating a more rapid evaluation and promotion process. Japanese employees with guaranteed lifetime employment have a much slower and deliberate evaluation and promotion process. A Japanese worker is evaluated internally by his or her work group, not externally by a supervisor. Not keeping up with group expectations is a very powerful motivating force for Japanese workers.

Japanese Management

Japanese managers do not specialize in a particular discipline as in the United States. After an extensive training period, they are assigned to a number of positions that, over a career, may span marketing, operations, finance, and accounting. This, along with a lifelong commitment to a single company, fosters an environment of strong interdependence with a high degree of coordination among managers within and among divisions. A Japanese manager knows that, with time, he will be promoted and be better compensated along with being provided job security. This reinforces a feeling of loyalty and dedication to the company. Having drinks after work is a means of cementing working relationships and a channel for open communications. Interestingly, a Japanese manager is free to assert his true feelings to his superior as long as he is deemed to be under the influence of you-know-what.

The manner of management control in Japan is subtle in nature. In the West, objectives are both specific and quantifiable for example, increase profits by 10 percent by the end of the next quarter. A Japanese manager is expected to direct his efforts in harmony with the general philosophy and overall mission of a company. Generally, this takes the form of making a superior product to be sold at a reasonable price to capture a greater market share without quantifying exactly what this means. A manager seeks to assign members to a group whose personalities, capabilities, and work habits will carry out the desired goals of a group without issuing a written directive as to what these goals are. The approach in the United States is far less subtle. A manager issues a detailed directive of what is expected from a group assembled without a great deal of forethought.

Japanese Decision Making

Japanese decision making is by consensus. No important decision is made without everyone's agreeing to the decision. Interviews and meetings are conducted with those who oppose the decision until consensus is reached. While gaining consensus for a decision can be extremely lengthy, implementation is swift, for there is no opposition. In the West decisions are made more rapidly but implementation is slow since those responsible for carrying out the decision had no part in making the decision. Moreover, in Japan the group remains responsible for carrying out decisions, and no single person takes credit for a decision. In fact, a group, rather than an individual, is rewarded for performance.

IS JAPAN OVER THE HILL?

Japan has been able to bootstrap itself from a war-ravaged economy where "made in Japan" was synonymous with junk, to the world's second largest industrial power, much of it at our expense. The late 1980s marked Japan's apogee, where commonly accepted opinion was that the United States would become an industrial colony of Japan.

Fortunately, it didn't happen. The United States has successfully stemmed the erosion of its industrial might by responding to the threat of better-quality Japanese products with better-quality U.S. products. While the United States has been in an economic resurgence of sorts, Japan has been in the economic doldrums for most of the 1990s, and its outlook remains dim. The cause is the price of success. Japan is suffering the consequences of transforming itself into a high labor-cost society. Japan must now compete against low labor-cost nations offering a broad range of products from consumer electronics, to automobiles, to industrial products. Many of these factories have been financed by the Japanese and taught Japanese management and production techniques by the Japanese. To remain price-competitive, Japan now imports components from Asia to control costs of its manufactured products. Moreover, Japan has taken steps to reduce labor costs by relying more on temporary employees at the expense of permanent employees with lifelong security. Imports of components hurt Japanese worker employment opportunities. Temporary workers receive less pay and can be laid off. Permanent workers' bonus pay has been presumably declining along with corporate profits. This triple threat to Japanese labor has eroded consumer confidence and dampened domestic demand.

In response to pressure on profits, there are now instances of the Japanese sacking managers who do not meet expectations now being expressed in not so subtle terms of growth in revenue and profits. Demotions, transferring permanent employees to remote locations without their families, and giving them meaningless assignments to drive them out of the company are beginning to take place. These newly instituted "American-style" practices may be necessary to cut costs, but they are also beginning to cause Japanese managers and workers to question why they typically work 14 hours a day, six days a week, plus attend mandatory company social functions. There is virtually no time for family or leisure in Japan. "Dropping dead at work" is an occupational hazard. Japan's high suicide rate reflects the internal stress within its society.

Japanese working abroad know that there are better job opportunities in America and Europe, where they can receive better pay for less effort, be promoted faster based on merit rather than seniority, and be given greater opportunities for personal freedom, creativity, and decision making. Upon their return from overseas assignments, some openly question the traditional Japanese management philosophy.

Traditional Japanese supplier relationships are based on a long-term, mutually beneficial relationship where price takes second place to performance and historical relationships. This is being weakened by a new requirement in some companies to switch suppliers if there is more than a 5 percent price savings. Japanese are taking a greater interest in management by objectives and modern marketing techniques, both radical departures from traditional Japanese practices that have served them so well in the past. Slowing business activity has visibly weakened the Japanese financial structure. Declining profit margins no longer support the past overreliance on debt to finance industrial expansion. Depressed stock and real estate values serving as collateral to loans compound Japanese financial problems. It is somewhat amazing to realize that Japanese financial institutions are in such trouble despite decades of massive positive trade balances.

What Is to Be Done?

While one can at least appreciate Japan's ready acceptance of Juran and Deming and America's rejection, the point is that we must compete with Japan and other nations that have adopted the Japanese management philosophy. If we are to compete successfully, and if another value system provides superior performance, then we have no choice but to copy some aspects of what the Japanese are doing. Unfortunately, our cultural values make it difficult for us to emulate Japanese management styles and Japanese management-worker relations. The irony is that as we wrestle with adopting Japanese management styles, the Japanese are beginning to adopt the very American management styles that have been blamed for our poor performance.

SELF-MANAGING WORK TEAMS

The Taylor system succeeded in a world of simple technology based on easy to understand mechanical tasks with untrained and uneducated workers. It was the right system for its time. Businesses today are faced with intense international competitive pressures, complex organizational structures, rapidly evolving technology, swiftly changing markets, and an explosion of information. We have a world that is, as previously quoted from Matsushita, "now so complex and difficult, that their continued existence depends on the day-to-day mobilization of every ounce of intelligence. Management is precisely the art of mobilizing and pulling together the intellectual resources of all employees in the service of the firm."

The cartoon Dilbert well illustrates the manager who does not have a clue as to what is going on but who insists on micromanaging his workers. Any input from Dilbert and friends is considered a threat to his authority. He resorts to inane slogans, budgetary subterfuge, and endless rounds of meetings to control a process about which he has no understanding. He blithely carries out the corporate policy to "initiate the description of the criteria for requirements by developing a framework for the application architecture consistent with the planning corridor specified in our strategic initiative" without any idea what it means.[1] Who does? The manager's effectiveness is limited to those occasions when Dilbert and his coworkers successfully manipulate his decisions. The most pathetic aspect of Dilbert is the realization that many of the cartoon's episodes are submitted by readers.

The Dilbert corporate environment cannot face the challenges of the modern world. Most, if not all, successful global companies have adopted some form of self-managing work teams if only to ensure their survival. Work teams improve the quality of life for the employee as well as the quality of a company's product or service. Improving a company's productivity and competitiveness should enhance its profits, although there is a body of evidence suggesting that enhanced productivity and competitiveness do not automatically translate into enhanced profitability.

Teams are led by worker-leaders, not management-bosses. Team leaders are often selected by the workers themselves and may be referred to as team coordinators, facilitators, or coaches. Typical responsibilities for work teams include timekeeping, analyzing quality problems, assigning jobs, training team members, setting team goals, and assessing internal performance. They are expected to record measures of quantity and quality, solve technical problems, resolve internal conflicts, prepare budgets, elect the team leader, and select new members.

Self-managing work teams are a win-win situation for both the employer and the employee. Increased productivity, competitiveness, and profitability are clear benefits for the corporation. Work teams allow a corporation to be more flexible in adapting to change. Work teams empower workers by fostering initiative, creativity, sense of responsibility, and internal problem solving. Empowered workers take pride and ownership in their efforts engendering greater motivation and commitment to their work. Theory Z employees develop a sense of control over their working environment and destiny. They learn to manage and lead themselves. Conflicts decrease along with the absentee and turnover rates. Product innovation advances as employees contribute to the process of making a better product. Teams can take advantage of the individualism and diversity inherent in our culture and enhance the quality of life in the workplace.

The traditional boss must give up presiding at meetings where his or her voice is the only one heard. He or she can no longer hide in a private office issuing memorandums and awaiting a written response. This is a waste of time and talent. The traditional boss is now needed to facilitate, coordinate, and lead in setting goals, resolving conflicts, and thinking of new opportunities. Leaders exercise their imagination rather than their authority. Leaders activate the minds and hearts of the workers, resolving difficulties beyond the workers' abilities, and dealing with the external world of upper management, suppliers, and technology. For work teams to succeed, management must endorse the concept and not feel threatened by giving employees more autonomy. Many traditional managers are loath to give up the traditional personal control over the workers. Increased trust and cooperation between management and labor actually enhances managers' personal control when they transform themselves from bosses into leaders.

Kaoru Ishikawa is credited with combining Deming's statistical quality control with Juran's concepts of quality management to create the first quality control circles. His intention was to create an organization whereby lower-level employees could increase their contribution to a company. In 1962 the first quality circle appeared in Japan, with over a million now operating in Japan. The first quality circle in the United States was established by Lockheed Aircraft in 1970, with an estimated 200,000 quality circles, or work teams, now in operation. Work teams have contributed to America's resurgence.

Setting up Self-Managing Work Teams

Employee involvement must be voluntary. Team spirit must be encouraged. The group, rather than individuals, should be recognized for success. An open and nonthreatening atmosphere should be fostered to stimulate creativity and innovation. Training in problem-solving techniques is needed to give workers tools to fulfill both organizational and personal goals. Implementing self-managing work teams represents a major change in organizational culture. Management should ensure that change progresses at a slow pace over a period of several years. Forced change creates resistance and conflict within an organization. Management should become involved at all levels as they plan for change. Short-term profit goals must give way to long-term performance goals.

Implementing work teams passes through several stages of development. At first, a team is a diverse group of individuals uncertain about what to expect and not clear on goals for the group or their roles within a group. The second stage is workers beginning to become involved with planning, problem solving, team meetings, and other duties while essentially maintaining their original jobs. At times team members feel overwhelmed, confused, and under pressure. Team members may struggle over who will handle various tasks. New demands and challenges frequently appear and beg solution. This is the stage where the process of setting up work teams is most vulnerable to failure.

The third stage entails an increasing focus on goals and routines to deal with crises, new situations, and problems. Team members have sorted out their mutual responsibilities and begin to rely more on one another. Individuals begin to emerge as leaders and as experts in certain aspects of an overall task. The team learns to tap the various skills and talents of its members to the team's advantage. Cross-training begins to enable individuals to perform a larger number of individual tasks. Differences in personal styles become more accepted. One potential problem at this stage is team members' becoming more devoted to the team than to the company.

The fourth stage is the team's becoming more proactive in anticipating demand, improving performance, conducting peer assessments, and accepting new forms of responsibility. Fully empowered, self-managing work teams assume responsibility for virtually everything that impacts on the group. They no longer tolerate autocratic supervision. They take on the responsibility of hiring new members, ask for information about the company's overall performance, and seek incentive awards based on the profits generated by their efforts. Team members feel less threatened if management is open and straightforward in presenting future plans. Involving workers in the process of change gives managers more insight into which methods work best and gives workers an incentive to make the new program successful.

Management Role in Setting up Work Teams

Top management defines organizational objectives, which fall into two broad categories. The first category includes those objectives related to cost savings, productivity and quality improvement, and error reduction. The second category includes those objectives related to developing worker skills in leadership, self-confidence, teamwork, and increased knowledge. Both sets of objectives require continuing attention and commitment from management throughout the process of setting up work teams. Once objectives are defined and communicated, responsibilities are delegated for actual implementation. The sponsor, a senior level manager, plays a key role in setting up work teams. He or she should be a highly visible person, well respected by all, who has the power to make strategic decisions to ensure that the transition avoids roadblocks. The next key player is the coordinator. The coordinator directs and documents the process and markets the concept of self-managing work teams to both management and labor. The coordinator should be knowledgeable of the daily operations within the company, a good communicator, and able to influence decisions.

The advisory board or steering committee is formed from representatives of top management and other key positions within a company. Its functions are to:

- control the rate of implementing work teams,
- arrange training of leaders and facilitators,
- measure the progress of making the transition to work teams, and
- establish a reward system.

The advisory board also guides individual managers in direct contact with work teams. These managers:

- work with team leaders,
- are responsible for ensuring that team leaders are adequately trained,
- act on work team requests and recommendations, and
- ensure progress in setting up work teams.

Team leaders play important roles in setting up self-managing work teams. Team leaders must be trusted by management to mold an effective problem-solving team from a diverse group of individuals. Team leaders must be trained in planning, coordinating, group dynamics, teaching, and communicating. A team leader is expected to:

- obtain management support when necessary,
- plan with other work teams concerning the functions of his or her team,
- provide progress reports,
- participate in the training and developing of other leaders,
- activate the team and ensure that the team gains recognition for its progress,
- be aware of trouble signs both within and without the team, and
- take action in damage control to keep the process on track.

Training is a major aspect in the ultimate success of setting up work teams, and should include program coordinators, managers, team leaders and members. Training can be handled by outside consultants or by internally developing trainers, or a combination of both. Usually one team is ahead of others and becomes a pilot group. A pilot group acts as a role model, clearing a path for others by identifying common pitfalls. The transition to self-managing work teams must be carefully coordinated in order to avoid failure. Data gathering, graphing, Pareto analysis, brainstorming, and cause-and-effect analysis should be initially confined to relatively simple workplace problems. This enables team members to learn creative problem-solving techniques and effectively present their conclusions and recommendations to management. Early successes build confidence and experience to prepare the team to tackle more difficult and ambitious problems.

Once a team is set up, a measure of performance is necessary in order to judge its success. Work teams have to be continually nurtured. An award system is set up along with a means of communicating work team accomplishments throughout the company. Management should demonstrate its commitment by encouraging people to continue participating and by investing in training and education.

IS THERE REALLY A CHOICE?

Is there really a choice in having self-managing work teams? Compare two companies. One has a work force that reports to the factory and awaits directions. They are not expected to think; that is the prerogative of the bosses. They do only what they are told. The other has self-managing work teams able to function as a factory within a factory, a company within a company, motivated and eager to perform for the best interests of the company. Both companies compete with one another. Who'll win?

Quality no longer resides in some small office in manufacturing but now permeates an organization. Quality is everyone's business. But that is not enough. Continuous improvement in quality is necessary for a company to remain competitive in the global marketplace. *Kaizen* comes from the efforts of work teams. Openness and trust toward work teams can build a bridge of confidence and cooperation with management. Self-managing work teams allow workers to achieve their desire for growth and self-fulfillment, gaining recognition and approval from those around them. Self-managing work teams allow corporations to compete globally with quality products that people want to buy.

Setting up self-managing work teams, while a necessity, is not an easy process. It requires planning, dedication of effort, resources, and time. The benefit in increased productivity and, ultimately, for many companies, greatly increased profits. That's the lesson to be learned from NUMMI, Saturn, Harley Davidson, Motorola, and a host of other successful American companies and from all of Japan.

ENDNOTE

1. As published in the *Newark Star-Ledger*, December 27, 1998.

Chapter 6

From Forecasting to the Master Schedule

FORECASTING

Forecasting is both unavoidable and a challenge. It is unavoidable because a sales forecast is necessary for production and financial planning. Production planning requires a forecast to ensure that adequate production capacity is available to satisfy anticipated demand, arrange delivery of material and components from internal and external suppliers, set up production schedules, and make appropriate arrangements for delivering finished goods to customers. Financial planning requires a forecast to ensure adequate liquidity (cash inflows covering cash outflows) and adequate funds for capital improvements, debt servicing, and dividend disbursements.

Forecasting is a challenge because humans are being asked to peer into the future, a preserve of the gods. One begins to understand the nature of the challenge that forecasting poses with the realization that management has little control over future sales. Those factors under its control that affect future sales are product design and characteristics, marketing and distribution, customer service, and price. While these may seem important in determining future sales, consider the imponderables over which management has no control:

- competitors' actions,
- business and product life cycles, and
- changes in product perception, demographics, and government regulation.

There is only one time when a company can make a sales forecast with confidence where its actions directly affect future sales. That is when a company produces a poorly designed product of bad quality and attempts to sell it at a high price. A forecast can now be made with near certainty: sales will plummet. Other than that, all a company can say in effectively marketing a product whose design, quality, service, and price meet consumer expectations is that the company is still in the game. If a company is doing a better job than its competitors, it may gain market share. If not, it may lose market share. All one can conclude in doing the right things is that future sales may be above or below current levels. This is not a very useful forecast for planning purposes.

Competitors' Actions

Every competitor determines its version of a product in terms of design and characteristics, marketing and distribution, customer service, and price. A company has no control nor, presumably, any idea over what its competitors will do in product design, quality, service, and price. Oftentimes, a company is taken by surprise by competitors' actions and is forced to react after the fact rather than plan in advance. Even if a company knows what a competitor is up to, it is not in a position to judge its eventual success or failure.

A famous journalist was asked whether his intimate knowledge of current events helped him predict the course of future events. His response was that almost invariably the expected never occurred and what did occur was entirely unexpected. Historians have noted that those most affected by a major turning point in history, such as the French and Russian Revolutions, had no inkling that history was about to take a sharp turn. Foretelling the future has never been easy except for the friends on the psychic hot line.

The Business Cycle

A forecast is affected by the business cycle. If business activity is expanding, sales may grow regardless of management actions. Conversely, if business activity is contracting, sales may plummet despite vigorous actions to the contrary. Companies catering to discretionary spending by Wall Streeters have seen sales evaporate overnight after a sharp setback in the stock market.

A forecast has to consider where business activity is in terms of the business cycle plus any perceived change to business activity and its impact on future sales. Business activity can be measured in real and psychological terms. Real measures include gross domestic product, new home construction, and a host of other economic indicators published by the U.S. Department of Commerce, financial institutions, and trade organizations. Psychological measures include surveys of consumers and purchasing managers where past spending patterns are compared to anticipated spending patterns in order to construct indices for consumer and purchasing manager confidence. Positive confidence indices pointing to greater purchases by consumers and purchasing managers bode well for future business activity, and vice versa.

Another psychological measure of business activity reflecting the optimism or pessimism of businesspeople is help wanted ads. Businesspeople do not add to their workforce unless they feel confident that business will expand. The greater the number of help wanted ads, the greater the optimism of businesspeople. Advertising expenditures likewise follow the business cycle, although one would expect that businesspeople would increase advertising expenditures to counteract falling sales. They don't. The better they feel about business prospects, the more they advertise.

Unemployment and employment data fall within both camps. They are real measures of business activity but also have a profound affect on business psychology, particularly the unemployment rate. Rising unemployment is a warning sign to consumers that their jobs may be in jeopardy. In response to feeling more insecure about the future, consumers rein in spending to put more money into their nest eggs. A greater savings rate sounds virtuous, but spending is the ultimate source of revenue for companies. If consumers saved all their income, there would be no spending and therefore no revenue for companies supplying goods and services. Companies are forced to lay off workers if the shift to savings is too dramatic—too much saving can destroy an economy.

Most consumers do not realize that their spending and savings habits heavily influence the business cycle. The Great Depression of the 1930s was brought about by the 1929 Wall Street crash. This instantly affected consumer confidence, savings increased, spending decreased, corporate sales fell, and inventories rose. Factory owners were forced to curtail production and lay off workers. This heightened the fear of losing one's job and set off another round of less spending leading to more layoffs. This positive feedback system transformed a robust economy into a full-fledged depression in a matter of months.

The Great Depression lasted until World War II. Roosevelt's priming of the pump during the 1930s was not sufficient to induce consumer spending. Government deficit spending simply ended up in consumer savings accounts. World War II cured the malady behind the Great Depression when deficit spending for military procurement overwhelmed the penchant for consumers to save. Many who lived through the harrowing experience of the Great Depression bear a permanent scar: they are more apt to save than spend. The Wall Street plunge in 1987 was another close call that could have inaugurated a depression. For a period of time, purchases in capital goods such as houses, automobiles, and appliances nearly ceased. Fortunately, the stock market quickly recovered, and the blow to consumer confidence did not last long enough to start a round of production cutbacks and worker layoffs.

Product Life Cycle

Another factor affecting future sales over which management has virtually no control is the product life cycle. A product passes through the introduction, growth, maturity, and decline phases. A forecast is affected by where a product is in its life cycle.

Introduction Phase

The introduction phase is marked by intense entrepreneurial activity to develop a new product for consumer consumption. While some biotechnology and internet companies have developed commercially successful products, others have little in sales. They are financially sustained by stock offerings to investors who hope that these companies will eventually develop commercially successful products. No forecast for production planning need be performed until a product takes its first step into the growth phase of its life cycle.

Growth Phase

The growth phase is marked by initial consumer acceptance of a product. Many corporate entities compete with one another to establish a market for a new consumer product if not protected by a patent. If protected, then competition is among variants of a new product that do not infringe on the patent. In the 1880s with the introduction of the first cereal (Kellogg's), about 100 cereal companies were founded to establish a foothold in a new industry by introducing different brands of cereal. In the 1900s about 60 automobile companies competed for another new consumer product, many operating out of a garage. The digital camera is in its growth phase as a product. The cellular phone is still in its growth phase in some parts of the world and entering its maturity stage in others.

The United States was the most inventive nation in the world and led the world in filing new patents. The nation that invented and manufactured the radio and the television set is not the nation that invented and manufactured video cassette recorders (VCRs), compact disks (CDs), and digital cameras. This hurts the U.S. economy in that production rights belong to the patent holder. To be fair, the United States is still a bastion for entrepreneurial activity in biotechnology, computer, communications, and information technology, and other areas. Still, it has lost some of its ability to commercialize inventions.

Bell Labs invented the transistor, but Sony made it a commercial success (Walkman). RCA and Ampex invented the VCR, but Matsushita made it a commercial success. RCA's initial price for a VCR, based on production cost, was about $2,500. At that price, RCA considered the VCR market to be thousands of corporate boardrooms where the VCR would be used in boardroom presentations. Matsushita, on the other hand, saw the potential market for VCRs not as thousands of corporations but as millions of individuals if the cost of the VCR could be substantially reduced. Matsushita invested in product and process development and was able to cut the cost of VCRs from $2,500 to less than $400 if made and sold in the millions. Matsushita succeeded in making product and process improvements to substantially cut costs, set up large-scale plants to make VCRs by the millions, and eventually sold them by the millions. The Japanese continue to dominate the VCR market to this day.

An American invented the robot. A trade show held in the United States drew little interest. Factory owners considered robots an expensive capital investment, and labor unions threatened to strike if they were installed. Like Deming, after the inventor's show died in America, he packed his bags and went to Japan. The response to the trade show in Japan was overwhelming. Factory owners saw robots as a means to increase productivity and unions supported robots since they knew that displaced workers would be retrained and reassigned. The inventor licensed his patent rights to Kawasaki, which now dominates the world robot market. The untold thousands of scientists, engineers, technicians, managers, and workers designing and manufacturing robots are mainly Japanese, not Americans. The transistor, VCR, CDs, digital cameras, and robots stand as an indictment of the failure of U.S. management to do their job; "we've identified the enemy and the enemy is us."

The growth phase starts with a few consumers' owning a product and ends with most consumers' owning a product. Sales depend on how fast the product permeates the market and what a company and its competitors are doing to enhance their respective shares. Forecasting sales of a product in the growth phase is relatively easy: sales will continue to rise. Sales may continue to rise even with a loss in market share or a business slump; they simply rise at a slower pace.

Maturity Phase

The maturity stage is marked by market saturation. Most consumers who intended to own a product already own one. Sales are primarily for replacement. The market for automobiles is primarily replacing existing automobiles plus growth in population. A forecast for automobile sales takes into account the age profile of existing automobiles to gauge replacement needs, population growth, consumer confidence, and changes in market share. A product in its mature phase can revert back to its growth phase by expanding the market. Coca-Cola is in its maturity phase in Europe and North America and in its growth phase in Russia, Asia, South America, and Africa. Coca-Cola has been a corporate leader in becoming a global company in terms of management outlook and operations, serving as a model for others on how to successfully tap the world market.

Besides Coca-Cola, other brand-name products that have been in the maturity phase for over a century are Tide, Ivory Soap, Kellogg's, Quaker Oats, and Hershey chocolate. As its name implies, Coca-Cola's initial addictive properties helped to make it America's favorite drink. Today, it contains only the flavor of the coca leaf. Hershey chocolate is an interesting case in advertising. Up to 1905 Hershey advertised heavily and achieved market domination. Then it ceased advertising for about 80 years while maintaining market dominance despite its ugly brown wrapper.

An observation for products in their maturity stage is the relative paucity of companies compared to the number during the growth phase. For instance, there were 100 cereal companies during the growth phase in the late nineteenth century, and today a few companies dominate in the United States, such as

Kellogg's, Quaker Oats, Post, and General Mills. "General" suggests the company's formation as a conglomerate of once-competing companies. Ford competed with 60 companies and today, in the United States, there are 3. General Motors is a conglomerate of former competitors as are Chrysler, and, to a lesser extent, Ford itself. A half dozen firms dominate the computer, chemical, steel, and a host of other industries. Corporate concentration continues with the globalization of commerce such as the Daimler-Chrysler merger.

A few companies dominating a mature industry can be traced to the rise of trusts during the nineteenth century. Business cycles during the nineteenth century were particularly severe because a large number of competitors in basic industries could not avoid the temptation to add too much productive capacity during the good times of a business cycle. The inevitable business contractions were marked with worker layoffs, corporate bankruptcies, and banking crises. The intent of the trust makers, like Rockefeller, was to gain control over an industry in order to rein in excessive additions to productive capacity, the Achilles' heel of Adam Smith's free market. The trust makers felt that they were doing society a favor in controlling the degree of capacity expansion and output in order to stabilize prices, which, in turn, stabilized employment. Stable employment was good for workers. A stable price was good for paying suppliers for their services, repaying bank loans, and disbursing shareholders' dividends. Naturally, this was also good for the trust makers, although the trustbusters felt otherwise. Nevertheless, the legacy of the trust makers has survived the efforts of the trustbusters. A few large companies are in a better position to control capacity additions than a flock of small companies. Large companies can "coordinate" their activities without direct communication through third party trade publications. Top executives in all major industries read the same trade publications that detail what is going on among the industrial giants. There are no secrets, no surprises. This allows for an "armed truce" among competing corporate giants not to rock the boat too much by aggressive additions to productive capacity. Naturally, this is not a foolproof system, as seen by industries' periodically suffering from the effects of overcapacity.

Whereas control over capacity additions in the United States is indirect, in Japan it is direct. Japanese *keiretsus* are an outgrowth of the *zaibatsus* existing before World War II. The major difference between the two is in shareholdings. A powerful and influential Japanese noble family owned a *zaibatsu*. A *keiretsu* is owned partly by external shareholders such as individuals and financial institutions but mostly by internal holdings within the *keiretsu* and among other *keiretsus*. Since only a small portion of the shareholdings of a company can be purchased on the open market, the Japanese *keiretsus* are immune to raids by outsiders and forced mergers and acquisitions. Internal shareholdings are not for investment purposes, but to maintain managerial control.

The six principal *keiretsus*, which include Mitsubishi, Mitsui, and Sumitomo, control much of Japan's commerce. They are horizontally integrated with activities under centralized control within the *keiretsu*'s bank and its associated trading company. Horizontal integration means that the *keiretsu* participates in a broad range of industries. Manufacturing companies associated with a *keiretsu* cover nearly every facet of the Japanese economy such as chemicals, oil refining, consumer products, textiles, drugs, automobiles, construction, shipbuilding, and many others. Companies within a *keiretsu* do not compete as they are in separate industries. In addition, these "industrial core" companies are closely linked to thousands of suppliers. The galaxy of companies making up a *keiretsu* is controlled through mutual share holdings, common financial ties to a single bank and insurance company, and interlocking boards of directors. Moreover there is a sharing of managerial personnel among companies within a *keiretsu*, which fosters strong business and social ties. These various means of corporate control assure strong conformance of executives and managers to *keiretsu* policies. In other words, to an outsider, the galaxy of corporate entities making up a *keiretsu* behaves as a single entity.

There is intense competition among the *keiretsus* in the Japanese domestic market. The competition is so intense that Japanese companies feel that survival in the domestic market virtually assures them victory in the global market. Although the *keiretsus* compete with one another, they also coordinate their international and domestic activities through the Ministry of Trade and Industry (MITI). The *keiretsus* agree among themselves, under the guidance of MITI, on what products are to be championed in the global market and which *keiretsu* will lead the way. Once this decision is made, banking support automatically follows. There is no need for a loan application, another major difference in business practices between Japan and the United States. The *keiretsus*, coordinating their activities through MITI, also agree on additions to productive capacity. The *keiretsus* do not always succeed in preventing too much productive capacity from being built, but they certainly have a direct means to coordinate their activities, quite unlike the United States.

Since World War II, newly organized manufacturing groups in Japan have been vertically integrated. Vertical integration means the same degree of control over suppliers as with a *keiretsu*. Unlike *keiretsus*, these manufacturing groups are not organized around a bank and have a much narrower product line. They include Nippon Steel (steel), Matsushita and Hitachi (consumer electronics), Toyota and Nissan (automobiles), and others. Nevertheless, these manufacturing groups also coordinate their activities with MITI and each has a close banking tie to one of the *keiretsus*. A Western company may think that it competes against a Japanese company, but it doesn't. The competition isn't even the company's associated *keiretsu* because the *keiretsus* coordinate their activities through MITI. The competition is actually a corporate state known as Japan, Inc. Korea and other Asian nations have organized their industrial, government, and financial institutions with Japan as a model.

Whether companies restrict their numbers through mergers or acquisition or coordinate their activities through a government agency, the impact is the same. A few dominating companies in a mature market are in a better position to ensure that additions to productive capacity are kept within reasonable bounds to stabilize price and employment, service debt, and provide a return to shareholders. While not always successful, this practice is exactly what was promoted by the trust makers a century ago to deal with corporate anarchy.

Decline Phase

The decline phase of the product life cycle is often the result of a technological advance. Canals died with the advent of railroads. The number of passengers on railroads and ocean liners declined with the advent of the airlines, as did short-haul railroad freight with the advent of trucks. Mainframe computers lost business from the development of personal computers, advances in computer memory, and networking. Record players fell victim to tapes and CDs.

These are instances of decline over which management has no, or very little, control. There are instances of product decline where management has direct control. The introduction of a new model of an existing product line pushes the old model into its decline phase. The timing of the introduction of a new model is under the control of management. Production of the new and old models has to be carefully coordinated. The new model must be produced in sufficient numbers to replace the old. Production of the old model has to be cut before a new model is introduced to avoid a write-off of obsolete inventory.

Product Perception

The buying public's having a change of heart in product perception has a major impact on future sales. Years ago a shift in the public's perception of the relative health consequences of drinking hard liquor versus beer and wine caused hard liquor sales to slump as beer and wine sales soared. Both were beyond the control of marketing managers to influence sales. Sometime later, a shift in consumer preference from red to white wine brought great distress to those growing red grapes. Again, no expenditure in advertising on the virtues of red wine could stem the shift in product preference.

Cigarette companies should be suffering from declining sales as the U.S. government wages war against smoking. Dire warnings, prohibition of smoking in public areas, and enormous hikes in taxes have changed the American public's perception on smoking. One would reasonably forecast a decline in cigarette sales in the United States, but certainly not in China. The Chinese have discovered the joy of smoking. A few discretionary dollars in their pockets instantly go up in a cloud of cigarette smoke. Opening up the market to 1 billion Chinese more than compensates for any loss in a market one quarter its size.

Demographics

Demographics affect sales. The United States went through a 10-year or so spell when women had fewer babies. Hence, sales of baby products fell despite attempts by marketing managers to expand sales. No babies, no need for diapers. Therefore, diaper sales were projected to fall, along with a declining birthrate. It made sense, but it didn't happen. Diaper sales expanded in response to growth in another segment of the population: the incontinent aged.

A cigarette company in reviewing multifaceted attacks on its business in the United States would forecast a decline in sales. So would a diaper manufacturer in reviewing data on a falling birthrate. Yet reality was just the opposite, illustrating the nature of imponderables affecting a forecast.

Government Regulation

Government regulation affects future sales. Consider gasoline additives mandated by environmental legislation. The market for gasoline additives was nonexistent prior to a government edict and ballooned after it was issued. Thus, the sales forecast is either zero or some huge figure. Does forecasting the timing of a government regulation fit into the definition of an imponderable? If not, then what does?

FORECASTING BY MARKETING

Forecasting can be done either by marketing or by production. A marketing forecast generally consists of a survey or poll, starting with those in charge of sales in a territory. A territory salesperson is the individual most knowledgeable about what is happening in an area under his or her responsibility. The salesperson is in constant contact with buyers and knows their intentions and what competitors are doing. No one is better positioned to do a sales forecast for the panhandle of Texas than the territory salesperson. All the aforementioned imponderables become integrated into a single number when the salesperson submits his or her forecast for each item in a product line.

A forecast for Texas is obtained by combining the forecast for the panhandle of Texas with the other territory sales forecasts within Texas. The southwest region sales forecast is obtained by combining the forecasts for Texas, New Mexico, and Arizona. The U.S. sales forecast is obtained by combining the regional sales forecasts. The North America sales forecast can be obtained by combining the forecasts for Canada, United States, and Mexico. A global sales forecast can be obtained by adding the forecasts for other parts of the world.

Every company does a marketing forecast, so what is wrong with a marketing forecast? A territory salesperson may be biased and may intentionally over- or underestimate sales. The bias is partly caused by a forecast's being revisited on a forecaster. Suppose that a territory salesperson forecasts widget sales at 10,000 units and actual sales are below the forecast. The following conversation is apt to take place between a territory salesperson and his or her superior.

"I see that you projected sales at 10,000 for this quarter."

"Yes, I did."

"The quarter is almost over, and it looks like your actual sales will be around 8,000."

"That's about right."

"So?"

"So what?"

"So why are your sales below what you projected?"

Then follows an explanation of the territory salesperson on how one customer after another failed to live up to his or her earlier expectations.

"So what are you going to do about it?"

"About what?"

"About getting sales up to where you said they would be in your forecast?"

Then follows another painful explanation on what actions the salesperson is taking to rectify the situation.

"Oh, by the way, what is your sales forecast for the next quarter?"

What would you say if you were the territory salesperson?

A forecast being revisited on the forecaster introduces bias into a forecast. Under these circumstances, the territory salesperson may be strongly tempted to "lowball," or purposefully underestimate his or her forecast in order never to experience the previous conversation again. Another reason to lowball is any perceived connection between a forecast and a sales target that generates an incentive bonus.

However, there are reasons for "highballing" a forecast. One is unintentional, reflecting the natural optimism of salespeople to overestimate their ability to consummate a sale. The other is an intentional inflating of a sales forecast for recognition. Personnel promotions in marketing are based on sales performance. Suppose that the salesperson in the panhandle of Texas wants to be promoted to head of sales for Texas when this position opens up in the near future. The first step in nailing down a promotion is establishing eligibility. This starts with being noticed. How does a salesperson become noticed? The best way is to set a high performance goal and meet it. How this is done is immaterial. Maybe the salesperson inveigles friends among the company's customers to make future purchases now and be billed later to artificially inflate current performance. Maybe prices are discounted aggressively to build up sales volume. Perhaps the salesperson is spending 20 hours a day stealing business from competitors. It doesn't matter as long as he or she gets noticed, the first step to being promoted.

Another cause for highballing marketing forecasts is confusion between what will actually be sold and a marketing goal. The marketing goal may be a 10 percent increase in sales. That doesn't mean that sales will go up by 10 percent. Marketing may expect sales to go up by no more than 1 percent, but forecasts 10 percent because that is their goal. Sometimes marketing gives a high forecast in order to ensure that there is plenty of inventory to instantly gratify customers. Highballing a forecast may serve the interests of marketing, but not those in production and financial planning.

Therefore, bias or a hidden agenda is introduced in a marketing forecast because a forecast can be revisited on the forecaster or be influenced by an incentive program or be a step toward advancement. Hardly anyone is telling the unvarnished truth. The irony of salespeople' lowballing and highballing is that one tends to balance the other. Thus, an aggregate forecast for sales may be more accurate than the individual forecasts that constitute it.

FORECASTING BY PRODUCTION

The great advantage of a marketing forecast is that the forecasters look forward into the future. They are intimately familiar with the market and the many imponderables that affect sales. The great disadvantage of a forecast done by production is that production has no contact with the market. Rather than looking forward, a production forecast looks backward, relying on the "past being prelude to the future." A production forecast is a mathematical massaging of historical sales figures to divine the future. If the past actually determines the future, as is inferred in a production forecast, then there would hardly be a need for managers. Fig. 6.1 illustrates past sales for widgets. Sales have been trending upward, but the recent dive is disturbing. What is the production sales forecast?

Figure 6.1
Past Sales Volume

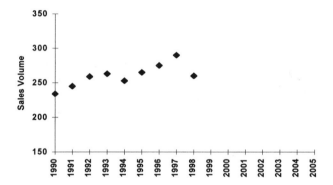

Microsoft Excel can fit trend lines to data, and a forecast can be obtained by extrapolating a trend line. Trend lines are obtained by clicking on the data in Fig. 6.1, right click and select *FORMAT DATA SERIES* and *INSERT TRENDLINES*. After choosing a trend line, click on the *OPTIONS* tab and select trend line formula and its associated R-square. Table 6.1 lists the various types of mathematical expressions along with their respective R-squares for the historical data in Figure 6.1. The various trend lines are illustrated in Fig. 6.2. A numerical forecast of sales can be obtained using the applicable formulas generated for each trend line (not shown). When substituting into the Excel trend line formulas to obtain numerical results, the appropriate entry for the first year is "1," not, in this case, "1990."

Table 6.1
Trend Lines

CURVE	MATHEMATICAL EXPRESSION	R-SQUARE
A	Exponential	60%
B	Linear	59
C	Logarithmic	67
D	Power	69
E	Polynomial 2nd Power	68
F	Polynomial 3rd Power	70
G	Polynomial 4th Power	88

Figure 6.2
A Plethora of Choice

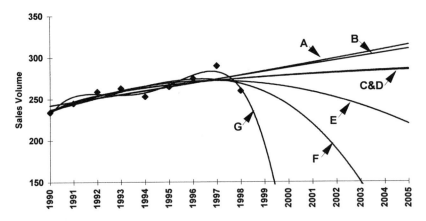

Mathematically speaking, the best-fitting curve is the one with the highest R-square, which is curve G. Notice how the oscillation in curve G more closely fits past data than the other curves. Although curve G is the best-fitting line mathematically, should this be the basis for doing a forecast? If so, then the future spells doom for the company as sales dive into oblivion. Oh, you don't like curve G; then which one would you select?

The problem of doing a forecast in Microsoft Excel is the relative ease of generating a family of trend lines. This leaves the forecaster with the chore of selecting the appropriate trend line. Microsoft Excel essentially negates the value of a production forecast by providing such a wide ranging choice of rising and falling trend lines. Yet one must be selected. Faced with this predicament, an individual performing a production forecast must confer with marketing to get a sense on the future direction of the market. This necessity leads to the following observation concerning forecasting: first do a production forecast. This quickly provides a set of mathematically valid forecasts. With these in hand, sit down with marketing and identify which one best fits their sense of the future direction of the market.

A production forecast must be submitted to marketing for comment because the forecast is independent of what is being sold. The same set of historical data leads to the same forecast whether the product is widgets, elephant tusks, or illegal contraband. A production forecast not only does not consider what the product is but has no allowance for business factors affecting future sales such as the award or loss of a major business contract or opening up a new or losing an existing market. Nor is there any allowance for what a company is doing to enhance sales, what competitors are doing in response, changes in business activity, and a product's transition from one life cycle phase to another. Nor is there any allowance for changes in product perception by consumers, demographic factors, and possible government regulation. Only in discussing a production forecast with marketing can this vital information on imponderables be integrated into the forecast.

AGGREGATE PLANNING

Aggregate planning is the next step in the production planning process to sense the relationship between overall productive capacity and the sales forecast. Suppose that the annual forecast for air conditioners in the coming year is 60,000. Further suppose that sales are primarily in Canada and are concentrated in the summer months: 20 percent of annual sales in June, 30 percent in July, and 50 percent in August. One approach to aggregate planning is to match production with actual demand. Suppose that goods produced in one month are sold the next. Fig. 6.3 illustrates production, sales, and inventory under these circumstances.

Figure 6.3
Match Production with Actual Demand

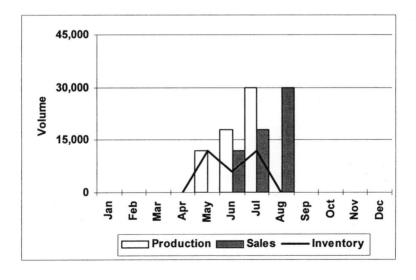

The advantage of this production strategy is a minimum amount of finished goods inventory. If production exactly matched demand, there would be no inventory. The disadvantages are twofold, labor and financial. Workers are hired in June, more in July, and even more in August, all to be let go in September. This hire-and-fire labor policy has definite drawbacks. Good workers seek work elsewhere. There are high training and severance costs (in the United States, companies fund state unemployment benefits). The quality of the product suffers when workers barely beginning to learn their jobs are then laid off. There is a financial reason not to pursue this production strategy. The plant has to be sized to peak demand, which, in this case, is 30,000 units per month. Hence, the plant is fully utilized one month per year, partly utilized two months, and idle nine months. Offhand, it sounds like a waste of capital resources.

A better alternative may be to match production with average demand of 5,000 air conditioners per month. Here, the plant is one-sixth of the capacity of a plant sized to match production with actual demand, hence one-sixth the investment. The plant is fully utilized throughout the year, and the workforce is stabilized. Work teams can be organized for continuous product improvement. The benefits are a smaller-sized plant producing a better product. The disadvantage, seen in Fig. 6.4, is the cost of carrying a considerable amount of inventory.

Figure 6.4
Match Production with Average Demand

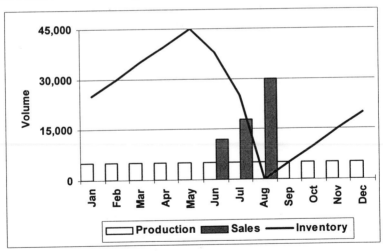

A third alternative is to introduce overtime during the peak sales season to reduce inventory. Figure 6.5 shows the spreadsheet for producing 5,000 units per month, normal time only (eight-hour working day), illustrated in Figure 6.4. Normal time production is annual production less total overtime production divided by 12 months. The formula in cell D6 is =($F$1-SUM(E6:E17))/12. The remaining cells in column D reference cell D6. Ending inventory in January is the initial ending inventory for the previous year less what is shipped out in

January plus what is made in normal and overtime. The formula in cell F6 is =F5-C6+D6+E6, replicated down. Initial inventory in cell F5 has been manually adjusted in order to minimize inventory holdings (zero inventory at the end of August). Total inventory carrying cost is $3 per unit in inventory per month. Cell F19 totals January through December inventory and multiplies the sum by $3 to determine the cost of $864,000 for following this aggregate plan.

Figure 6.5
Aggregate Plan with Normal Time Only

	A	B	C	D	E	F
1	SALES FORECAST FOR AIR CONDITIONERS:					60,000
2						
3				MONTHLY PROD		INVENTORY
4		SEASONAL	MONTHLY	NORMAL	OVER	STARTING
5		FACTOR	SALES	TIME	TIME	20,000
6	JAN		-	5,000	0	25,000
7	FEB		-	5,000	0	30,000
8	MAR		-	5,000	0	35,000
9	APR		-	5,000	0	40,000
10	MAY		-	5,000	0	45,000
11	JUN	20%	12,000	5,000	0	38,000
12	JUL	30%	18,000	5,000	0	25,000
13	AUG	50%	30,000	5,000	0	-
14	SEP		-	5,000	0	5,000
15	OCT		-	5,000	0	10,000
16	NOV		-	5,000	0	15,000
17	DEC		-	5,000	0	20,000
18						
19			TOTAL:	60,000	-	288,000
20			COST ELEMENTS:	$	10	$ 3
21			COST:	$	-	$ 864,000
22			TOTAL COST:			$ 864,000

Fig. 6.6 shows the same spreadsheet with overtime. Six hundred additional units can be made in overtime per month. Overtime has been arbitrarily selected for May through August. The formula for monthly normal time production takes into account overtime production to keep annual production at 60,000. Inventory in cell F5 was adjusted until August's ending inventory became zero. Suppose that units made in overtime generate an incremental charge of $10 per unit for work done in overtime. The total cost of $859,200 with four months of overtime is preferable over the previous total of $864,000 with no overtime. While this is better, it may not necessarily be the best. The best policy for minimizing total overtime and inventory carrying costs can be obtained through What's Best linear programming.[1] What cell was being watched when evaluating different overtime scenarios? This determines the objective cell. The objective cell is total cost in cell F22, which is to be minimized. What cells were being adjusted when manually evaluating the different scenarios? The beginning inventory in cell F5 and the overtime cells E6:E17 were the only ones being changed. These are designated adjustable cells. The more difficult part of the exercise in setting up a linear program is identifying constraints. Often, the human mind leaves constraints neatly buried in the subconscious. These are raised to the level of consciousness when reviewing the results of a linear program without the appropriate constraints.

Figure 6.6
Aggregate Plan with Normal Time and Overtime

	A	B	C	D	E	F
1	SALES FORECAST FOR AIR CONDITIONERS:					60,000
2						
3				MONTHLY PROD		INVENTORY
4		SEASONAL	MONTHLY	NORMAL	OVER	STARTING
5		FACTOR	SALES	TIME	TIME	19,200
6	JAN		-	4,800	0	24,000
7	FEB		-	4,800	0	28,800
8	MAR		-	4,800	0	33,600
9	APR		-	4,800	0	38,400
10	MAY		-	4,800	600	43,800
11	JUN	20%	12,000	4,800	600	37,200
12	JUL	30%	18,000	4,800	600	24,600
13	AUG	50%	30,000	4,800	600	-
14	SEP		-	4,800	0	4,800
15	OCT		-	4,800	0	9,600
16	NOV		-	4,800	0	14,400
17	DEC		-	4,800	0	19,200
18						
19			TOTAL:	57,600	2,400	278,400
20			COST ELEMENTS:	$ 10	$ 3	
21			COST:	$ 24,000	$ 835,200	
22			TOTAL COST:		$ 859,200	

Overtime has to be limited to 600 per month. In an empty cell, the constraint =WB(E6,"<=",600) is entered and replicated down for the remaining months. The program was run, and it became evident that another constraint was needed: =WB(F5,">",0) replicated down, to prevent What's Best, in seeking to minimize costs, from generating a solution with negative inventory. The optimal solution in Fig. 6.7 shows that the best course of action is to have three months of overtime from June through August.

Figure 6.7
Optimal Aggregate Plan

	A	B	C	D	E	F
1	SALES FORECAST FOR AIR CONDITIONERS:					60,000
2						
3				MONTHLY PROD		INVENTORY
4		SEASONAL	MONTHLY	NORMAL	OVER	STARTING
5		FACTOR	SALES	TIME	TIME	19,400
6	JAN		-	4,850	0	24,250
7	FEB		-	4,850	0	29,100
8	MAR		-	4,850	0	33,950
9	APR		-	4,850	0	38,800
10	MAY		-	4,850	0	43,650
11	JUN	20%	12,000	4,850	600	37,100
12	JUL	30%	18,000	4,850	600	24,550
13	AUG	50%	30,000	4,850	600	-
14	SEP		-	4,850	0	4,850
15	OCT		-	4,850	0	9,700
16	NOV		-	4,850	0	14,550
17	DEC		-	4,850	0	19,400
18						
19			TOTAL:	58,200	1,800	279,900
20			COST ELEMENTS:	$ 10	$ 3	
21			COST:	$ 18,000	$ 839,700	
22			TOTAL COST:		$ 857,700	

MASTER SCHEDULE

The forecast is generally done in terms of a nominal product. For instance, a forecast for air conditioners is simply the aggregate forecast for air conditioners, not specific models. The master schedule takes into account different models of air conditioners and can be easily calculated when production is kept constant all year. Suppose that model A is 60 percent of sales, model B is 30 percent, and model C is 10 percent. The market share for each model is derived from actual sales data. Market shares should be adjusted to take into account any underlying trend. For instance, model A may be gaining market share at the expense of model B. The market shares should include an extrapolation of this trend. The master schedule for daily production in Table 6.2 is based on an annual aggregate forecast of 60,000 air conditioners and 20 working days per month.

Table 6.2
Derivation of Daily Master Schedule

	MODEL A	MODEL B	MODEL C
Market share	60%	30%	10%
Annual sales	36,000	18,000	6,000
Monthly production	3,000	1,500	500
Daily master schedule	150	75	25

Annual sales' being confined to three summer months results in a massive accumulation of inventory in Figure 6.4. Any action to enhance sales during the slack season of nine months of the year would reduce the extent of inventory accumulation necessary to stabilize the workforce. In this case, one could expand the market from Canada to southern U.S., where air conditioner sales are more even throughout the year. This still leaves a summer seasonal peak. Expanding the market to the Southern Hemisphere, where seasons are the opposite of the Northern Hemisphere, would tend to level out annual sales and reduce the need for inventory accumulation. Another alternative is to build furnaces along with air conditioners, as both are contraseasonal. Air conditioners can be built during the spring and summer and furnaces during fall and winter. However, the master schedule becomes more complicated because the mix of air conditioners and furnaces to be manufactured changes monthly.

Master Schedule Derived by Linear Programming

Wells Industries makes air conditioners and furnaces year-round.[2] Monthly seasonal factors are obtained by comparing sales of a particular month with a running average plus and minus six months about a particular month. If possible, this analysis should be done on a multiyear basis to find out whether the monthly seasonal factors are reasonably consistent one year to the next. For no seasonal variation in sales, a comparison of monthly sales to a running annual average would result in a "monthly seasonal factor" of 1/12, or 8.33 percent, of annual sales. This monthly seasonal factor of 8.33 percent would not hold if sales were seasonal. Monthly seasonal factors below 8.33 percent are associated with the slack season; while those above with the busy season. For example, suppose that annual sales are expected to be 120,000. With no seasonal variation, monthly sales are 10,000 units. With seasonal variation in sales, a monthly seasonal factor during the slack season may be 5 percent, or anticipated sales of 6,000, not 10,000 units. A monthly seasonal factor during the busy season may be 10 percent, resulting in anticipated sales of 12,000 units. Monthly seasonal factors must total 100 percent over the course of the year. Projected monthly sales for an annual forecast of 120,000 units for air conditioners and 60,000 units for furnaces for the indicated monthly seasonal factors are listed in Table 6.3.

Table 6.3
Seasonal Factors for Air Conditioners

	A	B	C	D	E
1	WELLS INDUSTRIES MASTER SCHEDULING CONTROL BOARD				
2			A/C		FURN
3	SALES FORECAST:		120,000		60,000
4		A/C		FURN	
5		MONTHLY		MONTHLY	
6		SEASONAL	MONTHLY	SEASONAL	MONTHLY
7		FACTOR	SALES	FACTOR	SALES
8	JAN	1%	1,200	12%	7,200
9	FEB	1%	1,200	6%	3,600
10	MAR	2%	2,400	4%	2,400
11	APR	4%	4,800	8%	4,800
12	MAY	8%	9,600	10%	6,000
13	JUN	22%	26,400	12%	7,200
14	JUL	38%	45,600	8%	4,800
15	AUG	16%	19,200	4%	2,400
16	SEP	5%	6,000	4%	2,400
17	OCT	1%	1,200	10%	6,000
18	NOV	1%	1,200	10%	6,000
19	DEC	1%	1,200	12%	7,200
20	TOTAL	100%	120,000	100%	60,000

The annual cost of regular factory workers is $12 per hour paid whether a worker is at work or on vacation. In overtime, workers are paid a 50 percent premium. Overtime cannot exceed 20 percent of the normal monthly hours (seven hours per day, 20 days per month). During June, July, and August, the peak season for air conditioner sales, 20 percent of the regular workforce is on vacation and no one desires overtime work. During these months, a temporary workforce is hired made up mainly of local students and retirees. Summer workers are hired for the entire three-month period and are paid $8 per hour.

Each air conditioner requires 6 hours of labor, and each furnace 8 hours of labor. One component is manufactured internally, requiring 0.1 hours of labor. The remaining components are purchased from outside vendors. Inventory carrying cost is equivalent to 3 percent of the value (labor plus material) of the inventory per month. Machine and equipment limitations constrain maximum plant output. Unlike aggregate planning where the starting inventory was determined, in the master schedule, the starting inventory is the actual inventory. Equal starting and ending inventories restrict the factory to producing to demand; that is, a forecast of 120,000 units in sales results in factory production of 120,000 units. As in aggregate planning, inventory in any given month is the previous month's ending inventory, plus the current month's production less shipments, which is the monthly sales forecast. Safety stock, or minimum inventory to handle fluctuations in sales, is 1,000 for air conditioners and furnaces. The challenge is to set up a master schedule to answer the following questions:

1. What should be the size of the regular workforce given a maximum availability of 725 individuals?
2. When and how many hours should they work in overtime?
3. How many summer workers should be hired in June given a maximum availability of 100 individuals?
4. What is the master schedule for the production of air conditioners, furnaces, and the single component that is manufactured internally in order to minimize labor and inventory carrying costs?

Figures 6.8 through 6.10 are the solution spreadsheets. The adjustable cells initially had values of zero. In Figure 6.8, cell F5 is adjustable for determining the number of regular workers up to a maximum of 725, or =WB(F5,"<",725) in cell G5. Cells F8:F19 contain the hours available, which is 140 hours per worker per month, except for June, July, and August, where there is a 20 percent reduction for summer vacation. Overtime cells in column G are adjustable except for the summer months, where the cells are fixed at zero. Overtime, =WB(G8,"<",0.2*F8), cannot exceed 20 percent of regular time. The overtime constraint is replicated down to cover the remaining months other than the summer months where the cells are fixed at zero. Cell H5 is also adjustable with an associated constraint that the cell cannot exceed a value of 100, or =WB(H5,"<",100). Hours available are 140 hours per month per summer employee for the summer months only.

Column J contains the adjustable cells for the monthly production of air conditioners (again, as with other adjustable cells, the initial values were zero). Beginning inventory is 30,000 units. Subsequent inventory takes into account units made by normal, overtime, and summer labor less what is shipped out from the forecast. The formula in cell K8 is: =K7+J8-C8. Air conditioner inventory has a safety stock of 1,000 units, or =WB(K8,">",1000), replicated down. The ending inventory is desired to be the same as the beginning inventory, or =WB(K19,">",K20). An "equal" sign could have been used in this constraint, but a "greater than" sign was used. Since total costs are being minimized, one would expect that the ending inventory would be no more than the desired inventory. The "greater than" sign reduces the possibility of an infeasible solution if for some reason this condition cannot be satisfied.

Figure 6.8
Wells Industries Spreadsheet Part I

	F	G	H	I	J	K
3	REGULAR		SUMMER			
4	WORKERS		WORKERS			A/C
5	725	=<=	100			STARTING
6	NORMAL	OVERTIME	SUMMER		A/C	INVENTORY
7	HOURS	HOURS	HOURS		PROD	30,000
8	101,500	-			8,538	37,338
9	101,500	-			6,623	42,761
10	101,500	-			6,143	46,504
11	101,500	6,880			15,971	57,675
12	101,500	9,500			18,000	66,075
13	81,200		14,000		400	40,075
14	81,200		14,000		15,075	9,551
15	81,200		14,000		10,649	1,000
16	101,500	-			6,143	1,143
17	101,500	-			6,143	6,086
18	101,500	1,520			8,314	13,200
19	101,500	9,000			18,000	30,000
20					DESIRED	30,000

Fig. 6.9 shows the next portion of the spreadsheet. Columns M and P are adjustable for manufacturing the furnaces and the component. The inventory formula for the furnaces is constructed similarly to that for the air conditioners. The inventory formula for the component takes into account that the demand for the component is one for each air conditioner and one for each furnace. The formula in cell Q8 is: =Q7+P8-J8-M8. This formula can be edited to accommodate a multiple number of components in each finished product. The ending inventories for the furnaces and the component are not the same as the initial inventories to demonstrate that inventory adjustments can be incorporated in the model. As with air conditioners, constraints were added for the last month's inventory to be the same or greater than the desired inventory and to maintain a minimum safety stock of 1,000 for the furnaces and none for the component.

As yet, there is nothing linking labor to production. Labor hours required are the number of air conditioners made multiplied by 6 hours per unit plus the number of furnaces made multiplied by 8 hours per unit plus the number of components made multiplied by 0.1 hour per unit. Labor hours available are the sum of the hours of the regular workforce working normal and overtime plus the summer workforce. =WB(6*J8+8*M8+0.1*P8,"=",SUM(F8:H8)) is the constraint linking labor required to manufacture the indicated number of air conditioners, furnaces, and components with labor availability. The equal sign ensures that the workforce is always fully employed. Care has to be exercised when using equal signs in constraints to avoid an infeasible solution.

Machinery limitations are such that no more than 18,000 air conditioners, =WB(J8,"<",18000), can be made per month, and no more than 12,000 furnaces, =WB(M8,"<",12000), both replicated down. Moreover, the sum of air conditioners and furnaces cannot exceed a straight line connecting 12,000 on the y-axis, representing the number of furnaces manufactured, and 18,000 on the x-axis, representing the number of air conditioners manufactured, or =WB(M8+2*J8/3,"<",12000), replicated down.

Figure 6.9
Wells Industries Spreadsheet Part II

	M	N	O	P	Q
3					
4		FURN			COMP
5		STARTING			STARTING
6	FURN	INVENTORY		COMP	INVENTORY
7	PROD	2,000		PROD	8,000
8	6,200	1,000		6,738	-
9	7,543	4,943		14,166	0
10	7,905	10,448		14,048	0
11	1,352	7,000		17,324	-
12	-	1,000		30,000	12,000
13	11,600	5,400		-	-
14	400	1,000		15,475	-
15	3,733	2,333		14,383	0
16	7,905	7,838		14,048	-
17	7,905	9,743		14,048	-
18	6,457	10,200		14,771	-
19	-	3,000		25,000	7,000
20	DESIRED	3,000		DESIRED	7,000

Another constraint is that the manufacturing component line must be shut down for one month for maintenance. This is accommodated in Fig. 6.10 where cells Q24 through Q35 are adjustable binary integers that can have the value of only 0 or 1. A constraint was added for the sum of these cells to be 11. This forces the line to be shut down for one month when linked to the production constraint for making the component. The constraint in cell P24, =WB(P8,"<",30000*Q24), replicated down, ensures that production of the component cannot exceed a maximum of 30,000 per month subject to the production line's being available that month. Referring to Figure 6.9, the solution is to schedule the component's production line maintenance for June.

Figure 6.10
Wells Industries Spreadsheet Part III

	L	M	N	O	P	Q
22					MAX PROD	
23					COMP	
24					<=	1
25			COSTS ($000)		<=	1
26	NORMAL TIME		$ 14,616		<=	1
27	OVERTIME		$ 484		<=	1
28	SUMMER		$ 336		=<=	1
29					=<=	0
30	INVENTORY COSTS				<=	1
31	AIR CONDITIONERS	$	1,982		<=	1
32	FURNACES	$	502		<=	1
33	COMPONENTS	$	15		<=	1
34					<=	1
35	TOTAL COSTS		$ 17,935		<=	1

In minimizing total cost, the solution incorporates as much low-cost summer labor as possible backing out fulltime employees. Inventory carrying cost is 3 percent of the value of the labor and material per month per unit in inventory. The objective cell to be minimized is total cost in cell N35. The master schedule of production for the air conditioners, furnaces, and components contained in Figures 6.8 and 6.9 minimizes total labor and inventory carrying costs. If a production manager deviates from this schedule, costs will be higher. By substituting the actual schedule into the spreadsheet without violating any constraints, a production manager can obtain the incremental cost for following a nonoptimal schedule.

ENDNOTES

1. What's Best software available from www. lindo.com.
2. Case taken from *What's Best Linear Programming (Fifteen Cases)*, available from www.palisade.com and www.nerses.com.

Chapter 7

Inventory and Purchasing Practices

Materials and inventory management overlap in many areas even to the extent where one manager may be responsible for both. This chapter focuses primarily on managing inventory and on inventory and purchasing practices. However, there are elements of materials management in this chapter, as there are elements of inventory management in the next.

Inventory is the second largest investment after plant and equipment, which, if effectively managed, enhances a company's competitive position. The traditional purposes of inventory in the United States are to:

1. service customers,
2. protect against raw material and component shortages,
3. permit truckload purchases for largest discount,
4. hedge against a potential strike or price hike,
5. level production activities to stabilize employment,
6. decouple successive stages of production,
7. facilitate switching from one product to another.

While these purposes have traditionally guided U.S. inventory managers, not all apply in Japan. This chapter discusses both the similarities and differences in approach in inventory practices between the two nations.

SERVICE CUSTOMERS

Finished goods inventory services customers. Physical distribution managers are responsible for the storage and distribution of finished goods from the factory to wholesalers, retailers, and consumers. They are usually assigned to the marketing department or to a logistics department if one exists. Finished goods inventory management is undergoing a major transition from make, then sell to sell, then make. The transition started in Japan not so much by inspiration as by necessity. Land is too valuable in Japan to park scores or hundreds of automobiles commonly seen in U.S. automobile dealers' lots. When land values peaked in the late 1980s, the Australian government fortuitously sold a lot next to its embassy in Tokyo for $500 million, enough to cover its budget deficit for that year. Acres of land cannot be dedicated to carrying an inventory of cars in a nation where a buyer must have a document attesting that he or she has a place to park the car before a car can be purchased.

A Japanese automobile buyer visits a dealer and makes a decision based on the dealer's finished goods inventory of one car per model, about a half dozen in number. Once a decision is made, the buyer sits down with the dealer to fill out an order form specifying the model, exterior color and interior design, option package, and other details. The order is then faxed to the factory, where it becomes a factory order. This need not necessarily be a factory order for one because a large portion of Japanese automobile production is exported. The factory order could be for a small number of identical cars. Nevertheless, the automobile is assembled and delivered within a week of placing the order. There is virtually no finished goods inventory of automobiles in Japan other than dealers' models.

This was a matter of necessity rather than a flash of inspiration, but finished goods inventory carrying costs are limited to just a few automobiles. A Japanese dealer does not have the expense that a large U.S. automobile dealer bears in financing, insuring, and maintaining 100 or more automobiles plus guarding against theft. Moreover, a U.S. dealer faces the inevitable loss of value with the passage of time (New Year's Day adds one year to the age of every automobile in inventory). These carrying costs, which may amount to 30 percent or more of the value of inventory per year, must be passed on to the consumer for the dealer to stay in business. Presumably, if automobiles in the United States could be ordered, then manufactured, and delivered within a week, their price would reflect savings in inventory carrying costs.

Automobiles depreciate in value in a fairly predictable fashion. Other types of inventories can lose value overnight. The introduction of a new personal computer model instantly cuts the inventory value of the old model in half. The owner of an inventory of any product where new models are being introduced faces the risk of obsolescence. A manufacturer has ample warning to dispose of an inventory before a new model is introduced. This is not true for independent wholesalers and retailers. All they know is that they must slash prices to get rid of a now-obsolete inventory when a new model is available. Sometimes there is no warning for anyone. The fickleness of the buying public can obliterate the value of inventory overnight. Clothes in fashion one day may not be in fashion the next. Inventory value for fashion clothes can even turn negative if the inventory has to be disposed of if it can't be sold. The fear of being stuck with a warehouse full of fashion clothes no longer in fashion has been a prime mover in the transition from make, then sell to sell, then make.

One fashion clothes maker has a centralized manufacturing facility in Europe linked via global telecommunications to checkout counters at its principal retail outlets. When a purchase is made, the checkout counter takes care of the payment details and records the sale to update the store's inventory. This is normal. What is unusual is that the sale is also recorded electronically at the factory. Suppose that 38 size 40 Star Spangled jeans are sold at all the company's outlets. The company's flexible manufacturing system can respond rapidly with minimal setup time and costs to replenish only what has been sold. Within a short time of the sale of 38 size 40 Star Spangled ugly-to-look-at and uncomfortable-to-wear jeans, the manufacturing system responds by producing exactly 38 size 40 Star Spangled jeans. This is quite unlike traditional manufacturing systems where response time is slow and setup costs are high. This forces a long production run of size 40 Star Spangled jeans, many of which are to reside in a warehouse.

With a flexible manufacturing system, 38 jeans are sold, and 38 jeans are made. The jeans are combined with other items already sold and shipped to the respective outlets. The time between selling first and making later is kept short by a quick response by the factory and a rapid means of transport. The factory has no warehouse, nor do the outlets have any stockrooms to store finished goods. Finished goods inventory is limited to what is on the retail outlet shelves and what is in transit, drastically reducing the risk of obsolescence.

This is a major departure from the traditional practice of first manufacturing a warehouse of goods and praying that consumers will eventually empty it. The transition in finished goods inventory practices is to reverse the sequence. First a sufficient quantity is made to fill the retail outlet shelves. From that point on, goods are made to replace those sold. After the first initial run to stock the shelves, purchases trigger factory orders. This trend is in its early stage of development and will grow with time. It requires an automatic and reliable means of collecting and transmitting information, a flexible manufacturing system, and a dependable and rapid means of transport. All these are costs, indeed, extra costs of doing business over the traditional method of manufacture, store, and pray for sales. The benefit is reduced carrying costs in having a small finished goods inventory suitable for servicing customers with minimal exposure to the risks of obsolescence and spoilage (aging of inventory).

The concept is spreading. A neighborhood hardware store has its entire inventory on its shelves without a stockroom. The shelves carry only a small number of each item. A wholesale service company van frequently visits the store to replenish what has been sold. The wholesale company does not know what needs to be replaced until the van arrives. The system is only a step away from the van's being loaded only with what is needed to replace that which has already been sold at each retail outlet. The missing piece is the wholesaler's electronically tapping into retail outlets' checkout counters. The system becomes even more integrated when manufacturers can electronically tap the wholesaler's inventory. If manufacturers can rapidly respond to replenishing the wholesaler's inventory, that inventory, too, can be sharply reduced.

Dell Computer has totally eliminated finished goods inventory by building computers in response to customer orders via telephone or the Internet. The computers are built after customers place an order and are shipped directly to the customers eliminating intervening layers of wholesalers and retailers. A hot-line number covers customers' questions and minor problems. Dell supplies the names and telephone numbers of independent consultants who will set up the computer and provide training if desired by the customer. Dell has an arrangement with designated independent service centers to cover hardware problems and warranty obligations. There is no finished goods inventory. Dell has complemented its rapid response to customer orders with rapid replenishment of small quantities of components from suppliers. The only inventory at Dell is limited numbers of components for assembly of computers that have already been sold. The competitive advantage to Dell of eliminating finished goods inventory, minimizing component inventories, and marketing directly to consumers is affecting inventory and materials management not only in personal computers, but other products as well.

PROTECT AGAINST COMPONENT SUPPLY SHORTAGES

Three forms of inventory are finished goods, raw materials and components, and work-in-process (WIP). Raw materials and components consumed by a factory in making finished goods fall under the purview of materials managers, who normally report to production managers. A materials manager and a physical distribution manager sitting side by side report to different departments, even though their functions are similar. One of the advantages of setting up a logistics department is to ensure that the materials and physical distribution managers integrate their shipping needs. For instance, a truck unloading components at one end of the factory could be sent to the other end of the factory to load finished goods. This reduces shipping costs compared to employing two trucks. Most times, materials and physical distribution managers do not integrate their activities. They, along with purchasing managers, consider themselves specialists, reinforced by their belonging to different professional societies each with its own certification program.

Materials managers are responsible for ensuring that factories are adequately supplied with raw materials and components. Inventories protect against uncertainty in delivery or availability. While this is the traditional U.S. approach, the Japanese have led the way in JIT delivery, where factory demand for 800 doorknobs per day is not satisfied from inventory but from daily delivery of 800 doorknobs, if not hourly delivery of 100 doorknobs. Some U.S. companies feel that distances between suppliers and buyers in the United States are too great to implement JIT delivery. Maybe so, but Japanese transplant factories in the United States receive daily container shipments of parts from Japan, halfway around the world, with relatively little safety stock. The greater the reliability and dependability of the logistics system of ship, rail, and truck, the less the need for inventory to cover unexpected contingencies.

An example of JIT manufacturing was already given with the manufacture of the seats taking place hours before their being installed in a New Jersey automobile assembly plant. Here, the reliability of shipping and manufacturing has been thoroughly proven, eliminating the need for an inventory of seats other than a truckload arriving some hours before the seats are to be installed. The Saturn plant in Tennessee has supplier plants located up to 200 miles away. Trucks pick up partial loads daily at four different suppliers for a full load back to the Saturn plant. Trucks arrive at a waiting area some hours before they are directed to multiple locations at the assembly line to unload the individual shipments. The truck driver also acts as receiver on behalf of Saturn. The driver's receipt of a shipment triggers an electronic transfer of funds from Saturn to the supplier. This eliminates the cost of submitting invoices, verifying receipt of shipments, and processing payments.

PERMIT TRUCKLOAD PURCHASES FOR LARGEST DISCOUNT

Another traditional U.S. purchasing practice is to buy a full truckload of goods to get the largest discount. Rather than receive 800 doorknobs a day, the manufacturer receives a truckload of 50,000 doorknobs. Eight hundred are used, and the remaining 49,200 placed in a warehouse. The buyer receives a large price discount for a full truckload shipment, here representing about a 2-month supply of doorknobs. An economic analysis of the discount should take into account the associated inventory carrying cost. More often than not, it doesn't.

One paper products distributor could not resist the price discount associated with full truckload shipments. Unfortunately, this represented a two-year supply. To take advantage of the price discounts, the distributor had to rent a larger warehouse. The distributor neglected to take into account not only the cost of extra warehouse space and two years of carrying costs but also the fact that paper products turn yellow after eighteen months. The paper distributor was throwing away one-quarter of the inventory from spoilage while wondering why he wasn't making as much money as he thought he should considering the large discount.

The traditional practice of full truckload shipments of parts and components to be stored in a factory warehouse is opposite to JIT manufacturing, where daily shipments are made directly to the assembly line. No inventory is needed other than shipment arrivals occurring some time element before the parts are consumed. Shipments are not stored in a warehouse but unloaded directly at the assembly line when needed. JIT delivery depends on a reliable and dependable manufacturing and transport system. Any uncertainties in manufacture and delivery must be covered by safety stock.

Determining Safety Stock

A complementary software to Evolver is RISKOptimizer. RISKOptimizer is similar to Evolver in terms of setting up a spreadsheet problem. The difference is that RISKOptimizer combines the simulation capability of @RISK software with Evolver's optimization algorithms.[1] RISKOptimizer can be used to determine the necessary safety stock to compensate for uncertainty in delivery.[2]

Suppose that a factory requires one container of parts per day. The record of past shipments shows that shipping time from the supplier to the factory is one day 90 percent of the time, two days 7 percent of the time, and three days 3 percent of the time. What safety stock is sufficient to prevent a stockout that would interrupt production?

Figure 7.1 is a spreadsheet setup for analysis by RISKOptimizer. The discrete probability function in column A is common to both RISKOptimizer and @RISK software. It creates values of 1, 2, and 3 in accordance with their respective probabilities. If a "1" is generated, a "1" is placed in column B, denoting delivery on the next day. If a "2" is generated, a "1" is placed in column C, two days in the future; for a "3," a "1" is placed three days in the future in column D.

Figure 7.1
Determining Safety Stock

	A	B	C	D	E	F	G	H
1	SAFETY STOCK TO ACCOUNT FOR UNCERTAINTY IN DELIVERY							
2								
3	SHIPPING				OBJECT			
4	TIME				CELL			
5	1					2	INITIAL	NEG
6	1	1					INVENT	INVENT
7	1	1	0		ARRIVALS	DEMAND	2	0
8	1	1	0	0	1	1	2	0
9	3	1	0	0	1	1	2	0
10	2	0	0	0	0	1	1	0
11	2	0	0	0	0	1	0	0
12	1	0	1	1	2	1	1	0
13	1	1	1	0	2	1	2	0
14	1	1	0	0	1	1	2	0

Columns B through D are added in column E to obtain daily arrivals of containers. Demand in column F is constant at one a day, reflecting manufacturing needs. Column G is the day's end inventory obtained by taking the previous day's inventory, adding arrivals, and subtracting demand. Negative inventory represents stockouts that are totaled in cell H7. Cell G7 is an adjustable cell to determine the initial safety stock to avoid stockouts. The applicable formulas are shown in Figure 7.2. These formulas have been replicated down to create a period of 100 days for the simulation.

Figure 7.2
Spreadsheet Formulation

	A	B	C	D
8	=RiskDiscrete({1,2,3},{0.9,0.07,0.03})	=IF(A7=1,1,0)	=IF(A6=2,1,0)	=IF(A5=3,1,0)
9	=RiskDiscrete({1,2,3},{0.9,0.07,0.03})	=IF(A8=1,1,0)	=IF(A7=2,1,0)	=IF(A6=3,1,0)

	E	F	G	H
8	=B8+C8+D8	1	=G7+E8-F8	=IF(G8<0,1,0)
9	=B9+C9+D9	1	=G8+E9-F9	=IF(G9<0,1,0)

The objective cell E5 to be minimized is the sum of initial inventory (cell G7) and total stockouts over the simulation period (cell H7). Adjustable cell G7 is restricted in integers between 0 and 5. RISKOptimizer runs a simulation for a given set of values for the adjustable cells (there is only one adjustable cell in this example). Based on the results of the simulation, RISKOptimizer selects new values for the adjustable cells and runs another simulation. This process continues until the objective cell is optimized. The solution, shown in Figure 7.1, is to have an initial safety stock of two containers when the plant starts operating and receiving regular shipments.

Another approach is writing a simulation program in Basic, Fortran, and other computer languages or using object-oriented simulation software. Suppose that a factory needs one container of parts per day but that the containers are shipped from a location halfway around the world. Delivery time can range between 50 and 75 days. The span of 25 days could be handled on a spreadsheet, although it would be somewhat cumbersome. An alternative is to write a simulation program to select the initial safety stock at the start of plant operations necessary to avoid a stockout from late deliveries.[3] A surprisingly small number of containers were necessary as safety stock at the start of operations to avoid a stockout with such a wide degree of variability in delivery times. With an initial safety stock of three containers, inventory varied mostly between one and three containers with a small probability of being either zero or four containers. No negative inventory occurred to interrupt production. This showed the feasibility of employing JIT delivery from halfway around the world as long as the ocean carriers and railroads operate in a reasonably reliable fashion.

The advantage of RISKOptimizer is that programming is limited to setting up a problem on a spreadsheet. A computer simulation program or a simulation software package may have to be employed if spreadsheet formulation becomes too cumbersome or difficult.

Acme Appliances: Choice of Shipment Size

Managers are frequently guilty of suboptimizing. They select a course of action that best suits their interests, perhaps to the detriment of the company as a whole. This minicase illustrates suboptimization in the choice of shipment size to supply motors for an appliance maker. The traffic manager, Archy, optimizes his performance, but as his boss, Tom, finds out, Archy's choice is not the best one for the company.

Acme Appliances is currently purchasing 120,000 motors a year from White Motors. Flag Trucking operates a regular trucking service on the route between the two companies with a three-day transit time. Archy had a call from Flag Trucking. If Acme Appliances would accept full truckload shipments of 4,000 motors at a time, rather than the customary quantities between 3,000 and 4,000 motors, the shipping cost would be reduced to $36,000 per year. Flag Trucking charges according to shipment size as listed in Table 7.1.

Archy wrote a memo to Tom, materials manager at Acme Appliances, stating that he intended to shift to full truckload shipments of 4,000 motors, "which is close to what we are doing anyway. Flag Trucking is willing to give us a great deal if we take full truckloads. I checked with the warehouse, and this poses no problems. I am going ahead with full truckloads only. We really shouldn't pass up cutting our shipping costs by 25 percent."

Table 7.1
Annual Shipping Costs

Truck Shipment (4,000 motors full load)	Annual Shipping Costs
Less than half full	$96,000
More than half full	$48,000
Full (proposed)	$36,000

While Tom realized that Archy, as traffic manager, was doing his job in reducing shipping costs, he was a little piqued at the tone of Archy's memo. Archy was not practicing good corporate diplomacy when he informed Tom of what he was doing rather than asking his approval, which Tom would have freely given. Now, however, Tom wanted to "twist Archy's nose," but for what reason? Archy had just achieved a 25 percent savings in shipping costs. This prompted Tom to think about the broader issues of accepting larger-sized shipments. While Archy focused on one cost, shipping, Tom was about to focus on three, inventory carrying, ordering, and shipping. Inventory carrying costs consist of:

- capital and operating cost of a warehouse, including material handling, labor, building insurance, utility, property taxes, and so on,
- control system to keep track of inventory,
- inventory financing and insurance costs,
- risk of obsolescence (introduction of an improved model of motor),
- risk of spoilage (motors kept too long in inventory that must be scrapped), and
- risk of pilferage or costs to prevent pilferage (if anything can be stolen, it will be stolen).

Tom also knew that studies have indicated that 30 percent to 35 percent is the appropriate range to assess annual inventory carrying costs for many companies. He realized that keeping a warehouse full is a costly endeavor. For instance, $3 million in inventory generates about $1 million in annual carrying costs. Tom arbitrarily used 30 percent of the $120 price of a motor for a carrying cost of $36 per motor per year. Tom also brushed up on the economic order quantity (EOQ). The EOQ provides the optimal order size to minimize inventory carrying and ordering costs:

$$\sqrt{\frac{2 * \text{Ordering Cost} * \text{Annual Demand}}{\text{Unit Carrying Cost}}}$$

Tom's estimate of ordering cost is $50 per order, which he obtained by dividing the cost of the purchasing department (personnel, office, computer, communications, and overhead) by the number of orders processed. He then substituted the appropriate values into the EOQ formula:

$$\sqrt{\frac{2 * \$50 / \text{Order} * 120,000 \text{ Units} / \text{year}}{\$36 / \text{Unit} / \text{Year}}}$$

The EOQ was 577 motors, which shocked Tom. This was very close to daily usage of 480 motors per day (120,000 motors per year divided by 250 working days per year). According to the EOQ formula, Acme Appliances should be ordering the smallest possible quantity, whereas it is actually ordering the largest possible quantity. However, the EOQ formula does not incorporate price discounts. Here the price discount is not for large-volume purchases but for large-volume shipments. Tom decided that he better take a more detailed look at the various costs for daily shipments (500 per day) versus shipment sizes of 3,000 and 4,000 motors.

Fig. 7.3 shows the oscillation of inventory in a warehouse for shipments of 4,000 motors. The safety stock takes into account uncertainties associated with delivery. With a three-day transit time, Acme has a safety stock of two days, or 1,000 motors. Thus, a truck could be delayed by two days in arriving at the factory without interrupting production. Tom could not remember production ever being interrupted from a lack of motors. He also could not remember a late delivery by Flag Trucking. He wondered why a safety stock of 1,000 motors had been selected, who selected it, and when? Frequently, these questions are unanswerable.

Cycle stock sits on top of safety stock and oscillates with the arrival and consumption of a shipment. Average cycle stock is one-half of the size of the shipment, and average inventory is safety stock plus average cycle stock. It is interesting to note that the average amount in inventory is not dependent on the usage rate of the motors, but on the size of the shipment. As more motors are used, shipments become more frequent, but average cycle stock remains unchanged. For instance, in Fig. 7.3, doubling demand to 1,000 motors per day would reduce time between shipments to 4 days, but would not affect average cycle stock. Average cycle stock is affected only by changing the size of the shipment. If daily usage changes and shipment size remains the same, average inventory is affected only by changes in safety stock. Safety stock varies with changes in demand and its degree of variation.

Figure 7.3
Cycle and Safety Stock

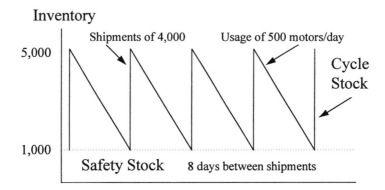

Tom calculated inventory carrying costs on the basis of $36 per motor per year. He reduced the safety stock for smaller-sized shipments partly as a gut reaction that safety stocks need not be as large for more frequent and smaller-sized shipments. He wasn't sure that this was correct but felt uncomfortable having two days' worth of safety stock for daily deliveries. (As already shown, the required safety stock for various-sized shipments and different demand and variations in demand can be determined by RISKOptimizer.) Table 7.2 illustrates the magnitude of inventory carrying costs for different size shipments at $36 per unit per year. Table 7.3 shows Tom's calculations for the ordering cost based on annual demand of 120,000 motors and $50 per order.

Table 7.2
Inventory Carrying Cost

Shipment Size	One-half Shipment Size	Safety Stock	Average Inventory	Inventory Carrying Cost
4,000	2,000	1,000	3,000	$108,000
3,000	1,500	800	2,300	82,800
500	250	500	750	27,000

Table 7.3
Ordering Cost

Shipment Size	Orders Per Year	Ordering Cost
4,000	30	$1,500
3,000	40	2,000
500	240	12,000

Tom looked at the ordering cost for shipment sizes of 3,000 and 4,000 of about $2,000. He knew that the economic order quantity formula minimizes the total of inventory carrying and ordering costs. But in comparing ordering costs with inventory carrying costs in Tables 7.2 and 7.3 for the larger shipping quantities, ordering costs are minuscule. So what was the point of minimizing the total? Tom also examined the ordering cost for daily orders. While the purchasing department was involved with placing individual orders for large-sized shipments, they would not be cutting daily purchase orders. Daily shipments would be covered by some sort of blanket purchase order. Tom decided to use $5,000 to better reflect the administrative burden of daily shipments with less involvement by purchasing. He was now prepared to total inventory carrying, ordering, and shipping costs, in Table 7.4.

Table 7.4
Total Costs

Shipment Size	Inventory Carrying Costs	Ordering Cost	Shipping Costs	Total
4,000	$108,000	$1,500	$36,000	$145,500
3,000	82,800	2,000	48,000	132,800
500	27,000	5,000	96,000	128,000

Tom was somewhat surprised at the results and wondered why he had not performed this analysis before. He relished the idea of pointing out to Archy that his attempts to minimize shipping costs were actually maximizing company costs. But this did not last long. Other matters loomed in his mind such as the inventory carrying cost of $108,000 for shipments of 4,000 motors. If that was his inventory carrying cost, wouldn't that also be White Motors' cost to accumulate 4,000 motors in inventory in expectation of Acme's order? Tom knew that Acme's orders were mixed in with others, and therefore White Motors' did not have to accumulate 4,000 motors for Acme alone. Nevertheless, White Motors had to have some incremental amount of inventory to cover fluctuations in orders that included Acme's.

Tom took a quantum leap in thinking about Acme's inventory policy for the motors. White Motors and Acme Appliances were located on an important trucking route for Flag Trucking. Tom guessed that Flag Trucking would be in a position to dedicate one truck per day to pick up a part-shipment of other freight and then stop at White Motors to fill the truck with another part-shipment of about 500 motors. Since the motors would be the last loaded on a truck, they would be the first unloaded when the truck arrived at Acme Appliances three days later. Tom thought that he would probably want the trucks to arrive about 8 to 12 hours before the production line started operating. The motors would not be off-loaded at the warehouse, which was customary, but directly at the assembly line.

Some motors could be kept at the assembly line to cover the contingency of the truck's being late. If Flag Trucking demonstrated the necessary reliability, even these would be unnecessary. Enhancing shipping reliability would necessitate Flag Trucking arranging with other trucking firms to pick up a trailer if one of Flag Trucking's rigs broke down. Unknown to Tom, Flag Trucking already had such arrangements. A near tripling of Flag Trucking's revenue to handle daily shipments would be a strong incentive for Flag Trucking to essentially guarantee performance. If Acme Appliances could live with little safety stock, inventory carrying costs for the motors would virtually disappear. Perhaps space saved in the warehouse could be dedicated to a more productive use, perhaps even rented out to a third party.

Tom thought about White Motors. If he entered into a single-source contract with White Motors where about 500 motors went straight from its production line into a Flag truck each day, there would be inventory carrying cost savings for White Motors in not having to accumulate 4,000 motors. Moreover, White Motors' safety stock could be reduced somewhat by substituting certainty for vagary in sales. This should be worth something in the form of a price reduction.

A single-source deal would also remove purchasing and its associated costs from the picture. Production would call White Motors daily to stipulate the number of motors for each shipment. The shipment would be direct from White Motor's production line for delivery three days later to Acme Appliance's production line. On receipt of the motors, Acme Appliances could wire transfer funds to White Motors. This would eliminate associated invoicing and other administrative costs. White Motors' receiving daily payments of $60,000 rather than waiting 60 days after delivery of a shipment of 4,000 motors for payment of $480,000 should also be worth something in terms of a price concession.

Tom was contemplating the unthinkable–an alternative that no one had offered him. Archy's memo of taking matters into his hands had triggered a train of thoughts in Tom's mind far different from what Archy could possibly imagine.

HEDGE AGAINST A POTENTIAL STRIKE OR PRICE HIKE

There was a time when U.S. automobile companies bought steel for inventory in anticipation of a strike by the United Steel Workers. Hedging against a strike in Japan by building up inventory is unheard of–strikes very rarely occur. In the United States strikes have been occurring less frequently and are settled more quickly than in the past. Part of this is a consequence of the globalization of production. Once a steel strike in the United States could shut down the automobile assembly lines. All that a steel strike now accomplishes is create a larger market for steel imports. The same can be said for price hikes. Unless price hikes are globally coordinated, all a price hike does is induce the buyer to seek supplies elsewhere. Elsewhere, today, is the entire world. Automobile companies do not have to accumulate steel in anticipation of a steel strike or a price hike when they have so many alternatives.

Another reason for labor being more cooperative is the willingness and ability of a company to shut down its domestic operations and move overseas if labor becomes too obstinate. Still another reason why strikes are less common is that companies are relying more on external, rather than internal, suppliers. This is a consequence of the growing popularity of a business strategy for companies to identify what they do best and buy the rest. External suppliers risk losing their contracts if they strike; therefore, workers risk losing their jobs by striking. This is a powerful inducement for labor at external suppliers not to strike that does not apply to internal suppliers.

LEVEL PRODUCTION ACTIVITIES TO STABILIZE EMPLOYMENT

As discussed under aggregate planning for air conditioners, the workforce is employed throughout the year manufacturing a constant number of air conditioners while fluctuations in demand is satisfied by accumulating or liquidating finished goods inventory. This is a common purpose of inventory both in the United States and in Japan. As also discussed, seeking contraseasonal products and expanding into the global market can flatten out demand, reducing the need to accumulate a large finished goods inventory. A flexible manufacturing system, while costly, can also reduce the amount of finished goods inventory by varying output more closely to demand. However, there are times when workers are not fully employed on the production line. During these times, workers can perform maintenance and dedicate time to thinking of, or experimenting with, ideas to improve quality or efficiency. The benefits of reduced inventory and improved quality and efficiency must be sufficient to compensate for the cost of having a more expensive flexible manufacturing system and excess labor.

DECOUPLE SUCCESSIVE STAGES OF PRODUCTION

So far the discussion has covered finished goods inventory handled by physical distribution managers and components and raw material inventory handled by materials managers. The third form is work-in-process (WIP) inventory. WIP inventory is partially completed goods within a factory under the control of materials managers. In Fig. 7.4, workstations A, B, C, and D are sequential steps in the process of making part X with WIP inventory outside each workstation. WIP inventory outside workstation B consists of parts that have already been through workstation A but not yet workstation B. WIP inventory outside C has been through B, and WIP inventory outside D has been through C.

Figure 7.4
WIP Inventory Single Part

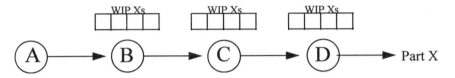

If workstation B suffered a machine breakdown that stopped or slowed production, workstation C could draw down on its WIP inventory and continue operating. System performance would not suffer from a breakdown in B as long as sufficient WIP inventory is outside C to provide enough time to fix the problem in B. This is sometimes called just-in-case inventory, inventory lying around just in case it's needed. Just-in-case inventory protects system performance from a workstation interruption. The larger the just-in-case inventory, the greater the degree of protection. In a way, just-in-case inventory is an insurance policy against the risk of an interruption in production. The larger the insurance policy, the greater the coverage–hence, the traditional U.S. management practice to have as much WIP inventory as possible.

The quintessential difference between Japanese and U.S. inventory practices is that the Japanese recognize that inventory is a cost to be minimized, not an asset to be carried on a balance sheet. As long as inventory is considered a balance sheet asset, what's the purpose of reducing inventory? The Japanese have taken the lead in reducing inventory to levels sufficient to ensure continuity of production and adequately service customers, and no more. U.S. management attitude toward inventory is changing. They are recognizing inventory for what it truly is: a cost of doing business.

How, then, do the Japanese handle a breakdown in workstation B? First, the Japanese do not depend on one large machine but on several smaller ones. If a machine does break down, the production line slows but does not stop. Second, the Japanese have a large number of industrial engineers and technicians whose desks are located on the production floor where WIP inventory was once stored. Industrial engineers in the United States reside in offices far from the noise and clutter of a production floor. Engineers and technicians sitting next to a production line can move quickly to resolve problems just as they begin to occur. In the United States, industrial engineers are informed of a problem after it has manifested itself.

It is true that the Japanese system requires a greater capital investment in a larger number of smaller-sized machines and a greater cost in engineering manpower. This is the cost side of the cost-benefit equation. The benefit is savings in WIP inventory carrying costs. One has to be weighed with the other to come to a conclusion, which for the Japanese has been to do away with WIP inventory. Nevertheless, even with a greater number of machines and having more technical personnel dedicated to keeping the production lines running, machine breakdowns are costly events since plant output slows. The last element is tender loving care of the machines.

Seiichi Nakajima

Seiichi Nakajima is the founder of total preventive maintenance (TPM), which he calls total productive maintenance, which consists of:

- maximizing the productive output of machines,
- a formalized system of preventive maintenance, and
- worker ownership of machines.

Maximizing Productive Output

Maximizing the productive output of machines can be likened to driving an automobile. A teenager may drive a car by alternately stomping down on the accelerator and the brakes, never bothering to check the oil in the engine. A car driven this way is not going to last long. An older person who nurtures a car by driving at reasonable speeds, accelerating and decelerating at a somewhat more leisurely pace, and changing the oil at regular intervals is going to get far more mileage out of a car. In like manner, the Japanese run their machines below their maximum output for sustained and reliable operation.

The Japanese view an older machine as having greater value in that it has been adapted to better fit into the manufacturing process. As a machine ages in Japan, it gains value, whereas in the United States, a machine is depreciated and thrown away. Interestingly, this same treatment applies to people. Older Japanese and other Orientals are accorded esteem and respect and are considered wise. In the West, they are depreciated and thrown away (nursing homes). The concept of a machine's gaining value as it ages is another example of the cultural difference in manufacturing practices between East and West. Another example is the Japanese view of inventory as a cost, which we view as a current asset on a balance sheet. Another is the Japanese view of labor as an asset to be maximized, which we view as a cost to be minimized.

Formalized System of Preventive Maintenance

The second part of TPM to minimize the occurrence of machine breakdowns is a formalized system for preventive maintenance over the life of the machine such as routine maintenance at given intervals based on time (every six months) or usage (10,000 hours of operation). Records are kept noting when parts begin to fail. Once known, parts are then replaced before they fail. Using the automobile as an example, suppose that fan belts begin to fail at 80,000 miles. Once this is known, the Japanese will routinely replace fan belts at 70,000 miles.

Replacing parts before they fail may not seem a way to minimize cost. Again using the automobile as an example, how much does it cost to replace a fan belt when the oil is being changed, another $20? The fan belt still may have many hours of life left when replaced. Now suppose that the operating policy is to maximize fan belt usage. This means that the fan belt fails not in a garage while the car is being serviced but while the car is being driven in the middle of a storm in the middle of the night in the middle of nowhere. Are a walk in a storm, a call to a garage, the tow, a stay in a motel, going to be less costly than replacing the fan belt before it failed? The same is true for a machine. The Japanese cannot afford for a machine part such as a bearing or a belt to fail because factory output slows. If this is the cost, then replacing parts before they fail makes a great deal of sense and cents.

Worker Ownership

The third step of TPM is developing a feeling of ownership between workers and their machines. Workers' operating habits influence the frequency of machine breakdowns, as seen in the first three principal causes of machine breakdowns:

1. failure to properly clean and repair machines,
2. exceeding machine operating specifications or limitations,
3. lack of worker knowledge in machine operation and maintenance,
4. deterioration of machine parts such as bearings and belts, and
5. poor choice of machine in terms of usage, capability, design characteristics, and quality.

Workers are familiar with a machine's capability, operating characteristics, and fit in the manufacturing process. Workers are in the best position to sense the start of machine problems and act in a timely and effective manner. Having workers responsible for simple preventive maintenance and minor adjustments and repairs promotes a sense of worker ownership. Workers should also assist repair and maintenance personnel in performing major or emergency repairs and machine overhauls. A work team should view machines and equipment under their control as owners, not temporary users. Some factories limit production to one shift so that workers cannot dodge responsibility by passing machine problems to the next shift.

FACILITATE SWITCHING FROM ONE PRODUCT TO ANOTHER

Another purpose of WIP inventory is to facilitate switching from making one part to another. This is done by having WIP inventory for all parts made by a line as in Fig. 7.5.

Figure 7.5
WIP Inventory Multiple Parts

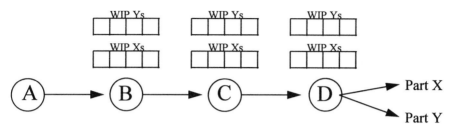

Suppose that the line is making part X, and there is an immediate need for part Y. If no WIP inventory for part Y is available, workstations B, C, and D cease operation while workstation A begins the process of making part Y. After a while, workstation B receives output from A to start its operation, while C and D remain idle. Output from B becomes input to C, and C is now in a productive mode. Output from C eventually becomes input for D. Production of part Y finally begins with output from workstation D, some time after the order was given to switch from part X to part Y.

The picture is entirely different when WIP inventory is available. Workstation D stops making part X and immediately draws on WIP inventory to start making part Y. The same is true for workstations B and C as A starts the process for making part Y. Thus, WIP inventory allows for the rapid switching of production. A new system had to be devised to rapidly switch from making one part to another before the Japanese did away with WIP inventory.

Setup Costs

Before describing this new system, a few words have to be dedicated to setup costs. Setup costs occur when there is one person operating one machine as in Fig. 7.6.

Figure 7.6
One Person One Machine

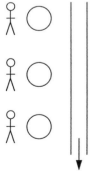

To change from making part X to part Y, the line must be stopped to make machine adjustments. Setup costs are the loss of gross margin while the line is stopped, the cost of idle workers, and poor quality of the first items before final adjustments are made. A production manager would not be anxious to shift production between part X and Y for a setup cost of $10,000. Therefore, the greater the setup cost, the less frequent a setup is made, and consequently, the longer the production run length. For a large number of part Y to be made before switching to part X, there must first be a large inventory of part X, as illustrated in Figure 7.7.

Figure 7.7
Production Run Lengths: High Setup Costs

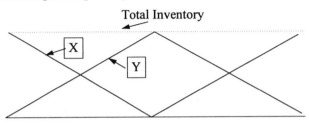

Now suppose that the setup cost is zero. When do you switch production? The glib answer is, Any time you want to. Now production runs can be short, and total inventory can be sharply reduced, as seen in Fig. 7.8.

Figure 7.8
Production Run Length: Low Setup Costs

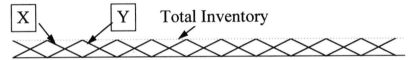

The necessary condition to shorten a production run in order to reduce WIP inventory is to cut setup costs. One way to do this is to employ machine clusters illustrated in Fig. 7.9.

Figure 7.9
Machine Clusters

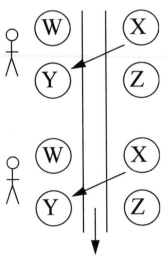

When it is time to switch from producing part X to part Y, the first worker shifts machines as he or she completes the last part X of a production run and orally communicates this to the next worker. When the last part X is completed by the second worker, he or she shifts machines, communicating this to the next worker, and so forth. Each machine is already set up to make a designated part. Since the line does not stop, there are no loss of gross margin and no idle workers, nor are any poor quality parts made because the machines do not have to be adjusted. With no setup costs, production can be changed whenever desired.

Of course, the major difference between Figures 7.8 and 7.9 is a quadrupling of the investment in machines. That is definitely a cost, but the benefit is a substantial cut in WIP inventory. The greater investment in machines has to be weighed against the benefit of savings in WIP inventory carrying costs. However, the same cost-benefit analysis done in Japan and the United States does not necessarily have the same result because interest rates in Japan are substantially less than in the United States. This reduces capital costs in Japan and swings the cost-benefit analysis in favor of machine clusters. Put another way, the benefit of savings in WIP inventory carrying cost can support a greater investment in machines in Japan than in the United States.

One reason for lower interest rates is that Japanese banks have large savings deposits to draw on to support their lending activities. Japanese housewives, who control family finances even to the extent of putting their husbands on allowances, save about 20 percent of family income. Savings are very important because Japanese companies do not provide retirement benefits other than a departing bonus and possibly part-time work. The Japanese do not have a government-sponsored social security program. Moreover, the Japanese feel that saving is a patriotic duty because a product not purchased is a product available for export–the Japanese sense Japan's vulnerability even if no one else does.

This source of funding for banks is not available in the United States, where most people save a negligible portion of their paychecks. Some maintain that Americans actually dissave if growth in consumer debt and home mortgages are taken into account. Another source of funding for Japanese banks is Japan's positive trade balance, which for the United States alone is in excess of $100 billion a year. This is a direct transfer of funds from U.S. to Japanese banks that impact interest rates in both nations. The Japanese also benefit in that the United States provides for most of their national defense, a provision in the treaty ending World War II. Money not spent on warships, helicopters, and tanks and technical expertise not dedicated to keeping them in operating order can be dedicated to ensuring Japan's competitive edge in civilian goods.

Kanban

Machine clusters give the Japanese the freedom to make what they need when they need it, but this hardly qualifies as a means of control. Ohno, production manager at Toyota, originated *kanban*, a Japanese word variously translated as signboard, sign, or card. The idea came to Ohno's mind when he was visiting a U.S. supermarket, where he watched an automatic reorder point system in operation. A card was revealed after buyers removed a certain number of, say, boxes of brand X cereal. Once the card was revealed, a store clerk would take the card to the stockroom. The stockroom clerk would read the card to identify the item, how many should be placed on the shelf, and the location of the shelf. The stockroom clerk would then place the requisite number of brand X cereal in a cart, go to the indicated location, replace the card in front of what was left and restock the shelf. After some time, the card was again exposed, and the cycle repeated. Ohno took this idea back to Japan and devised *kanban*. *Kanban* normally is a card attached to a container or a cart with the following information:

- identification of the part,
- the number of parts to fill the container or cart,
- workstation making the part, and
- workstation consuming the part.

A card need not be used. Sometimes a colored, geometric shape conveys the same information with little or no writing. One company uses a colored golf ball that rolls down a chute every time a container of parts is used. The colored golf ball becomes the authorization to manufacture a requisite number of replacement parts. The cart can be a container or box that holds the parts, although the container or box is moved about on some sort of wheeled conveyance. Fig. 7.10 illustrates a simple *kanban* system using a card on a cart where workstation M makes the part, and workstation C consumes it.

The process starts with workstation C's consuming a full cart of parts. As indicated on the card, the empty cart is pushed to workstation M, which makes the part. The presence of an empty cart at workstation M is the authority to shift production and fill the cart. As indicated on the card, the workers know what part to make and how many to fill the cart. When the cart is filled, a worker pushes the cart to workstation C, as indicated on the card, where the parts are soon to be consumed in the manufacturing process. When the cart is empty, it is returned to workstation M, where its presence again authorizes a shift in production to fill the cart and repeat the cycle.

Figure 7.10
Simple *Kanban* System

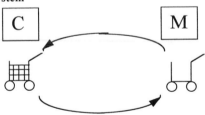

Kanban is a paperless system where the presence of an empty cart or container is the authority to shift production and fill it. It is also a visual system that does not depend on computer inputs and outputs or on management involvement once the system is set up and running. Ideally, a cart or container should be sized for about an hour's worth of production, necessitating the cart to be filled about 8 to 10 or so times a day. The number of carts or containers in the system to assure smooth operation takes into account the daily consumption of a part, the cycle time from manufacturing to consumption, the capacity of the cart or container, and a factor for system inefficiency. The *kanban* system automatically minimizes WIP inventory by ensuring that consuming workstations are adequately supplied by the requisite number of carts or containers for smooth operation, and no more. WIP inventory cannot be accumulated beyond filling the number of containers assigned to each part.

The *kanban* system was originally set up to control the output of the internal supplier, the workstation that makes parts within a factory. The concept has been extended to outside suppliers, or vendors. It doesn't matter—the system works the same. Toyota has central staging areas, called *kanban* stations, to handle the receipt and dispatch of thousands of containers of parts daily. A worker in need of replacement parts removes a "withdrawal" *kanban* from a container of parts that he or she is taking and deposits the card in a *kanban* mailbox. *Kanbans* are picked up by *kanban* postmen and taken to a *kanban* post office for automatic sorting for distribution to internal and external suppliers.

The internal and external suppliers have already manufactured a small number of containers of parts. These contain a "production instruction" *kanban*. A container of parts cannot be removed unless the production instruction *kanban* on the container is replaced with a withdrawal *kanban*. The production instruction *kanban* is then delivered to the workstation making the part where it serves as authority for the manufacture of a replacement container of parts. The production instruction *kanban* is attached to the container once the parts are made. Containers of parts with attached production instruction *kanbans* are picked up on a first-in, first-out basis to prevent parts from collecting dust.

A container cannot be removed unless the worker has a withdrawal *kanban*. A withdrawal *kanban* cannot exist unless a container of parts is in the process of being consumed. Replacing a production instruction *kanban* with a withdrawal *kanban* is the only way to "free up" the production instruction *kanban* to signal the manufacture of a replacement container. Withdrawal and production instruction *kanbans* lock production to consumption. In addition to withdrawal and production instruction *kanbans*, Toyota also has "intraprocess" *kanbans* and "signal" *kanbans* for special situations covering very fast set up times and lengthy setup times, respectively.

Regardless how the *kanban* system is set up, the essence is the same: it is a true pull system of manufacture. No cart or container can be filled until it has first been emptied or is in the process of being emptied. Production is limited to what is being consumed. Suppose that a problem is being experienced at a point in the manufacturing process. That point requires fewer parts and takes a longer time to empty a cart or container of parts. This slows the manufacture of the parts because a cart or container cannot be replenished until it is emptied. This slows production not only at the workstation making the part but also at preceding, or upstream, workstations supplying parts to this workstation. The *kanban* system automatically slows down the whole factory in response to operating problems at any point in the manufacturing process. The *kanban* system makes it impossible to accumulate WIP inventory beyond the stipulated number of carts or containers assigned to each part.

The traditional U.S. approach to a slowdown in one part of a factory is for the rest of the factory to keep operating at full capacity. Since the parts can no longer be consumed in the finished product, WIP inventory begins to accumulate. On the surface, this seems reasonable, as workers and machines are kept busy. Stacks of WIP inventory begin appearing on the production floor. The intent is to let the manufacturing process eventually absorb this inventory after the manufacturing problem has been resolved. The reality is that WIP inventory stacked willy-nilly in piles throughout the factory is largely unaccounted for and eventually forgotten and thrown away.

The homely kanban is an unlikely candidate for fame and usually are no more than printed pieces of cardboard sandwiched between clear plastic covers. Yet these nondescript items have become the best-known element of the Toyota Production System. Some people even think that the kanban system is the Toyota Production System.

Actually, the kanban is a tool that enables employees to operate the Toyota Production System by taking responsibility for managing their own jobs. Envision an employee who removes kanban from components before mounting them on vehicles. The employee sends the kanban back to the preceding process as orders for additional components to replace the ones he or she has used. That employee is shouldering an important part of the "management function" of ordering parts and managing inventory.

Employees use kanban to monitor continuously—by sight—the material that they withdraw from preceding processes and the finished items that they pass on to the next process. The employees thus manage the flow of their own work in accordance with the established work procedures for that work. And it is the employees themselves who establish the work procedures. Suppliers affix identifying kanban to the items they deliver. And they receive orders via kanban. The paperwork is minimal. The efficiency is maximal. And the employees themselves are completely in charge.[4]

Shigeo Shingo

Machine clusters cannot be economically justified for very costly machines. For instance, large metal presses that stamp out parts cannot be set up as a machine cluster. The financial cost of having three idle presses for every one in use is prohibitively high. On the other hand, changing dies in a press can be very time-consuming. Suppose that setup time to exchange dies is eight hours, or one working day. Switching production daily immobilizes the machine. Switching production every other day reduces machine utilization to 50 percent. Hence, an eight-hour setup time must translate into long production runs and high levels of WIP inventory.

Suppose that the eight hours to change the die in a press consists of a worker first shutting off the machine and spending the next two hours looking for the right die. The following six hours are used to exchange dies. This eight-hour operation can be reduced to six hours if the machine is not shut down until after the worker obtains the new die. This concept of differentiating between what can and cannot be done when the machine is operating is embodied in SMED, single minute exchange of dies. SMED was originated by Shigeo Shingo, also known as "Dr. Improvement." He was once one of the world's highest-paid consultants as he led efforts to reduce setup time from eight hours to as low as 10 minutes. SMED consists of:

- identifying internal and external steps. External steps can be accomplished while the machine is running, and internal steps require that the machine be shut down;
- converting as many internal steps as possible to external steps; and
- streamlining the remaining internal steps.

Under SMED, everything that can be done while a machine is running is accomplished. Then, on signal, the machine is stopped and surrounded by a group of about 10 people, like surgeons and nurses around an operating table. Each is assigned a particular task that has been streamlined to the point of being completed in minutes. By shortening setup time from eight hours to 10 or so minutes, dies can be exchanged whenever there is a need to shift production. There is no need to accumulate WIP inventory.

Shingo is also responsible for "zero quality control." This concept eliminates sampling, as espoused by Deming, and substitutes 100 percent inspection. But the inspectors are not just to find defects but to eliminate their causes. Zero quality control acknowledges that humans are fallible and prone to make mistakes. Even a conscientious worker will make mistakes when doing a repetitive task. The mind wanders, and mistakes ensue. Rather than waste time drawing statistical process control charts, Shingo maintains that it would be better to change the process to make it impossible for the mistake to occur. This is the essence of *poka-yoke*, mistake proofing in Japanese.

Suppose that a defect takes the form of installing an occasional automobile radio upside-down. Rather than chart the defect of upside-down radios, why not just make it impossible for a worker to install radios upside down? A worker cannot install the radio upside down once the shape of the radio frame is changed from rectangular to prismatic. This also eliminates the need to inspect. Another example is installing two springs in a switch. Suppose that the worker has a small pile of springs in front of him or her. The worker installs two springs as a switch passes by on the assembly line. No matter how conscientious the worker may be, he or she will occasionally install only one spring in a switch. Rather than taking samples and drawing statistical process control charts, rather than having 100 percent inspection, *poka-yoke* calls for making it impossible for this defect to occur. This can be done by moving the springs to the side of the worker and having the worker follow a checklist:

- use a specially designed tray that holds only two springs,
- fill the tray with two springs,
- install the springs in the switch, and
- make sure the tray is empty before letting the switch pass to the next workstation.

PURCHASING

Purchasing managers deal with outside suppliers or vendors, whereas materials managers deal with internal suppliers. Purchasing can be organized as an independent department or be part of the marketing, production, or finance departments. The latter is the worst place to have purchasing in JIT manufacturing, as price becomes central to the decision making process. In JIT manufacturing, price is just one element to be considered in purchasing; another is dependable delivery of shipments free of defects.

Purchasing practices differ depending whether a part is an "A," "B," or "C" item in the ABC inventory classification system. The ABC classification system takes into account both the price and volume of purchased parts. "A" items may not be necessarily expensive but are used in large volumes such as components in manufacturing. The ABC classification for an inventory can be obtained by using the spreadsheet sorting function on the price X volume column for each item in inventory. In Fig. 7.11, the lowest-priced items happen to be the most frequently purchased.

Figure 7.11
ABC Classification System

ITEM #	PRICE		VOLUME	PRICE*VOLUME		DISCRETE PROB	CUMULATIVE PROB	CLASS
519	$	4	150,000	$	600,000	77.8%	77.8%	A
428	$	1	100,000	$	100,000	13.0%	90.7%	A
357	$	36	1,000	$	36,000	4.7%	95.4%	B
496	$	43	350	$	15,050	2.0%	97.3%	B
324	$	4	1,500	$	6,000	0.8%	98.1%	B
789	$	33	150	$	4,950	0.6%	98.8%	C
378	$	76	60	$	4,560	0.6%	99.3%	C
213	$	567	5	$	2,835	0.4%	99.7%	C
624	$	45	20	$	900	0.1%	99.8%	C
357	$	21	40	$	840	0.1%	99.9%	C
738	$	51	10	$	510	0.1%	100.0%	C
			TOTAL:	$	771,645	100.0%		

Items 519 and 428 account for 90 percent of all purchasing expenditures and are therefore designated "A" items. About halfway down, item 789 and the following items account for only 1.2 percent of all purchase dollars and are designated "C" items. "B" items are what's left after "A" and "C" items have been identified. Purchasing managers should focus on "A" items and perhaps the high-end "B" items. "C" items should be removed from purchasing, as they consume valuable time that can be better spent on "A" and "B" items. "C" items, for instance, may be office supplies. Purchasing personnel should not be involved in occasional purchases of paper clips. Their focus should be on procuring parts that account for the bulk of a company's purchasing dollar expenditures.

Office supplies and other "C" items and "D" items such as an occasional can of paint can be removed from purchasing through arrangements with local wholesale or retail vendors. Vendor reps can visit a company's storeroom and replenish items that have been used. For instance, suppose that storeroom shelf space has been set aside for three one-gallon cans of paint. If the number of cans of paint falls to one, two cans of paint are added. The company is billed via a blanket invoice according to a previously agreed schedule of prices. Some effort has to be expended to ensure vendor honesty.

Many companies are dispensing with "C" and "D" inventory items altogether and depend on vendors to deliver supplies on demand. If the time to draw inventory out of a storeroom is the same as the time for a vendor to respond to a request, then there is no need to keep inventory. Buyers can join organizations that purchase "C" and "D" items in bulk and offer them to their members at reduced prices. The Internet is becoming a means by which companies can purchase office supplies and other "C" and "D" items.

There has been a long-standing trend for companies to shift inventory upstream from the retailer to the distributor or manufacturer. This affected who held the inventory but not necessarily the amount of inventory in the system. A more recent trend is a reduction in manufacturers' and distributors' inventory by their reacting faster to changes in demand. The benefit is savings in carrying costs. However, the cost is a system of production and distribution that has become more vulnerable to interruption from unforeseen events.

Best-Buy Costing

Purchasing managers may be motivated to get the lowest price, but the lowest-priced item may not be the best buy. Consider buying a carpet, one brand selling for $0.50 per square foot and another for triple the price at $1.50 per square foot. Which one should be purchased? Price alone is not sufficient to make the decision. Suppose that the cheaper carpet lasts 1 year and the more expensive one lasts 10 years. Now the carpet price per year of service is $0.50 per square foot per year for the first carpet and $0.15 per square foot per year for the second. Now which is the better choice?

The purchase of two machines for making a part cannot be made strictly in terms of the respective prices of the machines. Price is just one element of cost. The cost of making an item by either machine is the annual capital cost of the machine (initial cost less salvage value divided by the anticipated life of the machine). Each machine may have a different operating cost depending on its degree of automation, the amount of waste per unit production, and energy efficiency. The costs for repair and maintenance should take into consideration manufacturers' warranties and the machine's inherent quality. The machines may have a different output. The final decision is based on the unit cost of production, not on the price of the machine.

There is a classic story of how a purchasing manager crippled a city transit (bus) system. The purchasing manager measured performance in terms of minimizing costs under his direct control: the cost of carrying inventory and the cost of acquiring spare parts. He minimized inventory carrying costs by emptying the storerooms. When a bus broke down, it had to wait in a repair facility until a part could be procured. The procurement process took a long time because the purchasing manager scrupulously negotiated with as many vendors as possible to get the lowest possible price. The purchasing manager let the mayor know how successful he had been in cutting inventory carrying and procurement costs. He hinted about getting a raise.

The consequence of his inventory and procurement policies was a large number of immobilized buses, crippling the level of service. The transit manager was engulfed in complaints. His solution was to submit a request to the mayor to buy more buses. Rather than approve the request, the mayor decided to look more closely into the matter by getting out of his office and visiting the bus repair facility, a novel approach to problem solving. What he saw shocked him—repairmen standing about doing nothing in a huge garage jammed with buses in need of repair.

The purchasing manager, in optimizing costs under his direct control, was maximizing system costs. Revenue was being lost both temporarily and permanently. Immobilized buses can't pick up passengers, and discontented passengers were finding alternative ways of getting to work such as buying a car. Idle repair personnel waiting for parts are certainly a cost. City funds would have been wasted buying more buses than necessary to substitute for those waiting to be repaired. Buying the lowest-priced parts also meant buying the lowest quality parts with the shortest service life, increasing the breakdown rate. The purchasing manager wanted to be rewarded; he should have been fired.

Purchasing Practices, United States versus Japan

Purchasing practices in Japan and the United States for the all-important "A" items are diametrically opposed. No matter what is listed for the United States, Japan is the opposite.

	United States	Japan
Purchase quantity	By the truckload for the greatest price discount	By the wheelbarrowful
Price discount	The greater the better	None
Contract duration	Short (few months or a single or a few shipments)	Never-ending as long as supplier performs
Number suppliers competing	As many as possible	Few, if any, with supplier being in buyer's *keiretsu*
Selection criteria for supplier	1. Price 2. Price 3. Price 4. Ability to perform	Delivery (JIT)and quality (zero defects)

If anything illustrates cultural differences in performing the same managerial function, it is purchasing. Traditional American purchasing activities focus on price as the most important element, followed by availability of product, capacity to manufacture, on-time delivery, and other factors. The Japanese focus on reliability of delivery and quality, not price. We like truckload deliveries, they prefer small deliveries. We prefer short contracts, they prefer long. It doesn't matter, one is the opposite of the other.

In the United States quality is often handled on the basis of defects' being returned for full refund including shipping costs rather than the shipment's being defect-free. Contract duration is intentionally kept short in order for the buyer to be frequently in the market to get the best deal. Buyers want a large number of suppliers competing for their business in order to play one supplier off another in their single-minded pursuit of the lowest price.

In Japan a relationship between a buyer and a supplier is hypothetically never-ending as long as the supplier performs. Japanese companies take pride in pointing to supplier relations over a century-old. If a supplier is making something out of steel, and plastic is now desired, a Japanese buyer may work with a supplier to recast operations from steel to plastic to keep the relationship alive. This is practically unheard of in the West.

	United States	Japan
Attitude of buyer to supplier	Adversarial based on price	Long-term, mutually beneficial advantage
Attitude of supplier to buyer	Get even	Long-term, mutually beneficial advantage

My own experience illustrates the comparative attitudes between East and West toward purchasing. I've been associated with purchasing without realizing it by my involvement in the oil tanker business. Purchasing as a word was never used, but chartering was. Chartering is an oil company's purchasing the service of a vessel from a tanker owner to move oil. In common with manufacturing firms, there are a relatively few large buyers (oil companies) and many suppliers (tanker owners). How is purchasing (chartering of tankers) done in the West? Purchasing is based on price, price, price or, in this case, tanker rate, tanker rate, tanker rate, first and foremost. Once the rate is settled, then other aspects of moving oil are handled such as the condition of the ship.

The buyers tend to make mainly short-term and frequent purchases (single movements of oil between two ports). Low barriers of entry guarantee a large number of suppliers. This allows the buyers to continually churn the bidding-pot. The suppliers have a bad habit of overordering new tankers when rates are high. Consequently, good times in the tanker business scarcely last two years, the time necessary to build and deliver too many ships, the Achilles' heel of Adam Smith's free market. Thus, buyers enjoy low rates most of the time, say, 8 years out of 10. This makes life difficult for tanker owners. Many don't survive. Others survive by operating with cheap crews and deferring maintenance, practices that increase the chances of oil spills. The relationship between oil companies and tanker owners is adversarial, for the most part. There are, to be sure, counterexamples of strategic alliances between oil companies and tanker owners and long-term business deals where the relationship is not adversarial. But this is not how the preponderance of business is conducted.

The central question is, Why do so many tanker owners subject themselves to so much abuse? The reason why is to be ready to take advantage of the situation when the opportunity arises to get even. This happens when oil companies underestimate their shipping needs, and growth in oil demand transforms a surplus of tankers into a shortage. Sometimes this results from a war or the closing of the Suez Canal. Now owners are in the driver's seat. Before, oil companies would not respond to their phone calls; now, owners sit back and let their phones ring and ring. Every minute's delay in answering the phone means a higher rate for the owner's tanker. The well-publicized biographies on Onassis as they relate to his tanker business practices illustrate this phenomenon extremely well. Western tanker owners have become billionaires during the short "get even" period of time. The secret to success in tanker owning is to prepare for the coming bad times that always follow the good times from ordering too many tankers. This rapidly transforms a shortage into a surplus that takes another decade to liquidate, leaving the buyers, the oil companies, in the driver's seat. One owner went from $1 billion in net worth to $1 billion in debt and bankruptcy in the course of about 10 years, nicely illustrating the manner in which purchasing is conducted between buyers and suppliers in the West.

All this is rather exciting, but while this is going on in the West, the Japanese are conducting purchasing in a fundamentally different way. They do not normally enter into the spot market to move cargoes other than to straighten out scheduling difficulties. They satisfy most of their shipping needs by entering into long-term 15-year charters with owners. The deal is done for the long-term mutually beneficial advantage of both buyer and supplier. From the point of view of the buyer, a Japanese oil company, a rate is negotiated that covers the owner's crew, maintenance, and other operating costs plus financing costs plus a slim profit margin. The buyer can now ship oil for less cost than by owning the tanker because of the owner's lower cost crew, lower overhead, and lower profit margin.

The advantage to the oil company is clear in the form of lower shipping costs, but what about the owner? While the owner is making a meager return on the investment in the ship, the ship will be fully paid for in 15 years. Thus, the owner's return is primarily the residual value of a fully paid, 15-year-old vessel after the charter has expired. The benefit to the owner is that the owner would not have been able to acquire vessel were it not for the Japanese oil company charter. The charter assures a financial institution of the repayment of a loan taken out by the owner to purchase the vessel from a shipyard. The long-term charter insulates the owner from the threat of bankruptcy that looms over the heads of tanker owners in the West when their vessels no longer earn enough to support the underlying debt. While tanker owners serving Japan do not become billionaires, rarely do they go bankrupt. It is clear that both Japanese oil companies and their associated tanker owners have entered into an arrangement that actually does serve their long-term mutually beneficial advantage.

	United States	Japan
Value of market intelligence	Enormous; contracts are short and must be renewed or replaced	Who cares?, contracts are never-ending
Purchasing activities	Marketing for supplier, production or finance for buyer	Production only
Pricing	Name of game	Administered at cost plus slim profit margin

Purchasing activities in Japan are between production departments of buyer and supplier, as reliable and dependable delivery of shipments free of defects is the paramount consideration for JIT manufacturing. Price is administered based on cost plus a slim profit margin. The Japanese are obviously interested in price, but if price is basically cost plus, how do they control price? They do so by the buyer' placing a representative in the supplier's factories. The buyer's rep is to inform the buyer if the supplier is having any operating difficulties. This "friendly spying" activity is necessary when the buyer's factory depends on hourly delivery of parts. The buyer's rep also ensures that the factory owner is actively pursuing a cost reduction program. As costs fall, price declines, preserving the slim profit margin.

Hence, the buyer takes an active role in the operations of the supplier's factory and normally insists that the supplier restrict corporate activities to this single contract. Since a contract is never-ending, the buyer may as well become a shareholder in the supplier's company and sit on the board of directors and, possibly, arrange a marriage between a son of one and the daughter of the other. These are the ties that bind a *keiretsu* together. Thus, a strong case can be made that suppliers in Japan are not independent in the Western sense. Some Japanese suppliers feel smothered by the intrusive and all-embracing system and would prefer some of the freedom of action possessed by U.S. suppliers.

Negotiations in Japan between buyer and seller never cease. Price depends on cost, and cost-cutting actions are forever under negotiation. This is quite unlike Western practices, where negotiations cease with the signing of a contract. As an aside, the Japanese operate with relatively few lawyers, as sitting around a negotiating table is preferred over a courtroom confrontation. Bank lending to Japanese suppliers is much different from lending to U.S. suppliers. U.S. suppliers with short-term contracts have an element of risk to lenders not present in Japan, where contracts are never-ending and cover all costs, including financing. Moreover, Japanese suppliers, operating under a slim profit margin, cannot accumulate much in the way of equity in their firms. They must depend on debt as the primary method of financing their capital assets. Thus, Japanese suppliers carry a much heavier debt load than their U.S. counterparts.

This is part of the corporate banking problem in Japan. The large companies as buyers may make a lot of money, but not their thousands of suppliers. High debt loads coupled with slim profit margins push the breakeven point for suppliers dangerously close to operating at full capacity. Japanese output is slowing from the competitive onslaught of low labor-cost Asian nations in Japanese export markets and domestic economic stagnation. Cutbacks in needed supplies by Japanese manufacturers push suppliers below their breakeven points. In the past, manufacturers would raise prices on parts to keep their suppliers whole. This, then, required manufacturers to raise prices on finished goods. Nowadays, this makes Japanese products less competitive in the world market. Consequently, some Japanese buyers are no longer in a position, or willing, to protect their suppliers. Some suppliers are forced to adopt Western style layoffs. Some buyers are adopting the Western style business practice of shifting suppliers if a savings of at least 5 percent can be achieved. All is not well in corporate Japan.

The Xerox Story

In the 1970s many of Xerox's patents expired. Xerox concluded at that time that Japanese imports could not match Xerox in terms of quality, price, and level of service. Surprise! The prices of Japanese copier imports were much lower, their quality much higher thus reducing the need for copiers to be serviced. Xerox was in danger of bankruptcy unless it took drastic action. Inaugurating benchmarking was one action taken by Xerox. Another was revamping its purchasing activities.

The traditional American approach to purchasing is to focus almost exclusively on price. But price is made up of two elements, profit and cost. Of the 100¢ paid by a buyer to a suppliers, an average of 5¢ represents profits and 95¢ represents costs. If a supplier's profit is 5¢, then the lowest price a buyer can hope for is 95¢. A lower price carries the risk of bankrupting the supplier. The traditional American system of focusing on price can minimize only the smallest element of price: profit. Nothing is being done about cost.

Getting the price down to 95¢ was not sufficient for Xerox to survive. Japanese copiers were selling in the United States for what Xerox was spending to purchase parts, never mind the costs associated with manufacturing and distribution and marketing. Xerox had to cut the price of its purchased parts by half. Xerox was forced to abandon the American adversarial system based on minimizing price in order to reduce price! Xerox had to deal with the 95¢ in costs that the traditional American system of purchasing ignored.

Group technology is basically a minifactory, which could be set up as a cellular manufacturing unit, dedicated to making variations of a single part, called a family of parts. Group technology can produce a family of parts cheaply if there is sufficient volume to justify a large capital investment in modern manufacturing technology. In order to take advantage of the economies of scale afforded by group technology, Xerox had to issue a high-volume contract. In order for the supplier to finance the investment in modern manufacturing technology, Xerox had to enter into a multiyear contract. Xerox had to go from dealing with many suppliers on short-term contracts to dealing with a single supplier with a long-term contract if it wanted to cut purchasing costs in half.

Xerox called in its best-performing suppliers not for the potential award for a short-term contract for a part but for a long-term contract for a family of parts for all copiers made in all Xerox's factories for 5 to 10 years. The suppliers were not to bid on price alone, but on an "open book" basis where the supplier had to provide detailed plans for the manufacture of the family of parts. The primary reason for "open book" negotiations was for Xerox to assure itself about the supplier's capacity to perform. In reviewing proposed deals, Xerox learned that outside suppliers had lower labor costs and benefits, lower overhead, and a lower profit margin. If the suppliers proposed a high profit margin, then Xerox ought to make the family of parts itself and capture the profit. The only way a supplier can win a long-term contract is to present the buyer with a compelling case for the supplier to win the contract. The bid price has to be low enough to induce Xerox not to make the part itself. On the surface, a low profit margin may not seem attractive to a supplier, but the supplier's winning a huge single-source contract from Xerox is not exactly a punishment.

At some point, negotiations end with an award to the winner of a single-source contract. With a signed contract in hand, the supplier runs, not walks, to a friendly banker for a loan. The loan allows the borrower to buy the best technology to reduce variable costs by half as long as there is sufficient volume to take full advantage of its inherent economies of scale. Having a single-source contract for a family of parts provides the volume to lower costs using the best technology. Having a multiyear contract provides assurance of repayment to the bank financing the best technology.

By single sourcing, Xerox lowered the purchase price of components from 100¢ to 55¢, not by attacking the 5¢ of suppliers' profit but by attacking the 95¢ of suppliers' costs. Xerox then placed within the contract a cost sharing provision where a further 10¢ cost reduction would be shared, say, 8¢ going to Xerox in the form of a lower price, with the supplier keeping the remaining 2¢. The cost sharing provision provides a mechanism for the supplier to improve his or her slim profit margin. This is a strong incentive for the supplier to take whatever actions are necessary to reduce costs without Xerox having to hammer away at the supplier. As the price falls for Xerox, the supplier's profit margin improves. The supplier does exactly what Xerox wants him or her to do because the supplier is being rewarded accordingly.

Furthermore the basic relationship between buyer and supplier changes from adversary to partner. Single-source suppliers becomes good corporate citizens, visiting Xerox's factories and making helpful suggestions. The suppliers consider themselves part of the Xerox family because:

- they *are* part of the Xerox family,
- anything good for Xerox is good for the suppliers in the form of greater sales,
- the suppliers are concerned about contract renewals, and
- the suppliers are seeking other business opportunities with Xerox.

These are the "book" answers on the change in supplier attitudes. There is one other that I feel is just as important, if not more so. If a supplier does not comply with the contract, Xerox has the right to cancel the contract and award it to another. Who borrowed the money, usually amounting to millions of dollars, for the technology specifically tailored to suit Xerox's needs? Who is not going to be able to meet the debt servicing obligation in case the contract is canceled for nonperformance? Who may be forced into bankruptcy if he or she loses the Xerox contract?

Opponents to single sourcing used to argue that single-source contracts would place the buyer in an extremely vulnerable position where a supplier would take advantage of the situation. Experience has shown otherwise. What supplier is going to cause trouble with a buyer and jeopardize a contract that represents a large portion of the supplier's business and against which the supplier has borrowed a great deal of money?

In addition to single sourcing, Xerox gave suppliers access to its materials requirements plan. This permitted the suppliers to gear their production of parts and components with Xerox's manufacturing needs. This largely eliminated the need for Xerox and its suppliers to hold much in the way of inventories of parts and components. Single sourcing, cost reduction sharing, and reduced inventories for both Xerox and its suppliers gave Xerox a new lease on life. The Xerox story also illustrates the long-term mutually beneficial advantage for both parties. For Xerox, 100¢ in the price of purchased parts eventually was cut close to half. Single source suppliers won the largest contracts they ever had, were able to upgrade their plants with the latest manufacturing technology, and were put in a position to expand into other areas of manufacturing. Single sourcing based on a partnership relationship has proven to be a win-win situation for both buyer and supplier.

ENDNOTES

1. RISKOptimizer, @RISK simulation, and Evolver software available from www.palisade.com.
2. *RISKOptimizer for Business Applications (Twenty Cases)* available from www.palisade.com and www. nerses.com.
3. R. Nersesian and B. Swartz, "Just in Case Inventory for Delivery," *Computer Simulation in Logistics* (Westport, CT: Quorum Books, 1996).
4. *Toyota Production System* (Toyota City, Japan: Operations Management Consulting Division, Toyota Motors, 1992).

Chapter 8

Materials and Production Planning

The inherent economies of large-scale production can be best achieved in continuous flow manufacturing such as in chemical and food processing plants, and refineries. Linear programming and other optimization techniques can be utilized to identify the best mix or blend of raw materials or ingredients that maximizes profits or minimizes costs. Flow manufacturing can be discrete rather than continuous, as in an assembly line. The flow of parts and components can be controlled by *kanban*, covered in the previous chapter, or material requirements planning (MRP). *Kanban* is primarily a visual system of control whereas MRP is computer-driven. Material requirements planning has been expanded in function and scope to become manufacturing resource planning (MRPII). Computer-assisted manufacturing, flexible manufacturing systems, and demand flow technology provide manufacturers with the means to respond quickly and efficiently to changing market conditions.

BLENDING AND MIXING OPERATIONS

Blending and mixing operations provide a choice of ingredients or feedstocks. Each mix of ingredients affects the nature of the product slate as well as revenue and costs. Linear programming and other optimization techniques can be employed to maximize profits or minimize costs. In maximizing profits, a marketing manager provides a production manager with price information plus minimum and maximum limits to establish an acceptable range of output. The solution indicates which feedstocks should be purchased and how much of each product should be made to maximize profits consistent with constraints on product volume and characteristics, and plant capacity.

In minimizing costs, a marketing manager provides a production manager with a precise slate of products to be made. The production manager has discretion as to which raw materials or ingredients are purchased to minimize costs while satisfying constraints on product volume and characteristics, and plant capacity. The following three examples discuss the general aspects of applying linear programming to blending and mixing operations.[1]

Loving Dog

Loving Dog makes three brands of dog food, each with distinct nutritional guidelines with regard to ash, fat, protein, and fiber. The ingredients are two types of beef, chicken, and fish residues from processing plants. Each ingredient has a unique set of nutritional values. The two types of beef residue not only have different nutritional values but also require different amounts of drying agent. Two types of drying agents are available, one being twice as effective as the other and each having a different cost and set of nutritional values.

Setting up a linear programming model is a three-step process:

1. identify the objective cell to be minimized or maximized,
2. select the adjustable cells or variables that influence the value of the objective cell, and
3. construct the associated constraints.

In Fig. 8.1, the production manager has been told to make 10,000 pounds of Basic brand dog food and now must decide on a slate of ingredients that minimize cost. Hence, the objective is to minimize total cost in cell D13. The adjustable cells are those that change in value and, in so doing, affect the value of the objective cell. While prices for the ingredients certainly influence total cost, they cannot be changed. They are set by the market. What can be changed are the quantities of the various ingredients to be purchased. Thus, the adjustable cells are cells D5:D10.

Constraints are more of a challenge than selecting the objective and adjustable cells. The main difficulty with constraints is that they lie in the subconscious part of a human mind, and the computer doesn't have a subconscious, or a conscious mind for that matter. A computer is a calculator for doing simple arithmetic and logical functions. Logical functions are limited to comparing two values to determine whether one is equal to, greater than, or smaller than the other. A computer can store and retrieve information. Other than that, it must be told everything. For instance, the sum of the ingredients having to equal 10,000 pounds has to be explicitly stated as a constraint, even though it may be obvious to a human mind.

Figure 8.1
Solution Spreadsheet for Loving Dog

	A	B	C	D	E	F	G	H	I
1	LOVING DOG PRODUCTION PLANNING CONTROL BOARD							PRICE	
2	BASIC MIX							REDUCTION	
3						MAX		TO ENTER	
4		PRICE		LB		AVAIL		SOLUTION	
5	BEEF1	$ 0.35		-	<=	100,000		$ 0.15	
6	BEEF2	$ 0.17		5,871	<=	100,000		$ -	
7	CHICKEN	$ 0.22		1,867	<=	3,000		$ -	
8	FISH	$ 0.15		500	<=	2,000		$ -	
9	DRYAGT1	$ 0.12		1,761					
10	DRYAGT2	$ 0.02		-					
11				=					
12	QUANTITY			10,000					
13	COST			$ 1,695					
14	COST/LB			$ 0.17					
15									
16					MIN	MAX			
17				ACTUAL	SPEC	SPEC			
18			ASH	3%	0%	5%	>=	<=	
19			FAT	30%	0%	30%	>=	=<=	
20			PROTEIN	26%	20%	100%	>=	<=	
21			FIBER	6%	0%	10%	>=	<=	

Linear programming can be done with Excel Solver. In Excel Solver, each adjustable cell needs an associated constraint to ensure a positive value. In What's Best, adjustable cells are assumed to be positive unless indicated otherwise. This is simply a matter of convenience. As previously discussed, the advantage of What's Best is that constraints can be entered directly on a spreadsheet and can contain spreadsheet formulas. For instance, the "=" sign in cell D11 indicates the presence of a constraint. Clicking on cell D11 reveals the underlying What's Best constraint of =WB(SUM(D5:D10),"=",D12).

The constraint states that the sum of the ingredients in cells D5 through D10 must equal the amount of dog food to be made as indicated in cell D12. The constraint contains a SUM formula and does not have to reference a cell that contains the SUM formula as in Excel Solver. Other constraints in cells E5:E8 ensure that the amount of ingredients consumed is less than the quantity available in cells F5:F8. Constraints in cells G18:H21 ensure that the nutritional percentages of the dog food mix meets the minimum and maximum specifications in cells E18:F21. These percentages employ the SUMPRODUCT of the weight of the ingredients multiplied by their respective nutritional percentages (not shown). A constraint links the two drying agents to the quantity of the two types of beef and another constraint limits the amount of fish (also not shown).

If linearity can be preserved, the dual value for the adjustable cells provides useful information on what it takes for an adjustable cell to enter the solution. For instance, beef1 is not part of the solution. The $0.15 in cell H5 means that if the current price of $0.35 was lowered by $0.15 to $0.20, then beef1 would be part of the solution. Twenty cents is the proper response to the question by the beef1 supplier of what it takes for Loving Dog to purchase beef1. The quantity would be obtained by rerunning the program with the new price for beef1.

Evans Oil Refinery

Oil refineries and petrochemical plants have a choice of feedstocks to produce a slate of desired products. Evans Oil Refinery sells three brands of gasoline, distillates (diesel and home heating oil), and fuel oil burned in industrial plants and utilities. The marketing manager provides the production manager with minimum and maximum limits for the three brands of gasoline and distillates. The marketing manager also provides the selling price for each product including fuel oil, the waste product in the refining process.

The production manager has a choice of eight different types of crude oils, each producing a different slate of three blending stocks, distillates, and fuel oil. The blending stocks, in turn, have to be mixed in the right proportion to produce three brands of gasoline with different specifications on octane rating and vapor pressure. On top of this, the oil refinery has two modes of operation that affect the slate of products from each type of crude oil and the refining cost. For instance, the percentage of higher-valued blending stocks extracted from each type of crude can be enhanced at the expense of lower-valued distillates and fuel oil by changing the mode of operation. While this enhances revenues, it also adds to refining costs. Moreover, each mode of operation may also affect the productive capacity of the refinery.

This problem can be set up to maximize profits because discretion has been given to the production manager in the form of an acceptable range of output for each product. The solution often takes the form of producing some products at their upper limits and others at their lower limits, normally constraining profits. Revenue is the SUMPRODUCT of the sales prices of the three brands of gasoline, distillates, and fuel oil and their respective volumes. Costs are the SUMPRODUCT of the price and volume for each type of crude oil to be purchased and the operating cost of the refinery, which depends on the selected mode of operation. The difference between revenue and costs is profit, the objective cell to be maximized. Constraints have to be constructed to ensure that the mixing of the blending stocks produces three brands of gasoline that satisfy their respective octane and vapor pressure specifications. Constraints are also necessary to ensure that the volumes of the three brands of gasoline and distillates fall within their acceptable range set by marketing without exceeding the refinery's productive capacity.

While this is a more complex problem than Loving Dog, it follows a similar format. The objective is to maximize the spreadsheet cell containing profit. The adjustable cells are the quantities of each of the eight crude oil feedstocks to be purchased and the selector switch for the mode of operation. A selector switch is a binary integer with values of zero and one, which can be used to turn a mode of operation off and on. The constraints use the same SUMPRODUCT formulas as in Loving Dog but must reflect two "nutritional" tables—one for the octane rating and vapor pressures for the blending stocks and the other for the gasoline brands. The linear expressions reflect a double-step process of first producing three blending stocks from a choice of eight types of crude oil that are subsequently mixed to make three brands of gasoline. Moreover, the amount of blending stocks from each type of crude oil depends on the refinery mode of operation. While this makes formulation more complex than Loving Dog, the essence of setting up the linear program remains unchanged.

Mountain Utility Company

Mountain Utility produces electricity and must comply with environmental regulations on pollution emissions in Table 8.1. Mountain Utility has a choice of 11 different types of coals, each with its unique thermal content, the tons of coal to produce 1 percent power output, and pollution emissions in Fig. 8.2.

Table 8.1
Maximum Emissions

	% EMISSIONS FROM SMOKESTACK	ABSOLUTE LIMIT IN TONS
Sulfur	2%	100
Nitrogen	6%	300
Particulate	-	500

Figure 8.2
Coal Characteristics

	A	B	C	D	E	F
33	COAL	TONS PER	%	%	%	POWER
34	TYPE	% OUTPUT	SULFUR	NITROGEN	PART	CONTRIBUTION
35	A	80	0.5%	2.0%	5.0%	0
36	B	85	0.8%	4.0%	7.0%	0
37	C	90	1.0%	3.0%	6.0%	0
38	D	95	1.5%	5.0%	8.0%	0
39	E	100	2.0%	7.0%	9.0%	0
40	F	105	3.0%	5.0%	11.0%	0
41	G	110	5.0%	3.0%	7.0%	0
42	H	115	4.0%	4.0%	5.0%	0
43	I	120	3.0%	5.0%	8.0%	0
44	J	130	6.0%	7.0%	12.0%	0
45	K	150	8.0%	10.0%	15.0%	0

Column F is the contribution to the output for tons of each type of coal burned. For example, burning 80 tons of type A coal is equivalent to 1 percent power for the operating period. Burning 200 tons of type E coal contributes 2 percent to total power output. For 80 percent plant output, the total for column F must be constrained to equal 80.

In addition, pollution rights for sulfur emissions can be bought or sold. If the plant operates below the maximum allowed amount for sulfur emissions, the company can sell the difference as pollution rights to another company. The buying company can now legally pollute above its maximum allowed limit to the degree permitted by the pollution rights. The interchange of pollution rights among companies does not affect total pollution but simply shifts pollution among companies. Thus, it may pay to buy clean coals for low sulfur emissions and sell the difference between what is legally permitted and what is actually emitted to a third party. On the other hand, it may be in the utility's interests to buy dirty coal and purchase pollution rights from a third party in order to pollute above the permitted limit.

The conveyors for the 11 different piles of coal have individual maximum capacities of 3,500 tons for the operating period, and the main conveyor has a limit of 9,000 tons. Fig. 8.3 is the solution spreadsheet for purchasing the indicated amounts of coal to minimize the cost of producing electricity at 80 percent capacity. The solution is to burn clean coals and sell pollution rights to a another company.

Figure 8.3
Solution Spreadsheet for Mountain Utility

	A	B	C	D	E	F
1	MOUNTAIN UTILITY COMPANY CONTROL BOARD					
2						
3	POWER OUTPUT AS % FULL CAPACITY:				80	
4						MAX
5	COAL					CONVEYOR
6	TYPE	$/TON		TONS		CAPACITY
7						
8	A	$65		1,694	<=	3,500
9	B	$60		3,500	=<=	3,500
10	C	$57		-	<=	3,500
11	D	$53		-	<=	3,500
12	E	$50		-	<=	3,500
13	F	$47		-	<=	3,500
14	G	$45		-	<=	3,500
15	H	$40		-	<=	3,500
16	I	$37		2,118	<=	3,500
17	J	$35		-	<=	3,500
18	K	$25		-	<=	3,500
19						
20	MAIN CONVEYOR CAPACITY:			7,312	<=	9,000
21						
22	TOTAL COST ($000):	$ 398				
23						
24		RELATIVE			ABSOLUTE	
25		MAX	ACTUAL		MAX	ACTUAL
26	SULFUR:	2%	1.4%	<=	100	100
27	NITRO:	6%	3.8%	<=	300	280
28	PART:				500	499

The objective is to minimize cost in cell C22, the SUMPRODUCT of tons purchased for each type of coal and their respective prices, plus any additional cost for buying, or less any revenue (negative cost) from selling, pollution rights. The adjustable cells in column D are the amount of each type of coal to be purchased. These are constrained not to exceed the maximum capacity of the conveyers (column F). The absolute values for pollution emission is the SUMPRODUCT of the amount of coal burned and their respective pollution percentages. The relative pollution is the absolute pollution divided by the amount of coal burned. As seen in Figure 8.3, sulfur and particulate pollution are at their maximum limits. The reason sulfur is at its maximum value is that pollution rights have been sold (not shown) even though the plant is actually burning clean coals.

In Loving Dog, the relative percentages for nutrition involved division by the quantity of dog food, a fixed value of 10,000 pounds. Thus, linearity was preserved in the division process to obtain relative percentages. In this application, the measure of relative pollution is not linear because the total quantity of coal burned, the denominator in determining a relative measure of pollution, contains adjustable cells. Nonlinear relationships prohibit the use of the dual value in answering the question of how much the price of a nonselected coal has to be reduced to enter the solution. This question can be answered by constraining total cost to its present value and selecting the price of a nonselected coal as an adjustable cell. In rerunning the program, the solution shows not only the price of the nonselected coal that preserves total costs but also the quantity to be purchased. This methodology allows the utility manager to respond to a seller's request of what price is required for the utility to buy his or her coal.

Nonlinear expressions in the spreadsheet may lead to a local, rather than a global, optimal solution. This can be checked by rerunning the program with a different set of initial values for the adjustable cells. If the solution changes, then one solution has to be better than the other. One or both solutions are locally, rather than globally, optimal. This may be a reason to switch from linear programming to Evolver optimization. Another is that linear programming cannot handle Excel "IF" statements, logical functions, lookup tables, and other spreadsheet features. The Evolver optimization version of this problem in Fig. 8.4 shows that price depends on the volume of coal purchased.

Figure 8.4
Price Discounts for Volume Purchases

	A	B	C	D	E	F	G	H	I	J	K	L
1	MOUNTAIN UTILITY COMPANY											
2												
3	COAL						TONS PURCHASED					
4	TYPE	QTY	COST		0	500	1000	1500	2000	2500	3000	3500
5	A	-	$ 65	2	$ 65	$ 63	$ 60	$ 60	$60	$ 60	$ 60	$ 60
6	B	-	$ 60	3	$ 60	$ 60	$ 58	$ 58	$57	$ 57	$ 56	$ 56
7	C	-	$ 57	4	$ 57	$ 55	$ 53	$ 50	$50	$ 50	$ 50	$ 50
8	D	-	$ 53	5	$ 53	$ 53	$ 50	$ 50	$50	$ 50	$ 50	$ 50
9	E	-	$ 50	6	$ 50	$ 49	$ 48	$ 47	$46	$ 46	$ 46	$ 46
10	F	-	$ 47	7	$ 47	$ 47	$ 45	$ 45	$43	$ 43	$ 42	$ 42
11	G	-	$ 45	8	$ 45	$ 45	$ 45	$ 45	$40	$ 40	$ 40	$ 40
12	H	-	$ 40	9	$ 40	$ 38	$ 36	$ 35	$35	$ 35	$ 35	$ 35
13	I	-	$ 37	10	$ 37	$ 35	$ 34	$ 33	$32	$ 31	$ 30	$ 30
14	J	-	$ 35	11	$ 35	$ 35	$ 30	$ 30	$28	$ 28	$ 28	$ 28
15	K	-	$ 25	12	$ 25	$ 23	$ 22	$ 22	$20	$ 19	$ 18	$ 18

The lookup function is a handy way to express price in column C as a function of volume in columns E through L (column D is associated with the operation of the lookup function), but it rules out linear programming. Modeling a declining price with increasing volume is cumbersome in linear programming. For each type of coal, eight variables have to be set up for each segment of volume with corresponding constraints for the minimum and maximum limits. Then each adjustable cell has to be multiplied by an associated binary integer (0/1) with a corresponding constraint that the sum of the eight binary integers must be less than, or equal to, one. This constrains the solution to either no consumption of a particular type of coal or one of its price/volume segments. Multiplying binary integers with adjustable cells has to be done for the 11 types coal and the 8 price ranges, generating 88 nonlinear expressions. It may be difficult to obtain a globally optimal solution with this degree of nonlinearity. Price discounting can be better handled with a lookup table, but this eliminates linear programming. Evolver optimization, whose setup is similar to linear programming, can solve the problem.

MATERIAL REQUIREMENTS PLANNING

Material requirements planning (MRP) and *kanban* are ways to manage discrete flow manufacturing such as assembly lines. Both focus on ensuring an adequate supply of parts to avoid interruptions in production. Japanese manufacturers tend to prefer *kanban*, which they originated. Years ago, American manufacturers preferred MRP, which they originated. Nowadays both systems are accepted by world manufacturers to manage materials flow. The chief difference between the two systems was originally the degree of reliance on a computer. *Kanban* was a visual system with little reliance on a computer, whereas MRP and its descendant MRPII are computer-driven systems. *Kanban* can now be set up either as a visual system or be integrated in computer-driven demand flow technology.

A tentative master production schedule is first generated from a forecast (Chapter 6). The MRP then generates planned order releases (PORs), which are forwarded to external suppliers (vendors) and internal suppliers (factory workshops). The vendors and shop supervisors review their work schedule to ensure that they can comply with the PORs. If so, they sign the PORs, signifying their ability to deliver the right parts with the right quantity and right quality at the right time to the right place. Their assurance finalizes a tentative master schedule. If the external and internal parts manufacturers cannot comply, then the tentative master schedule must be revised until they can.

MRP is more adaptable to changes in production schedules because the external and internal suppliers must indicate their ability to perform before a change in the production schedule can be made. As originally designed, *kanban* did not contain a "forward" planning element to ensure that the suppliers could comply with a markedly different production schedule. Thus, changes in a production schedule had to be done in small incremental steps. Having said that, modern manufacturing can incorporate both *kanban* and MRP where *kanban* drives the system, and MRP serves as a planning tool forewarning suppliers of intended changes in production schedules. Suppliers do not build to the MRP but use MRP to prepare themselves for changes in the frequency and nature of *kanban* orders.

The essence of MRP is in Table 8.2, which shows the master schedule to assemble chairs over the next four days. The bill of material lists 4 brackets per chair. Thus, the demand for brackets is four times the master schedule to assemble chairs. Chairs cannot be assembled without the requisite brackets. The current inventory for brackets is 200. The day of reckoning is day 4, when the inventory is exhausted. If it takes two days to obtain more brackets, then action has to be taken on day 2 in order for a delivery to take place on day 4 to keep the workers busy.

Table 8.2
Simple MRP

Day	1	2	3	4
Master Schedule for chairs	10	15	20	20
Beginning inventory	200	160	100	20
Demand for brackets	40	60	80	80
Ending inventory	160	100	20	!

Fig. 8.5 is the bill of material for the finished products X and Y. To assemble one X, a worker needs one B and four Cs. To assemble one Y, a worker needs two Cs, two Ls, and one K. This is the first level of a bill of material. Suppose that all components and subcomponents are manufactured internally. The next level contains the subcomponents needed to manufacture components B, C, L, and K. To assemble one component C, a worker needs one E and two Ds. To assemble one component L, a worker needs three Ds and one N. Descending one more level in the bill of material, one G is needed to assemble one D, and two Gs are needed to assemble one N.

Figure 8.5
Bill of Material

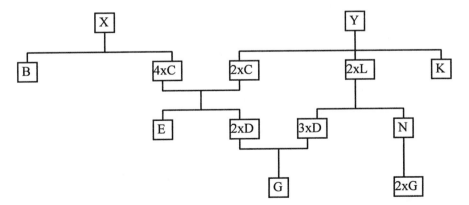

In addition to the bill of material and a master schedule, MRP requires an inventory status file as in Table 8.3.

Table 8.3
Inventory Status File

ITEM	LEAD TIME	INVENTORY	WEEK	ORDER QUANTITY	SAFETY STOCK
B	5	100	8	300	0
C	2	1,450	8	1,500	0
D	1	2,000	7	8,000	1,000
E	3	1,000	7	1,500	0
G	2	11,000	5	10,000	500
K	6	0	8	300	0
L	1	125	8	800	0
N	2	300	7	800	200

Lead time is the time in weeks from placing an order to receiving a shipment from either an external or internal supplier. Future inventory for parts within a factory is known with certainty because the beginning inventory and the master schedule, which creates the demand for a part, are known. For example, in Table 8.2, the starting and ending inventories for the brackets are known with certainty for the next four days. This is called time-dependent inventory, quite unlike time-independent inventory for finished goods inventory. Finished goods are manufactured and sold from inventory. Future inventory of finished goods, in this case chairs, depends on future demand, which is not known with certainty. Thus, a projection of the future inventory of chairs cannot be made with certainty, quite unlike projecting demand for the brackets. In Table 8.3, future inventory of each part is known for each week but is listed only for the indicated week.

The traditional approach to MRP is for the order quantity of parts to be a precise value for production of a batch lot. The quantity of a batch lot is determined from the economic run length (ERL) formula, which is similar in nature to the economic order quantity (EOQ) formula. Whereas the EOQ minimizes total order and inventory carrying costs, the ERL minimizes total setup and inventory carrying costs. The higher the setup cost, the greater the ERL. In Table 8.3, smaller order quantities for components B and K reflect their lower setup costs.

This is the major difference between the traditional and the Japanese version of the MRP. The Japanese version does not have an order quantity as a preestablished batch size. A great deal of effort has been expended in reducing both setup costs (machine clusters and SMED) and WIP inventory to absolute minimums. Under these conditions, there is little purpose in relying on the ERL formula to minimize costs that have already been virtually eliminated. The Japanese version of the MRP is to make only what is needed, not a predetermined batch size.

Safety stock is the trigger point to generate a planned order release. The traditional approach is to incorporate safety stock for those parts where the performance of the external or internal suppliers is uncertain. The Japanese remove uncertainty in supplier reliability and thereby eliminate safety stock.

MRP computer programs are written to fit the particular circumstances for manufacturing a product. As an instructional aid, an MRP can be incorporated in a spreadsheet. Fig. 8.6 shows the traditional MRP for part B.

Figure 8.6
Traditional MRP for Part B

	A	B	C	D	E	F	G	H	I	J	K	L
29	ITEM	B	L. TIME	5	ON HAND	100	WEEK	8	ORD QTY	300	S.STOCK	0
30	WEEK	1	2	3	4	5	6	7	8	9	10	11
31	BEG INV	0	0	0	0	0	0	0	100	0	100	250
32	SCH REC		0	0	0	0	0	0	0	300	300	0
33	DEMAND		0	0	0	0	0	0	100	200	150	100
34	END INV		0	0	0	0	0	0	0	100	250	150
35	P.O.R.		0	0	0	300	300	0	0	0	0	0

The master schedule has already been finalized for weeks 1 through 7. A tentative master schedule starts on week 8 and runs through week 11. PORs are derived for all components and subcomponents and are distributed to the various vendors and shop supervisors. If all signify that they can comply with the PORs, then the master schedule for weeks 8 through 11 is finalized. If the external and internal suppliers cannot comply with the PORs, the master schedule must be revised until they can. Sometime after the MRP has been finalized for weeks 8 through 11, the process is repeated for weeks 12 through 15.

The process starts with opening the inventory status file to fill out the information in row 29. This row contains the lead time of 5 weeks (cell D29), future inventory of 100 (cell F29) in week 8 (cell H29), order quantity of 300 (cell J29) to be ordered when the ending inventory falls below the safety stock, or trigger point of 0 (cell L29). The formula =IF(B30=$H29,$F29,0) in cell B31 states that if the week number is the same as in cell H29, then list the initial inventory in cell F29, otherwise enter a 0. This formula is replicated across the row. (For a full MRP working model, this row should contain the actual inventory for weeks 1 through 7.)

The next step is to fill out demand in row 33, which combines information from the master schedule and the bill of material. The portion of the spreadsheet listing the master schedule is in Fig. 8.7. From the bill of material in Figure 8.5, every product X requires one component B. Thus, the formula in cell C32 in Figure 8.6 is =1*C5, replicated to the right. The corresponding rows for the components making up the first level of the bill of material have the following formulas to determine demand.

Component K: =1*C6 (one for every Y)
Component L: =2*C6 (two for every Y)
Component C: =4*C5+2*C6 (two for every X and four for every Y)

Figure 8.7
Master Schedule

	A	B	C	D	E	F	G	H	I	J	K	L
1	MATERIALS REQUIREMENTS PLANNING (U.S. VERSION)											
2												
3	MASTER SCHEDULE											
4	WEEK	1	2	3	4	5	6	7	8	9	10	11
5	PROD X								100	200	150	100
6	PROD Y								225	180	210	250

Cell C32 in Figure 8.6 contains the formula =IF((C31-C33)<$L29,$J29,0) replicated to the right. This formula states that if the difference between beginning inventory and demand is less than the safety stock or trigger point, then a shipment whose size in cell J29 arrives that week. The formula in cell C34 is =C31+C32-C33, or ending inventory is beginning inventory plus shipments less demand. The formula in cell C35 is =G32, the planned order release that will start the manufacturing process whereby a shipment arrives five weeks later just in time to ensure continuity of production.

IBM was the first company to provide MRP software. After visiting the front office of a company to sell a computer to handle financial transactions, IBM salespeople would visit the back office to sell another computer to handle MRP. MRP predates computers but was not used because an MRP involving scores or hundreds of parts necessitated someone's manually performing the calculations. Even if the calculations could be performed within the time constraints, they would most apt contain arithmetic errors with potentially calamitous results. Since companies had no way to plan ahead for the parts that were needed for assembly operations, a huge WIP inventory insured against the risk of a shortage of parts stopping production. IBM justified a company's investing in a computer system for MRP by savings in WIP inventory. As seen in Figure 8.6, parts arrive just in time for incorporation in the product, greatly reducing the need for WIP inventory as insurance against stockouts.

Subsequent portions of the MRP for levels below the first level have one major difference. Demand is not determined by the master schedule directly but by the planned order releases for higher-level components. Referring to Figure 8.5, each component C requires one subcomponent E and two subcomponent Ds. These subcomponents have to be completed before component C can be assembled, not when component C is being consumed in the manufacturing process. Hence, demand for second- and lower-level subcomponents in a bill of material is the planned order releases for the manufacture of higher-level components. As an example, the planned order releases for component C of 1,500 units in weeks 7 and 8 becomes the demand for subcomponent E. The POR for subcomponent E takes into consideration its associated order quantity and lead time in order to be completed before component C is assembled. Fig. 8.8 is the planned order release summary for all components and subcomponents.

Figure 8.8
Traditional Planned Order Release Summary

	A	B	C	D	E	F	G	H	I	J	K	L
8	PLANNED ORDER RELEASE SUMMARY											
9	WEEK	1	2	3	4	5	6	7	8	9	10	11
10	B		0	0	0	300	300	0	0	0	0	0
11	C		0	0	0	0	0	1500	1500	0	0	0
12	D		0	0	0	0	8000	0	8000	0	0	0
13	E		0	0	1500	1500	0	0	0	0	0	0
14	G		0	0	0	10000	10000	0	0	0	0	0
15	K		300	300	300	0	0	0	0	0	0	0
16	L		0	0	0	0	0	800	0	800	800	0
17	N		0	0	0	800	0	800	800	0	0	0

The reason the first seven weeks have already been finalized is seen by examining component K, whose lead time is six weeks. Production cannot be increased for the first six weeks of the master schedule for anything that contains component K because of the six-week hiatus between ordering and delivering the component. Thus, the fixed portion of an MRP is linked to the component with the longest lead time. From this, one can also conclude that the longer the lead time to manufacture components, the less flexibility there is in changing a production schedule. Conversely, the smaller the lead times, the greater the flexibility of a manufacturing system to respond to changes in the market. To illustrate this point, suppose that two manufacturers are competing in the same market, but one has six-month lead times for its components and the other has two weeks. The market suddenly shifts away from model A to model B. The first company will be making too many model As and too few model Bs for the next six months. This is the earliest opportunity to get the parts necessary to make more model Bs. By this time, the company is drowning in model A inventory. In the meantime, the other company has been taking advantage of a shift in consumer preference for five and a half months. Hence, one can conclude that a company with short lead times has a competitive advantage over one with long lead times.

The traditional American approach of "if it ain't broke, don't fix it" is to leave lead times as they've always been. Don't disturb the status quo. The Japanese attack lead times head-on. If a component's lead time is six weeks, the manager in charge of manufacturing the component will either assume the responsibility or be told to reduce lead time to five weeks. The manager must examine every step of the process with the intent of shortening its completion time. Suppose that the manager succeeds in reducing lead time to five weeks. The manager is not content with the status quo. The next step is to strive to reduce lead time to four weeks. This constant effort to reduce lead times enhances the flexibility of a manufacturing system to respond to changing market conditions.

As mentioned, the Japanese version of the MRP is to make only what is needed, as seen for component B in Fig. 8.9. Comparing Figure 8.9 with Figure 8.6 shows that the Japanese have improved the traditional MRP by eliminating beginning and ending inventory, and their associated carrying costs, by only making what is needed. Furthermore it is a simpler system. The POR is demand backed off by the lead time as seen both in Figure 8.9 for component B and in Figure 8.10 for all components.

Figure 8.9
Japanese Version of MRP for Component B

	A	B	C	D	E	F	G	H	I	J	K	L
29	ITEM	B	L. TIME	5								
30	WEEK	1	2	3	4	5	6	7	8	9	10	11
31	BEG INV	0	0	0	0	0	0	0	0	0	0	0
32	SCH REC		0	0	0	0	0	0	100	200	150	100
33	DEMAND		0	0	0	0	0	0	100	200	150	100
34	END INV		0	0	0	0	0	0	0	0	0	0
35	P.O.R.		0	0	100	200	150	100	0	0	0	0

Figure 8.10
Japanese Version Planned Order Release Summary

MATERIALS REQUIREMENTS PLANNING (JAPANESE VERSION)											
MASTER SCHEDULE											
WEEK	1	2	3	4	5	6	7	8	9	10	11
PROD A								100	200	150	100
PROD T								225	180	210	250
PLANNED ORDER RELEASE SUMMARY											
WEEK	1	2	3	4	5	6	7	8	9	10	11
B			100	200	150	100					
C						850	1160	1020	900		
D					1700	3670	3120	3060	1500		
E			850	1160	1020	900					
G			2600	4390	3960	4060	1500				
K		225	180	210	250						
L								450	360	420	500
N					450	360	420	500			

The simplicity of the Japanese version of MRP is seen in the underlying formulas listed in Table 8.4. The formulas relate directly to the master schedule for first-level components or to the POR of higher-level components with a built-in delay for the respective lead times (a large portion of the spreadsheet has not been shown).

Table 8.4
Formula Support

		A	B
9	WEEK		1
10		B	=1*G5
11		C	=4*D5+2*D6
12		D	=2*C11+3*C16
13		E	=1*E11
14		G	=1*D12+2*D17
15		K	=1*H6
16		L	=2*C6
17		N	=1*D16

DISTRIBUTION REQUIREMENTS PLANNING

An interesting application of MRP is distribution requirements planning (DRP), originated by Abbott Laboratories in the late 1970s. DRP integrates factory production with distribution center needs, relying on the MRP model. Each distribution center makes a forecast of demand for each product. Referring to Figure 8.6, the forecast becomes demand in row 33. The POR becomes a factory order to produce a standard-sized shipment to replenish the distribution centers.

However, a forecast of demand is expected average demand. Actual demand fluctuates around average demand. Half the time demand will be higher than the average, and half the time demand will be lower. Initial inventory in DRP is the actual inventory, which reflects fluctuations of actual demand around the average. When demand is above average, actual (initial) inventory drops, expediting factory orders to replenish a distribution center. When demand is below average, actual (initial) inventory rises, delaying factory orders. Thus, fluctuating demand affects factory scheduling on a real-time basis by expediting or delaying replenishment orders. The result is less finished goods inventory in the distribution centers because replenishment is keyed more closely to the vagaries of actual demand rather than a forecast of average demand.

CAPACITY REQUIREMENTS PLANNING

Capacity requirements planning (CRP) provides suppliers with the means to decide whether they can comply with PORs. Suppose that a work center, along with others, is involved in the manufacture of components C, L, N, and G. Components G and L pass through the work center during the first week of their PORs, and components C and N pass through one week after the issuance of their PORs. Work cannot be done in advance because of the sequential nature of the manufacturing process. A delay in any workshop can lead to an interruption in manufacturing if a batch of parts is not completed in time for assembly in the finished product. Under these conditions, work must be completed as scheduled.

Suppose that a workshop has adequate machines and equipment and its capacity is constrained only by labor hours. The workload associated with the PORs for components C, L, N, and G cannot exceed the workshop's capacity to perform. Table 8.5 summarizes the demand on time in the manufacture of these components. Normal time is the actual time to complete a task. Standard time adjusts normal time to reflect a worker's not being physically able to work eight hours straight without taking time out for nourishment and rest. Fig. 8.11 is the spreadsheet portion related to this work center. The underlying formulas (not shown) relate the POR for the applicable components in Figure 8.8 to the data in Table 8.5 to generate the load demand for each individual component in terms of standard hours. The work center load demand for these four components is totaled in row 24. Net capacity in row 25 is the total capacity (2,000 hours) less any work already scheduled. Remaining capacity in row 25 is net capacity less demand that will be placed on the work center by the tentative master schedule.

Table 8.5
Work Center Demand of Components C, L, N, and G

Item	Week Work Done in Relation to POR	Standard Hours per Item	Order Quantity	Standard Hours per Order
C	1	0.5	1,500	750
G	0	0.1	10,000	1,000
L	0	0.8	800	640
N	1	0.5	800	400

Figure 8.11
Work Center Load Demand

	A	B	C	D	E	F	G	H	I	J	K	L
18	CAPACITY REQUIREMENTS PLANNING											
19	WEEK				4	5	6	7	8	9	10	11
20	C								750	750		
21	G					1000	1000					
22	L							640		640	640	
23	N						400		400	400		
24	TOTAL					1000	1400	640	1150	1790	640	
25	NET CAP					1300	1500	1700	1800	1800	1900	2000
26	REM CAP					300	100	1060	650	10	1260	2000

Positive values in row 26 indicate adequate resources to satisfy the PORs generated by the tentative master schedule. Thus, the shop supervisor can sign the tentative master schedule. The tentative master schedule is finalized when all the shop supervisors and vendors have signed off.

MRPII

Manufacturing resource planning (MRPII) pushes the involvement of the computer deeper into the manufacturing process. MRP explodes the bill of material to ensure an adequate supply of parts to support the manufacturing process. MRPII incorporates MRP as part of a management information and control system. Capacity requirements planning is not part of MRP, but is part of MRPII. Shop supervisors do not actually have to sign off on a tentative master schedule. Figure 8.11 can be generated for all workshops, and the computer can "view" the results for remaining capacity (row 26). If all entries for remaining capacity are zero or positive, then the computer can finalize the tentative master schedule. However, if a negative number appears, a human mind or a computer algorithm must alter the master schedule until every "row 26 value" is positive. This is part of MRPII's capacity to simulate a manufacturing environment to answer "what if" questions such as what happens if the master schedule is changed. Production managers can evaluate different operating strategies using MRPII with outcomes expressed in physical and financial terms.

In MRPII the inventory status file is expanded to include inventory usage forecasts, inventory control, purchasing, and receiving. The bill of material file is expanded to include field service reports and engineering activities that affect components and subcomponents. The master schedule is expanded to include sales, sales prospects, the forecast, and the generation of the tentative master schedule. As discussed, capacity resource planning is part of MRPII. Purchase orders are cut and sent electronically to vendors along with the applicable portions of the MRP. In addition, MRPII includes production activity control, batch planning and production, production posting, WIP inventory tracking, process control, and machine maintenance. This information is in terms of production units, but MRPII also includes financial information for sales analysis, payroll and personnel management, cost accounting, budget control, and forecasting cash flow. MRPII can run a factory from "soup to nuts."

COMPUTERS IN A MANUFACTURING ENVIRONMENT

A word processor does not save time over a typewriter in originating an initial draft. The saving in having a word processor over a typewriter is in making changes to a draft. Computer-aided design (CAD) is similar to a word processor. Once a design is entered into a computer, it can be easily altered with light pens, keyboards, and joysticks. A change of one dimension changes other associated dimensions automatically. A three-dimensional view can be generated, rotated to scrutinize a design from all angles. A database is needed to contain information on design tolerances and specifications. Once entered for one part, the database becomes a resource for designing other parts. Computer-aided engineering (CAE) incorporates engineering formulas in a design to evaluate performance without having to build a model to perform tests. For example, the performance of a designed diameter of an orifice carrying high-pressure hydraulic fluid through a part can be evaluated by CAE without having to build a model and test performance with different diameter orifices.

Numerical control machines have been around a long time. They are controlled by a paper tape with punched holes not unlike a player piano roll. Paper tapes require human coding of machine instructions. Computer aided manufacturing (CAM) lets the computer create the "tape." CAD-CAM is the computer integration of design and manufacturing. Group technology is the grouping of the necessary machines to manufacture a family of parts. A family of parts can be manufactured by adjusting the settings on the machines. This introduces tremendous economies of scale over manufacturing each part on an individual basis. A flexible manufacturing system (FMS) places group technology under computer control. A highly automated FMS has an automatic storage and retrieval system (AS/RS) to supply metal shapes at one end of a manufacturing line and remove finished parts from the other. Finished parts are placed in a container to be picked up by an automatic guided vehicle (AGV), a forklift truck without a driver. The container is then taken from the manufacturing line and placed in the correct bin.

Each machine in the FMS has some sort of "inspection robot" continually measuring the machine's output. The inspection robot provides feedback to the machine to change an adverse trend before parts have to be rejected. If parts are no longer within specifications, the inspection robot can pick them up and drop them into a nearby trash can plus send feedback information to the machine to change its settings. Computer-integrated manufacturing (CIM) combines production control and the operations of a FMS. The FMS receives computer instructions to make 1,000 type X parts followed by 3,000 type Y parts and so forth without human intervention. At the end of a production run, one metal shape is replaced by another and the settings of the machines are automatically adjusted to make a new type of part. The AGV delivers a container of completed parts to a new bin. CIM can integrate receipts of electronically formatted customer orders into its schedule of production for a rapid and automated response to current market requirements.

FMSs are economical for making high-quality parts in large numbers. The cost of labor is not critical in evaluating an investment in an FMS. Some FMS systems are essentially unmanned, operating 24 hours a day. What is critical is having sufficient volume to justify a rather costly investment in computers and computer support, machines and associated equipment, and automated storage, retrieval, and delivery systems.

JUST-IN-TIME MANUFACTURING

Just-in-time (JIT) manufacturing is a pull system where only what is required to be made is made. While JIT manufacturing or *kanban* sounds like a technique, it is really a manufacturing philosophy. This can be seen in examining the following requirements to successfully implement JIT manufacturing:

- a total commitment by managers and workers to JIT principles,
- an educational program for teaching JIT principles to managers and workers,
- a readiness to challenge traditional practices and methods,
- a commitment to eliminating waste on all levels,
- a change of management attitude to workers, and
- a change of worker attitude to management, their jobs, and their role in a company.

Initiating JIT manufacturing in a traditional manufacturing setting does spawn conflicts by bosses who want to remain bosses and union leaders who are opposed to anything that takes away from the power of a strike to settle grievances and increase pay. Unions have opposed cross-training and actions taken to increase productivity such as eliminating excess job classifications. These conflicts can be overcome by effective communication between management and labor and by educating both managers and workers to a new philosophy of manufacturing. If these conflicts cannot be resolved, a company may no longer be able to remain competitive and stay in business.

The transformation to JIT manufacturing is going to take place regardless of what bosses and union leaders may feel, because of its inherent competitive advantages. JIT manufacturing better prepares a company to deal with rapidly changing technologies, shortened product life cycles, and global competition. The following table summarizes the major differences in manufacturing philosophy between JIT and the traditional manufacturing approach.[2]

	JIT PHILOSOPHY	TRADITIONAL APPROACH
Inventory	A cost of doing business; get rid of it to the greatest possible extent.	An asset on the balance sheet that protects against errors in forecasting, problems with machines, and late deliveries from vendors.
Lot sizes	Minimum size to serve immediate needs only.	Based on ERL formula as a trade-off between setup and carrying costs.
Setups	Rapid changeover with minimal interruption to allow small lot size.	Maximizing output once a system has been set up has priority over reducing setup costs and time.
WIP inventory	Eliminate it to greatest possible extent.	The more the better just-in-case WIP inventory is needed to cover machine problems or production changes.
Vendors	Single source with a partnership relationship.	Many sources with an adversarial relationship based on price.
Quality	Zero defects as defects interrupt production.	Some toleration of defects for some acceptable level of scrapping.
Equipment maintenance	Continual to prevent machine breakdowns that interrupt production.	Just-in-case inventory covers machine breakdowns.
Lead times	The shorter the better for quicker response to changing market conditions.	The longer the better to give shop supervisors and vendors sufficient time to complete their work.
Workers	Everyone is critical to the functioning of the organization. They must be adequately trained and treated with respect as there are no unimportant workers. Workers are an asset to be maximized.	Issue orders and measure output. If output is not up to standards, take appropriate action to get output up to standards. Workers are a cost to be minimized.

DEMAND FLOW TECHNOLOGY

Demand flow technology is a departure from the traditional approach of the master schedule and MRP.[3] In MRP planned orders are created for standard batch lots and are pushed through the manufacturing system. Work orders are necessary to initiate the manufacture of a part and keep track of its progress through the manufacturing process. Demand flow technology integrates product engineering, demand management, shop floor design, production scheduling, material replenishment, and supply chain management into a single system. Its purpose is to produce the highest quality product at the lowest possible cost in the shortest possible time. Manufacturing cycle times are reduced to the greatest possible extent. Production is driven by actual demand, not a forecast of demand. A mix of products is manufactured with production scheduling responding to changes in actual demand, not by work orders anticipating future demand for a single product. Replenishing parts and components is driven by *kanban*. MRP serves as a planning tool for the benefit of suppliers. The chief characteristics of demand flow technology are:[4]

- a pull system based on customer demand,
- grouping of products into families based on shared processes,
- mixed-model production,
- incorporating total quality management into the manufacturing process,
- *kanban* replacement of parts and material procurement with automated communication of needs to suppliers,
- managing operations visually, and
- compressing bills of material to a single level.

John Costanza, an engineer consultant on President Reagan's Council of Productivity, traveled the world gathering information on successful and innovative manufacturing processes. Wearied of copying other companies' processes and doubtful of the capacity of U.S. firms to copy, Costanza decided to design a system of his own.

Demand flow technology can be compared to how the fast-food restaurant Subway responds to market demand. The normal practice for fast-food restaurants is to first prepare food, then sell it. A customer is served an already prepared hamburger that may have been sitting in a warming tray for hours, and tastes like it. Subway reverses the sequence by first taking the order, then making the sandwich, quickly and efficiently with fresh ingredients. Production is in response to actual, not anticipated, customer demand, reducing inventory and working capital costs.

Demand flow technology requires flexible, mixed-model production lines capable of rapid response to customer orders and a *kanban* system capable of rapid response by suppliers. Both manufacturing and materials planning is based on actual demand, not a forecast of demand. Simulation can analyze whether a chosen product mix can be optimally manufactured with full line balancing. The simulation matches work content with line capabilities and available resources to pinpoint operational bottlenecks needing management attention. Costanza himself best describes demand flow technology:[5]

> With the advent of global communication and worldwide logistics and distribution, the world is becoming a smaller and smaller place. Today companies must not only contend with domestic competitors but also with competitors internationally. Speed, response and flexibility with zero working capital are the keys to competing in the global marketplace. A major transition in manufacturing strategy relates to the ability of companies to adopt demand flow technology to design mix-model flow lines where volume and mix can easily be adjusted on a daily basis in the direction of actual customer demand.
>
> Many consultants were fascinated by the repetitive practices and techniques of the top Far Eastern manufacturers. These were then copied and implemented in the United States. Although short term gains were realized, the long term ability of these companies to compete was never achieved.
>
> Demand flow business strategy is based on the premise that in an increasingly competitive world, we as manufacturers can not predict or forecast what consumers will actually buy. Therefore, flexibility in manufacturing and in material management is key. With the technology based tools of mixed-model line design, demand flow technology manufacturers can adjust volume and mix across broad ranges of products without the common drawbacks of fixed volume, scheduled manufacturing. These other forms of manufacturing do not have the ability to adjust volume without redesigning lines. Short term schedule changes will typically create shortages of manufactured items and MRP planned material.
>
> The world continues to change, consumers continue to demand better delivery service and a greater breadth of product lines, features and options. We must accept that we cannot change our consumers' needs and wants and we certainly cannot dictate what they choose to buy. Once we accept that premise, demand flow technology provides the mathematically based tools and business strategy to transform manufacturing operations into a strategic competitive weapon.

ENDNOTES

1. What's Best linear programming software is available through www.lindo.com and Evolver optimization through www.palisade.com. Further details on constructing the three examples are available in *What's Best Linear Programming (Fifteen Cases)* and *Evolver-Applications for Business (Nineteen Cases)* at www.palisade.com and www.nerses.com.
2. Adapted from *Modern Material Handling* by Walter E. Goddard of the Oliver Wight Education Associations, 1982.
3. Extracted from *Flow Manufacturing-An Oracle White Paper*, available from Oracle Corporation through its Web site www.oracle.com.
4. Extracted from *Flowpower Manufacturing*, available from the John Costanza Institute of Technology through its Web site www.jcit.com.
5. Extracted *From the President,* published in The FlowLine (vol. 10) by the John Costanza Institute of Technology, Englewood, CO.

Chapter 9

Production Scheduling

Scheduling is an integral part of production planning. *Kanban* and MRP are means to schedule production of components consumed in the manufacturing process. Linear programming has long been used for scheduling production among plants and assigning the output to different regions in order to minimize manufacturing and shipping costs. Another application is project management. Many workshop and jobshop scheduling situations cannot utilize linear programming because their formulation require the use of "IF" statements, lookup tables, and other spreadsheet functions. These may now be handled by Evolver when demand is discrete (e.g. 100 units per day). If stochastic (e.g. 100 units per day plus or minus 10 percent), RISKOptimizer, a combination of Evolver optimization and @RISK simulation, may assist a scheduler. This chapter illustrates spreadsheet solutions to a variety of production scheduling situations.[1]

THE CLASSIC APPLICATION OF LINEAR PROGRAMMING

Linear programming can answer the universal question posed by manufacturers of what products are to be made in which plants to best satisfy regional demand. Suppliers can also be integrated into the picture. The following example demonstrates the efficacy of linear programming in scheduling production among several plants to satisfy regional needs on the basis of minimizing production, shipping, and procurement costs.

Suppose that a company makes three models of a machine and markets them in four regions. The forecast of demand for the individual models in each region is in Fig. 9.1.

Figure 9.1
Forecast of Demand

	K	L	M	N	O	P	Q	R	S	T	U
1											
2	REGION W DEMAND			REGION X DEMAND			REGION Y DEMAND			REGION Z DEMAND	
3	MODEL A:	2000		MODEL A:	1000		MODEL A:	1500		MODEL A:	500
4	MODEL B:	1000		MODEL B:	2000		MODEL B:	1500		MODEL B:	1000
5	MODEL C:	1000		MODEL C:	2000		MODEL C:	2000		MODEL C:	500

Each machine requires two bearings that can be supplied by two companies, F and G, with different selling and shipping costs to the company's three plants M, N, and O. Fig. 9.2 is the portion of the solution spreadsheet related to the suppliers and the manufacturing plants. The number of bearings sent by the two suppliers to each plant is twice the total production of machine models scheduled for each plant. Costs associated with the suppliers are the procurement costs for the bearings and their respective shipping costs to the plants. Constraints ensure that supplier and manufacturing plants do not exceed their maximum capacities.

Figure 9.2
Supplier Selection and Plant Production Schedules

	A	B	C	D	E	F	G	H	I
4		PART: BEARINGS							
5		2 PER MACHINE							
6									
7		SUPPLIER F			SUPPLIER G				
8									
9		COST	VOLUME		COST	VOLUME			UNIT
10	PLANT M				PLANT M			PLANT M	PROD	COST
11	$ 250	12000		$ 275		0 =	MODEL A:	500	$ 7,000
12							MODEL B:	4500	$ 6,500
13							MODEL C:	1000	$ 7,500
14							MAX CAP:	6000	
15								=<=	
16									UNIT
17	PLANT N			PLANT N			PLANT N	PROD	COST
18	$ 300	5000		$ 290		5000 =	MODEL A:	1000	$ 6,800
19							MODEL B:	0	$ 6,600
20							MODEL C:	4000	$ 7,300
21							MAX CAP:	5000	
22								=<=	
23									UNIT
24	PLANT O			PLANT O			PLANT O	PROD	COST
25	$ 325	0		$ 310		10000 =	MODEL A:	3500	$ 7,100
26							MODEL B:	1000	$ 6,700
27		<=			=<=		MODEL C:	500	$ 7,700
28	MAX CAP:	20000		MAX CAP:	15000		MAX CAP:	7000	

Fig. 9.3 shows the assignment of plant output to regions W, X, and Y only. Shipping costs vary between each plant and region. The constraint in cell C6 ensures that the supply of model A machines from all plants shipped to region W is equal to demand. Constraints in cells C7 and C8 do likewise for models B and C. The workings of these constraints can be seen in Figure 9.3, where what is shipped into the three regions from the three plants exactly matches demand.

Adjustable cells are those associated with scheduling production with suppliers and assigning plant production to regions. In Figure 9.2, the adjustable cells are cells B11, B18, and B25 and the corresponding cells in column E. In Figure 9.3, adjustable cells are L11:L13, L18:L20, and L25:L27 plus the corresponding cells in columns O, R, and U. The objective is to minimize the total cost of purchasing and shipping the bearings to the plants and manufacturing and shipping the machine models to the regions.

Figure 9.3
Plant Scheduling to Satisfy Region W, X, and Y

	K	L	M	N	O	P	Q	R
2	REGION W DEMAND			REGION X DEMAND			REGION Y DEMAND	
3	MODEL A:	2000		MODEL A:	1000		MODEL A:	1500
4	MODEL B:	1000		MODEL B:	2000		MODEL B:	1500
5	MODEL C:	1000		MODEL C:	2000		MODEL C:	2000
6		=			=			=
7		=			=			=
8		=			=			=
9	SHIPPING			SHIPPING			SHIPPING	
10	COST	SOURCE		COST	SOURCE		COST	SOURCE
11	$ 200	0		$ 300	0		$ 250	500
12	$ 200	1000		$ 300	2000		$ 250	1500
13	$ 200	0		$ 300	0		$ 250	1000
14								
15								
16								
17								
18	$ 250	0		$ 250	1000		$ 400	0
19	$ 250	0		$ 250	0		$ 400	0
20	$ 250	1000		$ 250	2000		$ 400	1000
21								
22								
23								
24								
25	$ 300	2000		$ 400	0		$ 450	1000
26	$ 300	0		$ 400	0		$ 450	0
27	$ 300	0		$ 400	0		$ 450	0

The constraints common for this application of linear programming are:

- output from suppliers must satisfy plant demand,
- output of each model from each plant must equal the total of what is being shipped to each region,
- the total for each model sent to each region by all the plants must equal the demand for that model in that region, and
- the maximum capacities of supplying and manufacturing plants cannot be exceeded.

SITING NEW PLANTS

The "dummy" plant is a plant that does not exist but is incorporated in the linear program. The dummy plant is kept out of a normal run for scheduling production among existing plants by having very high production costs. If aggregate demand exceeds existing plant capacity, then excess demand is assigned to the dummy plant. Thus, one benefit of the dummy plant is to avoid an infeasible solution when aggregate demand exceeds total existing plant capacity. The dummy plant also identifies which products are short and how many. With this information, a manager can take corrective action to either enhance production (overtime, subcontracting) or cut demand (canceling sales promotions, raising prices).

The prime purpose of the dummy plant is to evaluate potential sites for building a new plant. In this case, regional demand should not be a near-term, but a long-term forecast reflecting that a new plant is a 20-year or so investment. The associated production and shipping costs are entered for a potential site, and the program is run to obtain total cost. Then another site is entered, and the process repeated. The desired site for the new plant is the one that minimizes total costs. However, the previously described linear program model may concentrate all production at the new plant and close down the existing plants if the new plant has the lowest variable costs by utilizing the latest manufacturing technology. The model is incomplete by not including fixed costs. The fixed cost of a plant does not disappear when it is assigned zero production. Moreover, the fixed cost for the new plant should be related to its capacity by incorporating a formula coupling productive capacity to annual financing costs. The larger the plant, the greater the annual financing costs, although this relationship may not be linear from economies of scale.

Including fixed costs provides the optimal productive capacity of the new plant for each product along with the production schedules for the existing plants. It may be necessary to assign minimum production constraints at the existing plants to control the magnitude of plant cutbacks. This problem can also be laid out on a time sequence whereby the solution indicates the time to build the new plant in addition to its output.

Generally speaking, the capacity of the new plant is near a maximum or minimum size depending on its associated costs. It is advisable to experiment with small changes to the variable and fixed costs of the new plant. The optimal solution may be near a trigger point where a small change in costs radically swings the solution from one extreme to the other. If this is the case, then mention of this should be part of the findings. While the solution identifies plant location and size with the lowest system cost, numerous qualitative factors still have to be considered before a final decision can be made (see Chapter 4).

MANAGING A LINEAR PROGRAM

The size of linear programs grows exponentially when applied to more realistic situations where procurement is measured in hundreds of parts, where there is a score of models, and where shipments are made to numerous distributors. Aggregation of suppliers, models, and distributors is necessary to reduce the scope of the problem. Fifty distributors in Vermont can be combined into a single distributor as long as one is confident that all distributors in the area are going to be satisfied by the same plants. This may also hold for an entire region such as New England, which can then be treated as a single distributor. Essentially identical product types or models in manufacturing and shipping costs are going to have the same solution from the point of where they are manufactured and shipped. These can be combined into a single product type or model for planning purposes. Suppliers should be limited to those parts and components that make up much of the value of the product.

A linear program can be split into two segments—one for suppliers shipping parts to plants and one for plants shipping product to regions to further reduce its size. The latter is run first to identify plant production; then the former can be run to identify the optimal choice of suppliers. Moreover, it may not be necessary to continually rerun the supplier portion of the linear program once it is known that the best arrangement is for supplier X to ship part Y to plant Z. This also holds for assigning plant production to regions. The solution will essentially remain unchanged as long as the underlying supplier prices and shipping costs remain constant. However, significant changes in product demand may affect the nature of the solution even if underlying costs do not change such as exceeding plant capacities.

A manager responsible for setting up a linear program to schedule production is caught on the horns of a dilemma–too much detail may result in not achieving a working model, and too much simplicity robs a model of its usefulness. A pragmatic balance has to be struck between the two extremes.

MULTIMODAL SHIPPING

Linear programming can minimize shipping costs with different modes of transport. In this example, production costs are the same at three plants to focus on how to handle shipping from three plants to four regions where rail shipments are restricted to 80 tons and truck shipments to 25 tons. Moreover, truck rates are three times more costly than rail. Fig. 9.4 shows the assignment by rail and truck from the three plants to the four regions.

Figure 9.4
Multimodal Shipping

	A	B	C	D	E	F	G	H	I
3					TONS/SHIPMENT:		80		25
4						$/TON	R.R.	$/TON	TRUCK
5	PLANT 1	TONS			TO REG W:	$ 10.00	19	$ 30.00	1
6	MAX CAP	PROD			TO REG X:	$ 15.00	11	$ 45.00	0
7	2500	2425	<=		TO REG Y:	$ 30.00	0	$ 90.00	0
8					TO REG Z:	$ 40.00	0	$ 120.00	0
9									
10	PLANT 2	TONS			TO REG W:	$ 25.00	0	$ 75.00	0
11	MAX CAP	PROD			TO REG X:	$ 20.00	2	$ 60.00	0
12	1500	800	<=		TO REG Y:	$ 25.00	8	$ 75.00	0
13					TO REG Z:	$ 35.00	0	$ 105.00	0
14									
15	PLANT 3	TONS			TO REG W:	$ 40.00	0	$ 120.00	0
16	MAX CAP	PROD			TO REG X:	$ 30.00	0	$ 90.00	0
17	2000	2000	=<=		TO REG Y:	$ 20.00	7	$ 60.00	0
18					TO REG Z:	$ 15.00	18	$ 45.00	0

The constraints in column C ensure that tons of product output shipped by rail and truck from each plant to the four regions do not exceed each plant's maximum capacity. This linear program also allows interchanges between adjacent regions. The portion of the solution spreadsheet in Fig. 9.5 shows an interchange of a small truck shipment from region W to X and a regular truck shipment from region Z to Y.

Constraints in column D stipulate that rail and truck shipments from the plants, plus regular and small truck shipments from other regions, less regular and small truck shipments to other regions must be equal to, or greater than, demand for product in each region. The "greater than" requirement is necessary to avoid an infeasible solution, which would probably result if the constraint stipulated that regional demand had to be exactly matched with whole number shipments from the various sources. Adjustable cells are those in columns G and I denoting the number of shipments. The objective is to minimize shipping costs (not shown). Constraints ensure that maximum plant capacities are not exceeded and regional demands are satisfied. One problem facing a more realistic modeling of an actual situation is the length of the associated formulas. In this relatively simple situation, the number of tons shipped to region W in cell C22 is =80*(G5+G10+G15)+25*(I5+I10+I15)-25*G22-10*I22+25*G23+10*I23.

Figure 9.5
Regional Interchanges

	A	B	C	D	E	F	G	H	I
		TONS	TONS		TONS/SHIPMENT:		25		10
20		DEMAND	RECEIPTS			$/TON	TRUCK	$/TON	SMTRUCK
21									
22	REG W:	1530	1535	>=	FR W TO X:	$ 20.00	0	$ 30.00	1
23	REG X:	1050	1050	=>=	FR X TO W:	$ 20.00	0	$ 30.00	0
24	REG Y:	1220	1225	>=	FR X TO Y:	$ 30.00	0	$ 45.00	0
25	REG Z:	1390	1415	>=	FR Y TO X:	$ 30.00	0	$ 45.00	0
26					FR Y TO Z:	$ 25.00	0	$ 37.50	0
27					FR Z TO Y:	$ 25.00	1	$ 37.50	0

The size of the formulas greatly expands for larger numbers of plants and distribution centers. Aggregation of distribution centers may be necessary to reduce the scope of the problem to manageable proportions. The adjustable cells are general integers for whole-number shipments. These, like binary integers, are noncontinuous variables that greatly lengthen computer run time. Substituting continuous, rather than discrete, variables reduces run time but results in fractional shipments. While these can be rounded, they would most likely eliminate the more expensive interchanges among regions by substituting less expensive, but presumably not desired, partial shipments from the plants.

PROJECT MANAGEMENT

Another application of linear programming is as an aid in managing activities associated with a project such a building a new plant. The origin of performance evaluation review technique (PERT) was the Polaris submarine development program where the admiral in charge faced the daunting task of managing 3,000 separate activities. He turned to the operations research specialists for a management tool, who developed PERT. The same problem faced DuPont in building chemical plants. A management consulting firm developed the critical path method, which was subsequently merged into PERT.

Drawing a PERT diagram is a nontrivial exercise. Some degree of trial and error is necessary to lay out the PERT diagram to ensure both the proper sequence and precedence of activities described in Table 9.1. Critical activities are those that delay the entire project if they themselves are delayed. They form the critical path of a PERT diagram in Fig. 9.6 and demand more managerial attention than noncritical activities. Noncritical activities are those that can be delayed without affecting overall time to complete a project. Yet noncritical activities cannot be ignored because if delayed sufficiently, they will eventually delay the whole project, that is, become part of the critical path. Slack is the time element differentiating a noncritical activity from a critical activity. Knowledge of which activities are on the critical path and the slack associated with noncritical activities are valuable aids in managing large-scale projects.

Table 9.1
Activity Description

ACTIVITY	DESCRIPTION	MONTHS	PRIOR ACTIVITY
1	Design the plant	12	None
2	Select the site	8	1
3	Prepare site	12	2
4	Select vendor for generator	4	1
5	Manufacture generator	18	4
6	Install generator	4	3,5
7	Prepare operations manual	5	4
8	Select personnel	3	1
9	Train operators	9	7,8
10	Obtain license	6	6,9

Figure 9.6
PERT Diagram

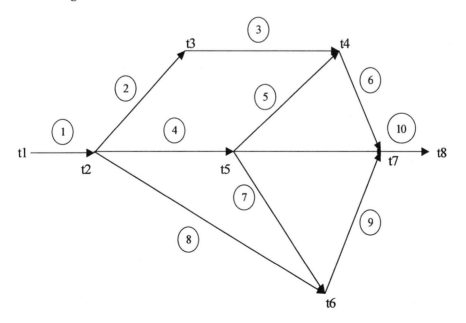

The linear relationships for the activities listed in Table 9.2 can be read directly off the PERT diagram. Listing (t2−t1) as (t1−t2) reverses the start and end points of an activity with dire consequences. The time element for each activity cannot be less than the stipulated, or minimum, time. The project starts at time t1 and ends at time t8. Thus, the duration of the project is (t8−t1), which a manager would like to minimize. Cells T1:T8 are adjustable. Fig. 9.7 shows the spreadsheet setup where column A contains activity descriptions, column C linear equations, column D constraint equations, and column E minimum times for completion. Cell C16 is the objective cell to be minimized.

Table 9.2
Activity Formulation

ACTIVITY	TIME ELEMENT	MUST BE	MONTHS
Design the plant	t2–t1	>	12
Select site	t3–t2	>	8
Prepare site	t4–t3	>	12
Select vendor for generator	t5–t2	>	4
Manufacture generator	t4–t5	>	18
Install generator	t7–t4	>	4
Prepare operations manual	t6–t5	>	5
Select personnel	t6–t2	>	3
Train operators	t7–t6	>	9
Obtain license	t8–t7	>	6

The solution shows that the minimum time to complete the project is 44 months. Incorporating dual values in the model reveals the critical path, which is designing the plant, selecting the vendor, manufacturing and installing the generator, and obtaining the license. Reducing the time to complete critical path activities shortens project time. This observation holds until the slack of an alternative noncritical path is consumed, resulting in a new critical path.

Figure 9.7
Spreadsheet Formulation for PERT

	A	B	C	D	E
1	PROJECT MANAGEMENT				
2					MIN
3					TIME
4	DESIGN PLANT		=T2-T1	=WB(C4,">=",E4)	12
5	SELECT SITE		=T3-T2	=WB(C5,">=",E5)	8
6	PREPARE SITE		=T4-T3	=WB(C6,">=",E6)	12
7	SELECT VENDOR		=T5-T2	=WB(C7,">=",E7)	4
8	MANUF GENERATOR		=T4-T5	=WB(C8,">=",E8)	18
9	INSTALL GEN		=T7-T4	=WB(C9,">=",E9)	4
10	PREPARE OPMANUAL		=T6-T5	=WB(C10,">=",E10)	5
11	SELECT PERSONNEL		=T6-T2	=WB(C11,">=",E11)	3
12	TRAIN OPERATORS		=T7-T6	=WB(C12,">=",E12)	9
13	OBTAIN LICENSE		=T8-T7	=WB(C13,">=",E13)	6
14					
15					
16	TOTAL PROJECT TIME		=T8-T1		

Shortening the time duration of project, or crashing a project, involves spending more money than planned to expedite the completion of critical path activities. Fig. 9.8 shows the solution spreadsheet for shortening the project from 44 to 38 months. The minimum cost corresponds to the maximum time to complete an activity, while the maximum cost corresponds to the minimum time to complete an activity. The relationship between cost and time to complete a project is linear; that is, the cost to shorten an activity by two months is twice that to shorten it by one month. Activities with the same minimum and maximum times cannot be crashed. Constraints in columns D and E ensure that the time to complete "crashable" activities lies between their minimum and maximum times. Project time is constrained to 38 months, and total cost is the objective cell to be minimized. Actual time for each activity can be calculated by examining the results in column J.

Figure 9.8
Crashing a Project

A	B	C	D	E	F	G	H	I	J
1 PROJECT MANAGEMENT									
2					MIN	MAX	MAX	MIN	ACTUAL
3					TIME	TIME	COST	COST	COST
4 DESIGN PLANT		8	<=	=>=	8	12	$ 200	$ 100	$ 200
5 SELECT SITE		8	=<=	>=	7	8	$ 30	$ 20	$ 20
6 PREPARE SITE		12	=<=	>=	6	12	$ 380	$ 200	$ 200
7 SELECT VENDOR		4		=>=	4	4		$ 10	$ 10
8 MANUF GENERATOR		16	<=	>=	10	18	$ 1,640	$ 1,000	$ 1,160
9 INSTALL GEN		4	=<=	>=	3	4	$ 350	$ 300	$ 300
10 PREPARE OPMANUAL		11		>=	5	5		$ 100	$ 100
11 SELECT PERSONNEL		15		>=	3	3		$ 10	$ 10
12 TRAIN OPERATORS		9	=<=	>=	6	9	$ 130	$ 100	$ 100
13 OBTAIN LICENSE		6		=>=	6	6		$ 80	$ 80
14									
15					REQUIRED MTHS:	38		TCOST:	$ 2,180
16 TOTAL PROJECT TIME		38			ACTUAL MTHS:	38			
17						=			

Utilizing PERT requires dedication of manpower to gather the requisite information to set up a PERT diagram and keep it updated as the project proceeds to completion. Costs have to be obtained for completing an activity for different time intervals if crashing a project is desired. A linear relationship may not hold between time to shorten a project and cost. For instance, the cost to shorten a project by two months is most apt to be more than twice the cost to shorten it by one month. A lookup table is a convenient way to identify costs associated with different time increments to crash an activity. A lookout table rules out linear programming, but not Evolver optimization. As a general rule, if a problem can be handled by linear programming, do so; if not, use other optimization methods such as Evolver or RISKOptimizer.

SCHEDULING PLANT LOADING

The classic formula in production planning is total cost equals fixed cost plus variable cost multiplied by production volume. As discussed in Chapter 4, fixed and variable costs are not constant, but are a function of production volume. A company may not know the exact relationship of fixed and variable costs to volume, but it always knows total costs and total production. Hence, a company knows its unit costs, which are total costs divided by total production, not to be confused with variable costs. Unit costs and their associated volume can be entered in a spreadsheet, and a cost curve can be obtained as a function of volume using Excel trend lines. It may be possible to get a better-fitting curve using Evolver. Fig. 9.9 shows the unit cost at different volumes of production obtained by dividing total costs by the production volume. The unit cost curve as a function of volume is assumed to take the general form, Unit Cost = Constant + $A*Volume^{-B}$, which is not available as an Excel trend line.

The Constant and A and B factors are not known and are designated as adjustable cells. Column C contains unit costs obtained by dividing total costs by total production. Evolver uses intelligent trial and error to select successive sets of values for the adjustable cells. For each set of values, unit costs are calculated in column D. In column E, differences between calculated and actual unit costs are squared and summed. The objective is to identify a set of values for the adjustable cells that minimize the sum of the squares of the differences in cell E35.

Figure 9.9
Obtaining a Unit Cost Curve

	B	C	D	E
21		CONSTANT:	0	
22		A FACTOR:	0	
23		B FACTOR:	0	
24	VOLUME	$/UNIT		
25	1000	200	=$D$21+$D$22*B25^-$D$23	=(C25-D25)^2
26	2000	150	=$D$21+$D$22*B26^-$D$23	=(C26-D26)^2
27	3000	133.33333333	=$D$21+$D$22*B27^-$D$23	=(C27-D27)^2
28	4000	125	=$D$21+$D$22*B28^-$D$23	=(C28-D28)^2
29	5000	120	=$D$21+$D$22*B29^-$D$23	=(C29-D29)^2
30	6000	116.66666666	=$D$21+$D$22*B30^-$D$23	=(C30-D30)^2
31	7000	114.28571428	=$D$21+$D$22*B31^-$D$23	=(C31-D31)^2
32	8000	112.5	=$D$21+$D$22*B32^-$D$23	=(C32-D32)^2
33	9000	111.11111111	=$D$21+$D$22*B33^-$D$23	=(C33-D33)^2
34	10000	110	=$D$21+$D$22*B34^-$D$23	=(C34-D34)^2
35				=SUM(E25:E34)

Scheduling Plant Loading from Cost Curves

To demonstrate how unit cost curves can be used to schedule plant loading, suppose that four plants have the unit cost curves indicated in row 21 of Fig. 9.10. Each plant can produce up to 10,000 units for a total of 40,000 units. Total desired output is 25,000 units. A manager desires to know the loading of individual plants to the nearest hundred that minimize costs with a constraint that no plant operates below 1,000 units. The initial set of values in row 19 has been intentionally selected to total 250. This allows the use of the budget method of solution, where Evolver examines only sets of values for the adjustable cells A19:D19 that total 250. Actual production in row 20 is 100-fold these values.

Figure 9.10
Plant Loading

	A	B	C	D	E	F
18		A	B	C	D	
19		70	70	70	40	=SUM(B19:E19)
20	VOLUME	=100*B19	=100*C19	=100*D19	=100*E19	=SUM(B20:E20)
21	U.COST	=150+300000/B20^1.5	=130+150000/C20^1.1	=90+100000/D20^0.9	=80+200000/E20^0.95	
22	T.COST	=B20*B21	=C20*C21	=D20*D21	=E20*E21	=SUM(B22:E22)

Row 21 contains the unit cost curves for the four plants, and row 22 contains their respective production costs. The objective is to minimize system cost in cell F22. After running the program, the manager knows that he or she should load plant A with 1,000 units, plant B with 4,000 units, and plants C and D with 10,000 each.

WORKSHOP SCHEDULING

Suppose that a workshop makes subassemblies used in building some form of capital equipment. Orders on hand for capital equipment call for delivery at specified times in the future. In order for this to occur, subassemblies must be finished at prescribed times before the delivery date for the capital equipment to be completed on time. Suppose that three orders for capital equipment have been received and that a workshop is responsible for manufacturing subassemblies X, Y, and Z. These subassemblies must be finished by the week indicated in Table 9.3 for the capital equipment to be completed on time.

Table 9.3
Latest Week of Completion

SUB X	SUB Y	SUB Z
26	24	20
30	28	24
32	30	27

The required labor-hours for each subassembly are in Table 9.4.

Table 9.4
Required Labor-Hours

WEEK BEFORE DELIVERY	SUB X	SUB Y	SUB Z
-1	100	150	50
-2	300	100	150
-3	400	50	200
-4	200	0	100
-5	100	0	0

The formula =IF(G7=1,100,0)+IF(F7=1,200,0)+IF(E7=1,400,0)+IF(D7=1,300,0)+ IF(C7=1,100,0) in cell B12 of Fig. 9.11 has been replicated to the right. A value of 1 was then entered into cell G7. The formula generates the hours of labor required in weeks 1 through 5 in order to deliver the subassembly in week 6.

Figure 9.11
Initial Spreadsheet Setup

	A	B	C	D	E	F	G
6	SUB X	1	2	3	4	5	6
7							1
8							
9							
10							
11	HOURS						
12		100	200	400	300	100	0

The spreadsheet was expanded horizontally for time and vertically to include subassemblies Y and Z. Fig. 9.12 illustrates the workload for the three subassemblies for completion scheduled at the due date. The workload is very uneven. The workers are either on overtime or idle. It would be a better use of manpower resources to complete some of the subassemblies prior to their due dates in order to even out the workload. The adjustable cells are the rows containing the delivery week of the subassemblies. Constraints are constructed for completion of subassemblies at, or prior to, their due dates. The aggregate workload for all subassemblies for each week is compared to the average workload throughout the period. The objective is to minimize the absolute difference between actual and average workloads. Evolver was able to schedule the completion of the subassemblies at, or prior to, their latest due dates with the resulting workload illustrated in Fig. 9.13. Comparing Figure 9.12 with Figure 9.13 demonstrates the efficacy of Evolver as a planning tool for workshop scheduling.

Figure 9.12
Projected Workload before Optimization

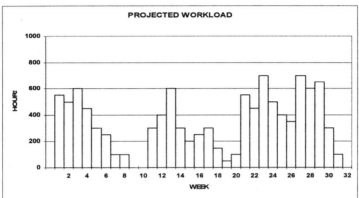

Figure 9.13
Projected Workload After Optimization

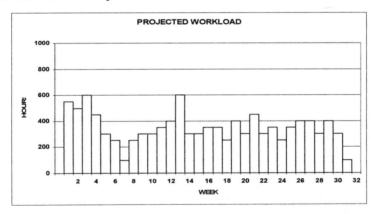

JOBSHOP SCHEDULING

A jobshop is characterized by individual jobs requiring different amounts of time to complete each operation. Suppose that a jobshop consists of four operations: sanding, varnishing, etching, and finishing. Every job is unique with regard to the amount of time required for each operation. The workload for six jobs is listed in Table 9.5.

Job 1 takes 1.5 hours to go through the first operation of sanding, 1.25 hours for the second sequential operation of varnishing, and 2.5 hours for the third sequential operation of etching, followed by 1.25 hours for the finishing operation. Once one job is sanded, the next job can be sanded without any intervening delay. If the jobs are sequenced in the order received: 1, 2, 3, and so forth, then job 1 is the first to be sanded. After sanding, job 1 can be varnished, etched, and finished without intervening delays. Once job 1 is sanded, other jobs can be sanded without intervening delays.

Table 9.5
Workload (Hours) per Operation

	SAND	VARNISH	ETCH	FINISH
JOB	1	2	3	4
1	1.50	1.25	2.50	1.25
2	2.00	3.00	1.50	1.00
3	0.50	2.00	2.50	1.00
4	2.25	1.25	2.00	0.50
5	0.75	1.25	1.00	1.25
6	0.50	2.00	1.50	2.00

All remaining jobs and operations must satisfy two conditions before an operation can commence. Before job 2 can be varnished, it must have been sanded, and job 1 must have completed its varnishing operation. Before job 5 can be etched, job 5 must have been varnished, and job 4 must have completed its etching operation. Thus, the starting time for operation X for job J is the greater of the completion time for the preceding operation X-1 for job J or the completion time of operation X for job J-1.

Evolver has the capability to generate a unique sequencing of numbers through the order solving method. Six jobs can be assigned 720 (6! or 6 x 5 x 4 x 3 x 2 x 1) unique arrangements such as 1, 2, 3, 4, 5, 6 or 6, 5, 4, 3, 2, 1. IF statements determine which of the two pertinent operations takes longer and a lookup table determines the duration of an operation. These rule out linear programming. For the initial sequence of 1, 2, 3, 4, 5, 6, depicting doing jobs in the order received, the length of time to do all the jobs would be 17.5 hours. Evolver was set up with the objective of minimizing total time, with the adjustable cells being the job sequence. The solution was to schedule jobs in the order of 3, 6, 1, 2, 5, 4 for a total completion time of 14 hours.

PRODUCTION FLOOR SCHEDULING

This approach can be expanded for production floor planning. Suppose that a factory makes 10 models of a machine that pass through four stages of production. There are orders for 10 model As, 4 model Bs, 7 model Cs, 2 model Ds, and so forth. Setup time between the four stages of production differ for each model. For instance, the setup time to switch from model A to model B at stage 3 may be 1 hour whereas to switch from model A to model C may be 2 hours. A lookup table can be created for switching production between each stage of production for every combination of models. With a spreadsheet setup very similar to that described for the jobshop, Evolver can determine the order of manufacture that minimizes total production time.

DETERMINING PRODUCTION RUNS (SINGLE PRODUCT)

Both linear programming and Evolver optimization require that a values be discrete, such as production demand being 100. Stochastic demand incorporates uncertainty such as demand being 100 units plus or minus 10 percent. RISKOptimizer combines the optimization algorithms of Evolver with @RISK simulation to handle stochastic values for demand or price or other factors affecting a business situation.

Suppose that demand is in the form of standard order sizes of 4,000, 3,000, 2,000, and 1,000 units. Table 9.6 shows the probability distribution for multiple orders for the variously sized orders. On a given day, there is a 5 percent chance of obtaining 5 separate orders of 4,000 units, a 15 percent chance of obtaining 4 separate orders of 4,000 units, and so on. Orders of the same size can utilize the discrete probability function provided by @RISK software. The formula =4000*RiskDiscrete({5,4,3,2,1,0},{0.05,0.15,0.15,0.15,0.2,0.3}) models orders for 4,000 units where the probability for five orders as 5 percent, four orders 15 percent, and so forth,.

Table 9.6
Order Size Probability Distributions

Order size:	4,000	3,000	2,000	1,000
# Orders	%	%	%	%
10				5
9				10
8				15
7			10	40
6			20	20
5	5	5	35	10
4	15	10	20	
3	15	15	10	
2	15	40	5	
1	20	20		
0	30	10		

The @RISK discrete probability function is used to model the probability distributions for other order sizes. Daily demand is the number of discrete orders multiplied by the order size. Daily demand is stochastic in that it cannot be predicted with certainty. This rules out linear programming and Evolver in determining the length of the production run, but not RISKOptimizer.

In Fig. 9.14, the stochastic demand formulas for the variously sized orders are in columns A through D and totaled in column E, then replicated down to create 100 days of operation. The task facing RISKOptimizer is to identify two levels of production and a cutoff or trigger point. If inventory falls below the cutoff or trigger point, production is increased to prevent stockouts. If inventory is above the cutoff point, then production is cut to avoid accumulating excess inventory. The optimal cutoff point and the two production levels minimize inventory holdings and the number of stockouts.

Column F is yesterday's inventory plus today's production in column G less today's demand in column E. Adjustable cells F2:F4 are limited to integers between 0 and 50 and are multiplied by 1,000 to determine the cutoff point and the two production levels in cells G2:G4. Column G determines production in relation to the cutoff point. If inventory is below the cutoff point in cell G2, then production is as indicated in cell G3; otherwise, cell G4. Column H contains stockouts (positive values of any negative inventory). The objective is to minimize both inventory and stockouts with a punitive charge applied to total stockouts. The formula =SUM(F8:F108)+100*SUM(H8:H108) is in objective cell B3. The solution in Fig. 9.14 is to produce 42,000 units per day when factory inventory is below 20,000 units and 24,000 units if above 20,000. These values minimize both inventory holdings and the number of stockouts. Since demand is stochastic, outputs are not discrete, but take the form of probability distributions.

Figure 9.14
Spreadsheet Setup

	A	B	C	D	E	F	G	H
2					CUTOFF:	20	20000	
3	OBJ:	2502000			PROD1	42	42000	
4					PROD2	24	24000	
5		ORDER SIZES						
6	4,000	3,000	2,000	1,000	TOTAL	INVENTORY	PRODUCTION	STOCKOUTS
7						30000		0
8	12000	9000	8000	7000	36000	18000	24000	0
9	0	9000	14000	9000	32000	28000	42000	0
10	12000	6000	8000	6000	32000	20000	24000	0
11	16000	6000	6000	7000	35000	9000	24000	0
12	0	3000	14000	6000	23000	28000	42000	0
13	8000	3000	14000	6000	31000	21000	24000	0
14	8000	6000	10000	7000	31000	14000	24000	0
15	8000	6000	10000	6000	30000	26000	42000	0

Fig. 9.15 is the discrete probability distribution for aggregate stockouts over the 100-day simulation, obtained from @RISK simulation software. There are no stockouts 68 percent of the time during the 100-day simulation period. Thirty-two percent of the simulations experienced stockouts, and the aggregate number of stockouts over 100 days was, for the most part, less than 30,000 units, or less than a single day's demand. This level of stockouts would not degrade customer service. The discrete probability distribution for total stockouts is handy for determining the appropriate punitive charge to be placed against stockouts. For a given punitive charge, RISKOptimizer strikes a balance between inventory holdings and the degree of stockouts when determining the optimal values for the adjustable cells. The perceived effect of stockouts on customer service influences the solution. Too great an aversion for stockouts (high punitive charge) results in large inventory holdings and carrying costs. Too small a punitive charge results in customer dissatisfaction from too many stockouts.

Figure 9.15
Total Stockouts Discrete Probability Distribution

DETERMINING PRODUCTION RUNS (MULTIPLE PRODUCTS)

RISKOptimizer can be applied to determine trigger points for multiple products being manufactured on the same line. Suppose that a line can make three products, but only one at a time. Daily demand for product A is a normal distribution with a mean of 300 and a standard deviation of 100. As seen in Fig. 9.16, if inventory for product A falls below 400 units, then the production run should be 1,100 per day until inventory rises above 400. This is a one-day production run as production stops when inventory rises above 400 units.

Figure 9.16
Trigger Points for Three Products

	A	B	C	D	E	F	G	H	I	J	K	L
3	TRIGGER:		4	400			12	1200			39	3900
4	RUN LENGTH:		11	1100			22	2200			9	900
5			INVENT A				INVENT B				INVENT C	
6	PROD A		66971		PROD B		177041				298154	
7	286	286	1000		742	742	1000		223	223	1000	
8	157	157	843	0	501	501	2699	2200	227	227	773	0
9	241	241	602	0	791	791	1908	0	255	255	1418	900
10	273	273	329	0	242	242	1666	0	471	471	1847	900
11	308	308	1121	1100	190	190	1476	0	435	435	1412	0
12	136	136	985	0	129	129	1347	0	558	558	1754	900
13	231	231	754	0	735	735	612	0	129	129	2525	900
14	258	258	496	0	522	522	2290	2200	279	279	2246	0

Daily demand for product B has a mean of 500 with a standard deviation of 200. Product B can be produced only if product A is not being produced. The trigger point to start production is 1,200 units with a production run of 2,200 per day until inventory is above 1,200 (another single-day production run). Product C has a daily demand with a mean of 400 and a standard deviation of 150. Product C can be produced only if products A and B are not being produced.

The trigger point to start production is 3,900 units, and the production run is 900 units per day until inventory is restored to 3,900 units (as seen in Figure 9.16, multiple-day runs are possible). The trigger points and production run lengths were obtained by running RISKOptimizer with the objective of minimizing inventory, stockouts, and days of idle production with punitive charges applied against the latter two. The order of setting up the spreadsheet does affect the solution as product A has the highest priority and product C the least priority. Nevertheless, RISKOptimizer does determine the length of a production run and the trigger to start production. Production runs continue as long as inventory is less than the trigger point.

A SUPPLIER'S PERSPECTIVE

With demand flow technology, a manufacturer changes production daily in response to demand. Thus, a supplier does not know the manufacturer's demand for parts with certainty, ruling out MRP as a means to schedule components. RISKOptimizer can determine trigger points and production runs for a company supplying parts to a manufacturer.

Suppose that a manufacturer makes two models (A and B) and that the supplier is responsible for two components (K and L). According to the bill of material, model A requires 2Ks and 3Ls, and model B requires 3Ks and 2Ls. The supplier needs three days to replenish the manufacturer's inventory of components L and K once they fall below their respective trigger points. Moreover, the supplier makes subcomponent E where the bill of material requires 4Es for every K and 5Es for every L. The subcomponent requires a two-day lead time between falling below its trigger point and being available for the manufacture of components K and L. Suppose that the manufacturer's production for model A varies between 700 and 800 per day and model B between 200 and 300 per day. These can be modeled with the @RISK histogram functions based on past data. RISKOptimizer is able to determine the trigger points and length of the production runs for components K and L and subcomponent E that minimize inventory for the supplier and avoid stockouts at the manufacturer's plant, listed in Table 9.10. A production run of the indicated length is scheduled when inventory falls below the trigger point and continues as long as inventory remains below the trigger point.

Table 9.10
Trigger Points and Production Run Lengths

	K	L	E
Trigger Point	8,600	6,800	66,000
Production Run	3,500	3,500	24,000

ENDNOTE

1. Cases are from manuals available at www.palisade.com and www.nerses.com.

Chapter 10

Quality and Continuous Improvement

A quality product or service is one that satisfies consumers' needs. No company can survive in today's globally competitive environment without a quality product or service. A preeminently positioned product cannot remain so without continuous improvement as an integral part of a company's business strategy and operations. Lotus once held a stranglehold on spreadsheet software, but no more. What happened? Lotus had a quality product but lagged in continuous improvement. The company rested on its oars and became a standing target for Microsoft to develop a superior product. Microsoft is not about to repeat the mistake made by Lotus, as it continuously upgrades its product line to maintain a competitive advantage. In so doing, Microsoft protects its competitive advantage by presenting a moving target to potential competitors.

Thus, survival in a competitive environment depends on continuous improvement to enhance or change the nature of a product. Continuous improvement goes under various labels such as *kaizen*, total quality control (TQC), and its latter variant, total quality management (TQM). Japan was the first nation to embrace the concept of TQC and bootstrapped itself to a world industrial power. Quality was Japan's competitive advantage up through the 1980s. To survive the Japanese onslaught, companies had to adopt the principles of TQC/TQM or go out of business. For the most part, quality products are a given. Quality differentials between Japanese, European, other Asian, and American-made products are far less discernible, eroding Japan's competitive advantage in the world market. Quality gurus Deming, Juran, Feigenbaum, Crosby, and Ishikawa expounded variations on the central theme of continuous improvement. Each had a unique approach that created a number of pathways for achieving a quality product or service. At times the pathways seem to run parallel to one another. They eventually merge at a common destination of corporate survival in an extremely competitive world where national boundaries no longer protect mediocre performance.

DEFINING QUALITY

Before a quality product can be made, quality has to be defined. The usual attributes of a quality product are performance, features, reliability, durability, serviceability, and aesthetics. Another attribute is the consumer's perception of quality. A buyer of a luxury automobile has a markedly different perception of quality than an individual who needs a cheap and reliable means of getting to and from work. The perception of quality for a person visiting a doctor's office is not the same as for a person taking a television set to a repair shop. Nevertheless, what consumers expect as a quality luxury automobile or as quality medical service is fairly consistent. Defining quality requires correct interpretation of consumer perceptions of a quality product or service. That interpretation was once in the hands of product designers who determined what constituted a quality product with little reference to consumer wants. Nowadays, consumers are the ultimate arbiters of quality.

INTELLECTUAL RESOURCES

Taylor captured the brains of management, but not the workers. Continuous improvement requires that the brains of the workers be captured along with their brawn. Successful companies operating in the global marketplace must be able to tap the brains of all their employees, including secretaries and janitors. Secretaries have proven to be quite effective in making suggestions to reduce administrative confusion or inefficiencies. Janitors see what is being thrown away and have contributed to reducing waste. Ultimately, how can a manager of 30 workers who do not think compete successfully against one whose workers do think? It is a matter of 1 brain against 31. It isn't even a contest. Successful companies are becoming learning institutions where employees are losing the luxury of working 40 mindless hours for a weekly paycheck.

The traditional purpose of a company was to transform capital, labor, and material resources into useful goods and services with profit as the feedback mechanism. Labor meant a worker's brawn in operating a machine, and capital meant financial funds. Now the resources for a successful company competing in the global environment include the intellectual capital of labor. The feedback mechanism still includes profits because a company cannot survive without profits, but profits for a global company depend on successfully:

- penetrating new regions of the world market,
- introducing new products or services,
- enhancing share of established markets,
- developing niche markets,
- focusing resources on a company's core competencies,
- maintaining leading edge technology, and
- entering into strategic alliances to further a company's objectives.

The virtual corporation minimizes material resources and maximizes intellectual resources to supply quality products and services to the marketplace. Dell Computer's principal physical asset is a building to assemble computers. Dell selects suppliers based on their products' technical attributes; builds to demand, eliminating finished goods inventory; and markets directly to consumers, bypassing wholesalers and retailers. Its principal asset is its intellectual capital to orchestrate being a major computer supplier with little in the way of physical assets. The virtual oil company buys crude oil and sells oil products without owning oil fields and refineries. Its principal asset is the intellectual capital to utilize other companies' assets for its own advantage. The virtual airline leases rather than owns aircraft, contracts out maintenance and baggage handling, and focuses its intellectual capital on route selection, flight schedules, ticket prices, and level of service.

HISTORICAL BACKGROUND TO QUALITY

Quality was neither invented by Deming nor first put into practice by the Japanese. Quality has been with us since the dawn of civilization. Quality by inspection was born with the first pottery jar. It is apparent in Egyptian pyramids and Inca fortifications–stones not cut to fit precisely in place had apparently been rejected. The master craftsmen before the Industrial Revolution personally inspected everything made in their shops. Workers in Ford's plant had to inspect everything that passed through their hands. What is different now is active worker involvement to improve not only the quality of a product but also the process that makes the product. The concept of eliminating the causes of defects was invented neither by Deming nor by the Japanese. It began with managerial encouragement for worker inspired suggestions. A suggestion comes from the brain, not the brawn, of a worker. A Scottish shipbuilder, Denny of Dumbarton, organized an early worker suggestion program in 1871. Rewards were given to employees who invented a new machine or introduced a new method that improved quality or productivity, cut waste, or prevented accidents. In 1887 William Proctor, grandson of the founder of Procter & Gamble, told his employees that their first job was to turn out quality merchandise that consumers wanted to buy. The willingness of consumers to buy coupled with worker productivity were responsible for the prosperity of the company and its employees. In 1894 John Patterson, founder of NCR, introduced mandatory daily exercises for his employees (shades of Japan) and a vigorous safety program along with encouraging workers to submit suggestions. He believed that the company pyramid is supported by a base of a "hundred-headed brain" to provide the top of the pyramid, management, with a source for new ideas.

The U.S. company that best symbolized what Japanese companies would eventually put into practice was Lincoln Electric Company. In 1915 Lincoln devised an incentive program to promote continuous improvement. He cultivated worker capabilities in order to tap their brains for the good of the company. He entered into long-term contractual arrangements with his employees to ensure job security. In return, Lincoln expected active worker involvement in making suggestions for improving operations. If a suggestion resulted in the loss of a job position, a worker was protected from loss of employment by being retrained and reassigned. Rewards were based on savings generated from improvements to the manufacturing process and bonuses on a share of corporate profits.

Employees were encouraged to improve output and originate suggestions because the bonus was a large portion of their pay. The same bonus that rewarded performance and actions to improve quality and productivity also penalized workers for absences, poor quality work, and low productivity. Lincoln created an environment of openness and respect between workers and managers. Managers did not retreat to private offices but were expected to spend most of the day on the factory floor. Workers were responsible for the quality of their output and were held accountable for their performance. An advisory board elected by the workers met with top management to identify and resolve problems.

Lincoln believed that customers and workers were responsible for creating profits and were therefore entitled to receive a large share of the profits. Customers, whose purchases generated the revenue for the company and ultimately its profit, should be rewarded with low-priced, high-quality products. Workers, who produced the goods, were paid twice the general wage level. Competing companies, with half the labor cost, found it difficult to survive against Lincoln's competitively-priced, higher quality products. Rather than switch and compete against Lincoln on his terms, they complained to the U.S. government, which initiated antitrust proceedings against Lincoln. The conflict between Lincoln and the government continued until World War II, when wartime regulations were imposed on labor-management relations and wages. These regulations essentially undid all that Lincoln had accomplished, and Lincoln was threatened with a prison sentence if he did not comply. It is ironic that the U.S. government was instrumental in preventing the spread of an idea in the United States that was eventually exported to Japan and led to the demise of so many U.S. companies.

It should not be forgotten that the basis for Japanese adoption of quality and the emphasis on continuous improvement was not that the Japanese were "nice-guys" but to ensure their economic survival after World War II. It was their only way to compete against the U.S. approach of high-volume, mediocre-quality production to satisfy pent-up postwar consumer demand. High-volume, mediocre-quality production was the right business strategy when the United States' had the only operating factories in the world; the mistake was American managers' belated reaction to Japan's gaining an edge on the market by making quality products.

U.S. managers viewed Japanese success as a zero-sum game where the Japanese gain in market share was at their expense. From the Japanese perspective, it was not a zero-sum game in that Japanese companies, in capturing a growing share of the U.S. market, were able to create another growing market for their products in Japan by raising worker living standards. The Far East

Industrial Tigers emulated the Japanese success story of using export earnings to develop their economies and raise living standards. China and India are following the same model of economic development. It is not a zero-sum game, but it is problematic whether the U.S. market, with 5 percent of the world's population, is sufficiently large to bootstrap both China and India, representing one-third of the world's population.

QUALITY BY REDUCING DEFECTS

Quality was once narrowly defined as a product's being free of defects. This was associated with the Taylor system of quality where defects were inspected out of the system. While 99.9 percent defect-free sounds fine, it really isn't. It is equivalent to:

- two unsafe landings at O'Hare International Airport per day,
- 16,000 lost pieces of mail per hour,
- 20,000 wrong drug prescriptions per year,
- 500 incorrect surgical operations performed each week,
- 50 newborn babies dropped by doctors each day,
- 22,000 checks incorrectly posted per hour, and
- 32,000 missed heartbeats per person each year.

After World War II, the War Department sponsored several trips by Deming to Japan to help revive its economy. Deming convinced Kenichi Koyanagi, a founding member of the Union of Japanese Scientists and Engineers, of the value of applying statistics to improve quality. Deming began teaching the same statistical quality methods that he taught to U.S. munitions suppliers during the war. He enhanced the quality of Japanese consumer goods just as he had enhanced the quality of U.S. military goods. U.S. managers chose to turn a blind eye to his success in Japan until they could no longer ignore his impact on their bottom line. In 1979 he received his first consulting assignment from a U.S. company when he advised Nashua, an office and computer products manufacturer, on how to survive the Japanese competitive onslaught. Nashua adopted Deming's advice and improved its profits dramatically. This led to Deming's 1980 appearance on a NBC show on quality called "If Japan Can, Why Can't We?" A top Ford executive watched the program and became interested in Deming's principles. This resulted in Team Taurus, a quality program that turned Ford around and started the belated change in emphasis from volume to quality production in the United States.

STABLE PROCESS

Deming's first lesson in Japan on statistical quality methods was the concept of a stable process. A stable process is one where the mean, or average, and the variation do not change. This was an important lesson in that Japanese industrial practices were not stable. As an example, suppose that the manufacturing processes for making the door of an automobile and the door frame in the automobile body are not stable. Thus, the average width of the door and the average width of the door frame change with time. For some automobiles, the door is wider than the frame and won't shut. For others, the door is narrower than the frame and won't stay shut. For a miraculous few, the door fits the door frame. What description does one give for the quality of a car whose doors can't be shut or won't stay shut? Deming taught the Japanese that manufacturing processes cannot be improved until they are first stabilized. Fig. 10.1 is a stable process with a mean of 100 and a standard deviation of 1 for sample sizes of 5.

Figure 10.1
Stable Process (Mean)

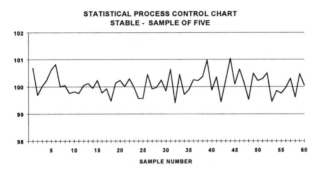

Fig. 10.2 illustrates a stable process in terms of variation, or the degree of scatter in the data. Here variation is expressed as the difference between the high and low readings in a sample.

Figure 10.2
Stable Process (Variation)

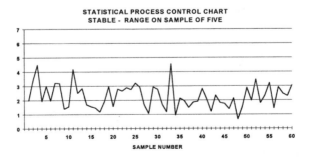

Figures 10.1 and 10.2 for the mean and range of variation in a sample of five readings can be simulated on an Excel spreadsheet by following the instructions in Table 10.1.

Table 10.1
Creating a Statistical Process Control Chart

Tools/Data Analysis/Random Number Generator	
Number of variables	5
Number of random numbers	100
Distribution	Normal
Mean	100
Standard deviation	1
Output range	Cell A5

This creates 100 samples of five readings starting in cell A5, where each reading is taken from a normal distribution whose mean is 100 and standard deviation is 1. The average of each sample of five readings can be obtained, =AVERAGE(A5:E5), along with the range, =MAX(A5:E5)-MIN(A5:E5), which can then be replicated down and plotted. Fig. 10.3 shows an unstable process where the mean has shifted.

Figure 10.3
Unstable Process (Mean Shifted)

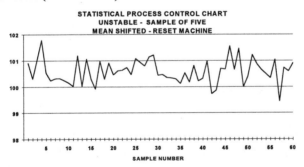

Visually comparing Figures 10.1 and 10.3 shows that the mean has shifted upward. This can be fixed by adjusting a machine setting. Figures 10.4 and 10.5 show an unstable process where the mean is unchanged, but not the degree of variation. Comparing Figure 10.4 with Figure 10.1 shows an increase in variation, or scatter in the data. Comparing Figure 10.5 with Figure 10.2 shows an increase in the range of values within each sample. Increasing variation is usually a sign of a worn part in need of replacement. There are a number of different types of statistical process control charts and different ways of establishing upper and lower control limits for variation, depending on the nature of the measurements.

Figure 10.4
Unstable Process (Increased Variation)

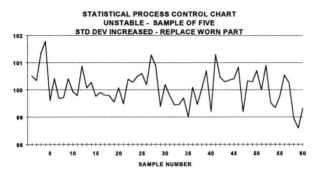

Figure 10.5
Impact on Sample Range

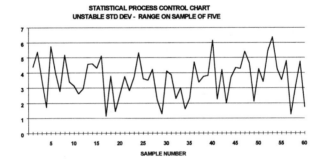

TWO TYPES OF VARIATION

Shewhart, Deming's mentor, divided variation into two types: chance causes and assignable causes. Deming used the words "common causes" and "special causes" while Juran preferred "chronic problems" and "sporadic problems." Using Deming's nomenclature, common cause variation is what is normally seen in a process. There is nothing workers can do to reduce common cause variation as long as they are operating the system as best they can. To reduce common cause variation, the process must be changed through new technology, new machines, or new suppliers. Thus, the primary responsibility for reducing common cause variation rests with management.

Special cause variation is identified as variation with a low probability of occurrence. The concept of special cause variation has been around for many decades. Meters in processing plants have a green band through the middle surrounded by two red bands. The green band is normally the mean plus or minus three standard deviations. Red band readings are more than three standard deviations above or below the mean. As long as readings are in the green band, the shift supervisor sits serenely in his or her console chair. This epitomizes the concept of common cause variation since variation in the green band is inherent in the process. There is nothing a shift supervisor and the workers can do to reduce it.

An alarm goes off when a reading is in the red band. The shift supervisor jumps from his or her chair and checks out possible causes. There are only a limited number of things a shift supervisor can do. A machine may have to be reset or a worn part replaced or a value or processing control knob turned. An operator may have become inattentive or perhaps is new at the job and requires training. Maybe the operator needs a new pair of glasses. What else can a shift supervisor do?

Why did the supervisor spring into action? The probability of a red band reading if the mean and standard deviation of a normal distribution have not changed is only 0.135 percent. So if the process is still stable, there is only about 1 chance in 1,000 of a red band reading. Red band readings have a low probability of occurrence, the identification mark of special cause variation. The supervisor jumping from his or her chair to take corrective action is on the basis that the variation is no longer common cause, highly probable readings within the green band but special cause, highly improbable readings outside the green band. It is true that an isolated red band reading may occur, even though the process is still stable. While a red band reading has a small probability of being common cause variation, it is treated as special cause as there is no real way to separate the two. Thus, variation is simply dubbed special cause because of its low probability of occurrence if the process is still stable. Workers are primary responsible for special cause variation since the reaction is to make an adjustment and check the operator.

Deming expanded on the meaning of special cause variation by including unusual patterns within the green band. He maintained that if a red band reading is deemed special cause variation simply because of its low probability of occurrence, if the process is still stable, then this should hold for unusual patterns within the green band. For instance, a pattern of two out of three readings being between two and three standard deviations from the mean is considered special cause, even though the individual readings are within the green band. The reason for considering this pattern as special cause is its low probability of occurrence, the same criterion applied to red band readings. A pattern of four out of five readings being between one and three standard deviations from the mean has a small probability of occurrence. A shift supervisor should react to this pattern and others as though they were red band readings.

Perhaps the easiest pattern to understand is eight consecutive green band readings above or below the mean. Suppose that the mean is 100. The probability of a green band reading above the mean is 0.5 (actually, 0.50 less the probability of a red band reading of 0.00135). The chance of 2 consecutive green band readings above the mean is very close to 0.5 X 0.5 or 0.25, or 1 chance in 4. The probability of 3 consecutive readings is one chance in 8; 4 consecutive readings, 1 chance in 16; and 8 consecutive readings, 1 chance in 256. Is it possible for the mean to be still 100 and have eight consecutive readings above the mean? Yes, and that chance is 1 in 256. But another, more probable explanation for the 8 consecutive readings above the mean is that the mean has shifted. Thus, the process is no longer stable, and an adjustment should be made to restore the mean to 100. However, in so doing, there is 1 chance in 256 that the process is still stable, and no adjustment should have been made.

ENHANCING QUALITY BY REDUCING VARIATION

Deming stresses the need to reduce common cause variation to improve quality. This can be demonstrated through the following simulation. Suppose that a component is made up of a shaft passing through four bearings. The bearings have an inner diameter of 100 units and an inherent variation (standard deviation) of 0.2 units. The shaft is made to a smaller outer diameter of 99.8 units with an inherent variation of 0.2 units. Quality is defined by how the shaft fits through the four bearings as listed in Table 10.2.

Table 10.2
Defining Quality

PHYSICAL CHARACTERISTIC	MEASURE OF QUALITY
Shaft larger than any one of the four bearings	Defective
Spacing between shaft and any one bearing larger than one unit causes excessive vibrations and exercise of warranty	Warranty
Spacing between shaft and all bearings less than 0.5 units	Superior
All others	Average

The simulation determines the diameter of a shaft by a random draw from a normal distribution with a mean of 99.8 and a standard deviation of 0.2. Four diameters are obtained for the bearings by drawing random samples from a normal distribution whose mean is 100 and standard deviation is 0.2. The spacing between the shaft and each of the four bearings is measured to determine the resulting quality as per Table 10.2.

Although the shaft has a smaller average outer diameter than the average inner diameter of the bearings, the chance of the shaft's being too large to fit through four bearings is actually quite high. The probability of a shaft's having a diameter greater than 100, or more than one standard deviation from the mean, is 15.87 percent. At the same time, 50 percent of all bearings will have an inner diameter less than 100. A shaft whose diameter is greater than the diameter of any one of the four bearings results in a defect. In Table 10.3, half of the output has a shaft diameter greater than the diameter of at least one of the four bearings.

Table 10.3
Relationship between Quality and Variation

	STAGE 1	STAGE 2	STAGE 3	STAGE 4
S.D. Bearings	0.2	0.1	0.1	0.05
S.D. Shaft	0.2	0.2	0.1	0.05
Defective	50.3%	32.8%	22.1%	0.6%
Superior	19.5	47.6	72.9	99.4
Average	29.5	19.6	5.0	0.0
Warranty	0.7	0.0	0.0	0.0

Parenthetically, this simulation can determine the optimal diameter for the shaft to maximize quality for the given variation in the manufacturing process by varying its diameter and observing the resulting quality measurements. More to the point, Table 10.3 illustrates the link between enhancing quality and reducing common cause variation. The percentage of defects falls from 50 percent to virtually nil, while superior performance climbs from 20 percent to virtually all by changing the process to reduce variation inherent in the process. Each of the four stages of progress in Table 10.3 involves an investment in terms of new technology and machines or a decision to switch suppliers. While this is primarily a management responsibility, participation by the workers should not be neglected. A manager who changes suppliers without the workers actually trying out the new supplies is tempting fate.

Suppose that Joe, a machinist, comes to work on Monday and is surprised to see a new machine for him to operate. What is his initial reaction? What would be yours if someone switches your personal computer to a better model without informing you? You're not sure of the differences in operating the new software and you may wonder what happened to your files, or if your files will be compatible with the new software. Thus there may be a distinct lack of enthusiasm over the introduction of new technology until these fears and reservations have been overcome. Why would it be any different for Joe? Suppose that Joe's new machine does not live up to the salesperson's promises or the manager's expectations. Joe's natural reaction would be to hold the manager responsible for the fiasco and make no secret of it. Joe would most probably do nothing to try to improve machine performance, as he now possessed prima facie evidence of management incompetence.

Now suppose that Joe was part of the process of selecting the new machine. His reaction will be quite different for the same circumstances: since he was part of the process of selecting the new machine, he would make the machine work. Even though a manager is primarily responsible for selecting new suppliers, technology, and machines, a manager operates in a partial information vacuum if he or she ignores workers' contributions in making the final selection.

While continuous improvement is never-ending, there does seem to be a limit. In Table 10.3, how much of an investment should be made once variation has been reduced to a point where nearly all of the output is superior? The Taguchi loss function can evaluate the benefit of achieving a higher degree of quality versus the cost of further reducing variance inherent in the process. Thus, there is an economic limit to investing funds to reduce variation in a process. However, a continuous improvement program is not discontinued even when further reduction in defects cannot be economically justified. It is redirected to other activities such as product delivery, pricing, and performance.

SIX-SIGMA QUALITY

The traditional approach to quality is to fix high and low specification readings beyond which a product is deemed defective. The manufacturing process is designed such that the acceptable range represents the mean plus or minus three standard deviations, or sigma. Defects are products whose measurements are above the mean plus three sigma or below the mean less three sigma. One would expect 0.135 percent of product output to be above three sigma from the mean and another 0.135 percent to be below three sigma from the mean. While total defects for "three-sigma quality" of 0.27 percent of product output may sound small, it is equivalent to 2,700 defects per million units of output. The problem becomes acute if the mean shifts off the target value. If the shift from the target value is equivalent to 1.5 sigma, then the number of defects will rise to 66,810 per million units of output. This increase in defects stems from the mean's no longer being at its target value, shifting a larger portion of a normal distribution's tail into the red band. Table 10.4 illustrates the reduction in defects by reducing variation, or sigma, in relation to product specifications. The reliability of a product made up of 10 components depends on all being free of defects.

Table 10.4
Quality Enhancement by Reducing Variance

Degree of Quality	Shift in Mean	Defects in Parts/Million For Components	Reliability of Product with 10 Components
3 Sigma	No	2,700	97.33%
3 Sigma	Yes	66,810	61.63
4 Sigma	Yes	6,210	95.73
5 Sigma	Yes	233	99.84
6 Sigma	Yes	3.4	99.9976

Six-sigma quality with the mean on its target value yields a defect rate of about two per billion, which is difficult to achieve because of variations inherent in a manufacturing process. Under Robert Galvin's leadership, Motorola

Corporation became a world leader in reducing variance to a point where parts, components, and the finished product are virtually defect-free. The process of continuous improvement for Motorola started in 1986 and was so successful that Motorola won the Malcolm Baldrige National Quality Award in 1988. By 1991 Motorola had reduced the defect rate 100-fold from its former level, achieving six-sigma quality in 1992. However, achieving such high standards of quality did not stem from simply reducing variance in the manufacturing process. The entire company, along with its suppliers, became involved with quality. Motorola used points and counterpoints in the form of old and new truths, summarized in Table 10.5, to impress its employees of the company's fundamental shift of emphasis to total customer satisfaction.

Table 10.5
Old Truths, New Truths

OLD TRUTH	NEW TRUTH
Quality is the primary concern of the quality control department.	Quality is everyone's concern.
Training is costly.	The benefits of a trained workforce far exceeds the cost of training.
Quality initiatives have high up-front costs.	The benefits of higher quality products far exceed the cost of quality.
Minimize measurements to cut costs.	There never is too much relevant data.
Tolerate some degree of human error and product defects.	Human error and product defects are to be driven from the system.
Quality is achieved in small incremental steps based on the existing system.	Quality is achieved in both small and large incremental steps by either improving the existing system or adopting a new system.
Improving quality takes time.	Improving quality saves time.
Haste makes waste.	Time is money, but thoughtful speed improves quality.
Quality programs are restricted to products and manufacturing.	Quality programs encompass all functions of a company including administration and services.
At some point, customers no longer detect quality improvement.	Improvements can always be made, if not in a better product, then in better pricing, delivery, and performance.
Quality ideas are developed internally.	Quality ideas are developed internally and externally through benchmarking and other means.
Select suppliers primarily on price.	Integrate company-wide quality program with suppliers, make them part of the team, and set up a system to transfer knowledge between buyer and seller. A world-class seller of goods better be a world-class buyer of parts and components.

Motorola never rested on its oars. The company is continually planning and taking action to reduce its defect rate down to parts per billion with the mean shifted off its target value. Motorola is a leading corporate exponent of quality and offers educational services to other companies through Motorola University.[1]

QUALITY IN TERMS OF MANAGING THE PROCESS

Inspection is not the answer to quality improvement. The focus must shift from the product to the process that makes the product by eliminating the causes of defects and reducing variance. The process of improving a product requires an educated and motivated workforce willing to originate and offer suggestions. Workers can no longer be considered an extension of a machine. This fundamental change in attitude toward workers requires top management commitment. Management support for continuous improvement cannot simply be voiced at a meeting or written in a mission statement. To achieve quality, managers at all levels must exert leadership to guide employee activities and create a corporate culture conducive to improving quality and productivity. Continuous improvement must be backed by the necessary funds, be permanently ingrained in the corporate culture, and involve the entire organization. A significant investment has to be made in training. Companies that have taken these steps are prospering on a global scale; those that haven't are lucky to be alive. This transformation of corporate culture from inspection for defects to a commitment to provide consumers with quality products and services is the result of the work of thousands of executives and operations managers who choose, willingly or not, to follow the teachings of the quality gurus.

JOSEPH M. JURAN

At Western Electric, Juran developed statistical methods for quality. He was sent to Japan in the postwar period to assist in teaching the managerial side of quality and is regarded as second only to Deming in his contribution to revitalizing Japan. Juran advocates quality cost accounting similar in structure to financial cost accounting in order for top management to more easily understand his principles. Juran is concerned with corporate leadership to develop a business strategy to attain, maintain, and ensure a quality product or service. He defines quality as fitness for use free of deficiencies in the form of defects, late deliveries, field failures, incorrect invoicing, and excessive engineering design changes. Fitness for use encompasses design, availability, safety, field use, and conformance to quality standards. Product features that meet customer needs define quality standards. These are identified through customer surveys. Quality products and services generate customer satisfaction, the ultimate source of a company's revenue and profits. Conversely, product deficiencies lead to customer dissatisfaction and financial losses.

Juran's quality trilogy is based on planning, control, and improvement. Specific goals and plans are established along with clear assignment of responsibility for meeting the goals. Rewards are given based on achieving desired results (management by objective). Elements of quality planning are to:

- identify the customers,
- determine the needs of the customers through an analysis of their behavior, by direct communication, and by becoming a customer,
- ensure that groups within a company correctly interpret customer needs,
- develop a product that responds to customers' real, stated, and perceived needs, and
- create and sustain a process that can manufacture a product with desired features.

Quality control is the means of directing activities to meet standards. Managers are responsible for observing and comparing worker performance to company standards and must act if workers do not meet standards. Elements of quality control are to:

- choose a control mechanism by which signs of a problem can be detected,
- select a unit of measure for a product feature or a process,
- decide on a goal for a group that is measurable, equitable, and has official recognition,
- create a means of measuring a product or process feature,
- compare actual performance with standards, and
- take corrective action on discrepancies between actual performance and quality standards.

Elements of quality improvement are to:

- establish a corporate infrastructure for annual quality improvement,
- identify what is in need of improvement,
- specify improvement projects,
- organize a project team for each improvement project with clear responsibility for bringing the project to a successful conclusion, and
- provide the resources, motivation, and training needed by the teams to diagnose causes, determine a remedy, improve quality, and establish controls to hold on to improvement gains.

Juran first used the Pareto chart to illustrate that only a vital few (20 percent) of the types of defects account for most (80 percent) of the defects. The chart is a simple device to determine priorities in dedicating resources to reduce defects. Juran tends to focus on top-down management to encourage quality. He feels that individual parts on an organization must be finely tuned before the whole organization can function smoothly.

Juran's 10-step process for achieving quality consists of:

1. building awareness of opportunities to improve quality,
2. setting goals for improvement,
3. organizing activities to achieve these goals,
4. providing necessary training,
5. creating problem solving teams to eliminate impediments to quality improvement,
6. reporting progress of these teams,
7. giving recognition to teams improving quality,
8. communicating results to all personnel,
9. keeping track of improvements, and
10. incorporating continuous improvement of quality and establishing new quality goals into the company's management program.

The Juran Institute educates managers on Juran's precepts on how to implement quality standards and strategies. His *Quality Control Handbook*, originally written in 1951 and subsequently updated, is considered a reference work.

ARNOLD V. FEIGENBAUM

Feigenbaum was manager of quality control for General Electric's manufacturing operations. He succeeded in getting all divisions within a plant (marketing, design, manufacturing, inspection, shipping and distribution) and all plants within the company to cooperate in a coordinated, company-wide quality program. This company-wide approach is at variance with Juran's dealing with individual parts of a company. Feigenbaum, in his book *Total Quality Control*, defines quality as "the total composite product and service characteristics of marketing, engineering, manufacture, and maintenance through which the product and service in use will meet the expectations of the customer." Feigenbaum coined the phrase "total quality control" and its acronym "TQC." He defines total quality control as "an effective system for integrating the quality-development, quality-maintenance, and quality-improvement efforts of the various groups in an organization so as to enable marketing, engineering, production, and service to function at the most economical levels which allow for full customer satisfaction."

TQC encompasses the integration of efforts by all the various groups in an organization to develop, maintain, and improve quality. The characteristics of quality must be identified in terms of reliability, durability, attractiveness, maintenance, and service. Quality must be understood by all. Quality improves a company's competitiveness, and improving quality requires continuous leadership by those in charge. This is done by first devising a way to measure quality characteristics. Then plans can be originated and placed in action to improve these characteristics to meet customer expectations. Control, defined as "the process of delegating responsibility and authority for a management activity while retaining the means of assuring satisfactory results," has to be established over quality activities.

KAORU ISHIKAWA

Ishikawa, an engineering professor at Tokyo University, was instrumental in introducing total quality control into Japanese manufacturing operations. He promoted company-wide awareness for quality based on statistical methods. He emphasized the bottom-up approach to quality management, starting at the worker level, quite unlike the top-down approach of Juran. He advocated the importance of educating the entire workforce and was instrumental in organizing the first quality circles. He delineated a manager's new role as a coach to encourage and enable workers to improve products and processes. He originated the cause-and-effect diagram, also known as the fishbone or Ishikawa diagram, as a brainstorming tool to encourage worker suggestions. He identified the importance of the customer in defining a quality product or service. He broadened the concept of the external customer to include the internal customer—the next work team or quality circle in the production process. His greatest contribution was to transform the concepts of Deming, Juran, and Feigenbaum into reality by his ability to present them in an easy and understandable way to operating personnel.

PHILIP CROSBY

Crosby started out at International Telephone and Telegraph at the bottom of a quality organization and worked his way to the top. Crosby points to the significant savings in time and effort if a job is done right the first time. Management is to establish requirements that employees can meet and provide the wherewithal and encouragement for employees to meet these requirements. He defines quality as conformance to requirements. He emphasizes prevention, rather than detection, of defects with a performance standard of zero defects. Crosby stresses motivation and planning with less emphasis on statistical methods and problem-solving techniques. Crosby feels that people should strive to achieve a zero defect (ZD) strategy by eliminating opportunities that compromise conformance. Thus, one has to become a "fanatic" to ensure the development, implementation, and continued success of a ZD strategy.

Crosby maintains that quality should not be described in terms of being "good" but in terms of conformance to requirements. Quality is not intangible and immeasurable but can be measured in terms of three costs: prevention, appraisal, and failure. Prevention costs are all activities undertaken to prevent defects in design and development of a product, purchasing components, training personnel, and manufacturing a product or providing a service. Appraisal costs are those necessary to ensure that a product does conform to standards. Failure costs are those associated with nonconformance to requirements such as dealing with dissatisfied consumers, product redesign, engineering and purchasing change orders, rework, scrap, warranty, service after purchase, and product liability. Quality is "free" because the savings in costs by having a product conform to requirements are greater than the costs of prevention, appraisal, and failure. Crosby states that a company should adopt four basic objectives to achieve quality:

1. establish a competent quality management program in every operation of a company where the definition of quality is conformance to requirements,
2. design an appropriate measure of quality in terms of the cost of nonconformance,
3. organize an effective quality improvement program that eliminates nonconformance, and
4. set a performance standard for a quality improvement program of zero defects.

Crosby's 14-step improvement program consists of:

1. management commitment–management must state a clear, understandable policy on quality. They must impress workers on their stand on quality to ensure that the workers take the concept of defect prevention seriously;
2. quality improvement team–form a quality improvement team within each department to run the quality improvement program. They should have different functional backgrounds, and their purpose, among others, is to change employee attitudes toward quality;
3. quality measurement–determine the status of quality throughout the company. Quality measurements must be obtained and nonconformance problems displayed in a manner that permits objective evaluation and corrective action;
4. cost of quality evaluation–define the elements making up the cost of quality to direct corrective action;
5. quality awareness–share with employees what nonconformance is costing and its impact on the reputation of a company;
6. corrective action–provide a systematic method of resolving problems identified through the previous steps and take corrective action to root out causes of nonconformance;
7. establish a committee for the zero defects program–a committee representing various groups within a company is set up to start the preparation for launching a ZD program;
8. training–all levels of management first, then the workers must be trained in order to actively carry out their part of a quality improvement program;
9. zero defects day–establish a ZD day to give everyone a personal experience in zero defects and to demonstrate that there has been a change in company operations;

10. goal setting–employees must be actively involved to transform a commitment to quality into action by establishing improvement goals for themselves and their groups on their way to zero defects;

11. error-cause removal–employees are given a line of communication to management for situations where they are experiencing difficulties in meeting their pledges to improve quality. Customers are asked about problems with a product or a service for quality improvement ideas;

12. recognition–recognize individuals or groups whose performance can be used as a model for others trying to improve quality;

13. quality councils–quality professionals and team leaders meet regularly to upgrade and improve the quality program and to learn from one another; and

14. do it over again–typical program takes from 12 to 18 months. Turnover and changing situations require redoing the program. The quality improvement program never ends.

Like Juran, he founded Philip Crosby Associates to provide training in his approach to quality. Unlike Juran, Crosby is pessimistic on converting U.S. top management to focus more on quality and less on financial reports. He feels that it may be necessary to promote those middle managers who are interested and knowledgeable about quality to top positions and retire those at the top who find it impossible to view corporate activities other than in financial terms. The excerpt on the next page is from a speech Crosby delivered at an American Management Association (AMA) meeting.

In the past, I spent most of the time rattling on about quality and giving little attention to leadership. That approach, I have decided, was a mistake. It tended to position quality out of the mainstream of executive life. Executives should concentrate on finance, relationships and quality. This emphasis should be equal. At the present time, executives typically concentrate 90 percent of their personal effort on finance. That consists mostly of manipulating numbers in order to understand the status of the business. Since they do not seem interested in making a genuine change, I essentially have given up on today's current senior executives, as well as the thought leaders of quality management. This group is never going to get serious about quality. They prefer to work around what they call TQM while convincing themselves that things must be getting better. They spend time trying to win awards that are meaningless, and they convince their customers that things are continually improving.

However, if 37 years in management has taught me nothing else, it absolutely has taught me that management measures everything it cares about in financial terms. It breaks down into money, without exception. Yet quality is given no such measurement in executive life. I know of no company that has placed the price of nonconformance into its accounting system and reports on it during management meetings. Inventory, compensation, depreciation and a hundred other things are measured down to two places to the right of the decimal point. I know of no company where this cost of quality is in the 10-K of the annual report. There, quality is a subjective item, usually only included in the chairman's remarks.

I am spending my time now on those who will be running companies in the future: the students, the middle management, the executive "wannabes" who are willing to have open minds on the subject. My contemporaries have not absorbed this quality business into their hearts. Just as they talk about the need for processed information and are computer illiterate, they rant about the need for quality and think it is ethereal goodness. I have given up on them ever changing.

GENICHI TAGUCHI

Taguchi, a well-known Japanese engineer, started with Nippon Telephone and Telegraph. During his career, Taguchi developed three concepts—robust design, the loss function, and design of experiments. Taguchi is a several-time recipient of the Deming Prize for his contributions to achieving quality products.

Robust Design

Robust design means that a product is designed not to fail in actual field conditions. A product designed not to fail in actual operation will automatically pass a factory inspection. A television set designed to work well where voltages vary or automobile brakes designed to work well under all road conditions will have few defects when tested in a factory. For instance, a television set designed to have a sharp picture between 90 and 130 volts will certainly pass a factory inspection at the specified 110 volts. Automobile brakes designed to work well in slush and mud will certainly pass an inspection inside a controlled environment of a factory. Taguchi moves quality upstream from the factory floor to product design. Taguchi is critical of Crosby's zero defects in that products successfully tested in a controlled environment of a factory can fail under actual field conditions. Since consumers experience field, not factory, performance, the former should determine quality standards.

Taguchi describes quality in terms of a sharp television picture where there is a high signal-to-noise ratio even when field operating conditions are not perfect. Taguchi uses this analogy in his philosophy on quality:

- quality is more a function of product design than complying with stringent manufacturing standards (direct opposition to the concept of zero defects);
- product design should be focused on strengthening the signal-to-noise ratio;
- components designed not to fail in the field lead to reduced defects in the manufacturing process;
- reduced variance in component design improves product performance;
- nothing more is gained in shipping a product that is just within specification than in shipping a product just outside specifications; and
- deviation from the target value should be minimized consistent with the outcome of a cost-benefit analysis using the loss function.

Taguchi Loss Function

In the traditional U.S. system of quality, as long as a product is within specifications, then the customer is assumed to be 100 percent satisfied. Suppose that the specification for the sharpness of a television picture is a rating between 7 and 13 with a target value of 10. If the sharpness of the television is below 7 or above 13, the television set does not pass inspection. This approach to quality presumes that a customer is 100 percent satisfied if the sharpness is between 7 and 13 and 0 percent satisfied if it is not.

Taguchi maintains that this is nonsense. A consumer cannot tell the difference between the sharpness of a television picture of 12.9 and 13.1. Both are fuzzy. Thus, there is no difference between selling a product just within specifications and selling one just outside specifications. Thus, any deviation from the desired target value creates a loss. The Taguchi loss function increases with the square of the deviation between the actual and target performance. The loss function can be quantified by estimating the deviation from the target value where a certain percentage of dissatisfied consumers are exercising the product's warranty. The loss function takes into consideration the:

1. cost of replacing a product with a new one,
2. loss of profit margin in not selling the replacement to another customer,
3. gain in reusing some portion of the parts of the returned product, and
4. loss of future business.

This last factor is essentially a qualitative judgment, but Taguchi feels that this loss may be several times worse than what most managers think. While the cost associated with the exercise of a warranty is quantifiable, the loss of future business caused by the circumstances surrounding the exercise of a warranty is not. A consumer's reaction to a mediocre performing product is likewise difficult to quantify. The loss of repeat business is not limited to a consumer switching to another manufacturer, but also includes sales lost from negative word-of-mouth advertising, and the greater effort in marketing products with less than a stellar reputation.

One can conclude from this that any deviation from the target value is bad. This is not true. The Taguchi loss function is an attempt to apply economic analysis on how much money should be spent to improve quality. Taguchi does not support spending huge amounts of money to marginally improve the quality of a product if it cannot be justified by a cost-benefit analysis. The cost of improving a product can be quantified. The benefit can now be quantified by the savings in the Taguchi loss function in narrowing the spread between target and actual performance.

Design of Experiments

Experiments with the manufacturing process may be necessary to improve the quality of a product. Suppose that there are 15 variables in the form of 15 knobs controlling various aspects of a process. The conventional approach to running experiments to improve quality is changing one knob setting at a time, keeping the others constant. A testing program to investigate all possibilities depends on the number of individual knob settings. This could result in anywhere from hundreds, to thousands, to millions of experiments to examine every possibility. Taguchi design of experiments uses a traditional statistical tool, analysis of variation (ANOVA), to analyze the results of a relatively few experiments where a number of variables (knob settings) are simultaneously changed. Taguchi's design of experiments can efficiently identify those variables most important in influencing quality and their optimal settings.

QUALITY TOOLS

Some of the "old" quality tools have already been discussed in Chapter 5, such as defect record keeping, the Pareto diagram, the Ishikawa or fishbone cause-and-effect diagram, and the Deming plan-do-check-act (PDCA) cycle. In 1988 Shigeru Mizuno proposed seven "new" tools for quality control.[2] The first is a relations diagram intended to clarify complex situations in order to identify causal relationships. The affinity diagram takes a large number of individual ideas and groups them according to their "affinity" to broader concepts. A horizontal or vertical tree diagram translates the results of the relations and affinity diagrams into an operational plan to carry out an objective. The matrix diagram clarifies items of interest by arranging elements in rows and columns to show the presence or the absence of relationships between pairs of elements. As an example, the row headings in a matrix diagram could be goals, and the column headings, actions. Symbols depicting strong or weak relationships are shown where the rows and columns for goals and actions intercept. Matrix data analysis is the only numerical analysis tool of the seven. It weights and ranks factors associated with, for example, customer satisfaction. A process decision program chart is a method of illustrating events and contingencies associated with a solution to a problem. The arrow diagram is similar to a PERT diagram depicting the end and start of a sequence of events to solve a problem.

Another visual tool originated in Japan is the quality function deployment (QFD). Before QFD, the sales force knew customer needs and preferences, but this information was not always communicated to those in product development. QFD ensures a line of communication from those who possess information on customer needs to those who design or improve a product. The visual presentation of QFD, called a "house of quality," ensures that product design remains focused on satisfying customer needs gleaned from sales personnel, customer surveys and interviews. Customer needs are matched against product characteristics to identify those characteristics most strongly correlated with customer needs. Customer satisfaction for each product characteristic is ranked in comparison with that for competitors along with listing information on competitors' prices, market shares, and profit margins. Benchmarks are then established to focus product development on product characteristics with the greatest impact on improving customer satisfaction.

Mizuno's seven tools are designed to enhance a company's ability to complete tasks, eliminate failures, exchange and disseminate information, and encourage the expression of new ideas. The QFD ensures a strong link between customer satisfaction and product design. The seven tools and the QFD help employees express their inner thoughts, allowing companies to more effectively tap their brains. These tools express the Japanese philosophy that all employees have intrinsic value in being able to make a contribution to improve quality and productivity.

TOTAL QUALITY MANAGEMENT

Total quality control focuses on the removal of the causes of defects. In the early 1980s Polaroid identified several areas of concern that affected quality not directly related to defects or their causes such as marketing, employee attitudes, supplier relations, and finance. Total quality management (TQM) focuses on continuously improving performance at every level of operation and functional area within an organization, using all available human and capital resources to achieve the highest degree of customer satisfaction. An argument can be made that the principles of TQM are implicitly embedded in Feigenbaum's TQC. Perhaps the advantage of TQM is its explicit emphasis on quality's being a company-wide activity, not restricted to the factory floor. Characteristics of a successful TQM program encompass:

- a focus on customer satisfaction backed by a holistic, balanced, and integrated system for ensuring that customer needs are met;
- a commitment to continuous improvement throughout all of management;
- a flattening of the organization by eliminating useless or bureaucratic layers of management in order to enhance response time to change;
- interdisciplinary collaboration among departments;
- a focus on the process rather than on the product or the results of a process by critically examining why things are done the way they are;
- empowering and involving everyone in a company-wide quality program, including suppliers and customers;
- a fluid and unfettered flow of communication both vertically within groups and horizontally between groups;
- an unending effort for continuous improvement of products and processes;
- the customer as final arbiter of quality;
- investment in people to improve their proficiency;
- team building and improving the work environment;

- stimulating and cultivating creativity;
- building a company infrastructure to support quality enhancement; and
- goal setting for both individuals and teams to achieve higher levels of quality and productivity.

Commitment to TQM by top management must be strong in intellectual and emotional terms. Lip service guarantees failure. Implementing TQM starts with building awareness among the employees and in establishing and training teams. A company may have to be internally reorganized in order to implement and integrate TQM in all aspects of its operations. The five key parts of TQM are product, process, organization, leadership, and commitment. The product is the focal point of an organization's purpose and must fit customer expectations. The desired product cannot be made without the right process that builds in the requisite degree of quality and productivity. The process, in turn, depends on having an effective organization stripped of excess layers of management. Managers must interact with those under their direction as leaders, not bosses. In short, committed managers must deal with committed workers.

While all this sounds reasonable, TQM is difficult to implement. First of all, people do not like change. TQM is a radical departure from conventional management practices, calling for a fundamental change in attitude. Many managers are really bosses who do not relish giving up control. They find it difficult to transform themselves into leaders willing to share information with others. Conventional management practices focus on quantitative measures such as production levels and profits and not on substantially qualitative measures as fostering a work environment conducive to improving quality. Under TQM, managers must learn to cope with:

- systems thinking and learning new ways of doing things,
- defining customer requirements,
- planning quality improvement,
- ensuring continuous improvement,
- building and coaching teams rather than ordering individuals,
- encouraging openness and trust while eliminating fear, and
- clarifying goals, resolving conflicts, and implementing change.

This is no small order for managers, but workers are also not eager for change. Many workers would rather obey instructions and fulfill quotas than think or plan or make the necessary commitment demanded by TQM. They have to be trained in new techniques and educated in a new way of thinking. Workers interested only in picking up their paychecks at the end of the week and abiding by union work rules are not going to be willing students eager to learn new ways of doing things and thinking about things. Yet they must if TQM is to succeed.

The Ford Motor Company developed an eight-step procedure for encouraging employees to adopt a new way of thinking about the nature of their jobs and themselves through employee involvement:

1. open up the company books to show employees that there are problems and to show the nature of these problems to start establishing a sense of trust;
2. organize steering committees of managers and workers to monitor progress;
3. bring in consultants and others who have had previous experience launching TQM;
4. look for opportunities to experiment with TQM;
5. publicize plans to implement TQM, letting workers know what is going on to encourage them to volunteer;
6. launch a pilot project by giving challenging, but solvable, problems to a small number of teams;
7. have the steering committees observe results with emphasis on the process more than the outcome; and
8. spread the word throughout the plant and to other plants that the process is working. Once one group embraces employee involvement, others will follow.

One of the potential drawbacks of TQM is concentrating on improving current practices without reflecting on the need to revamp or replace these practices. Many companies assume that current processes are correct and that it is simply a matter of improving them. Thus, TQM may result in marginal improvements in processes that are fundamentally flawed. There is little point in improving the wrong process. One example discussed in Chapter 3 was reengineering the IBM credit approval process. The existing system that originally took days to approve a credit application could not be improved. It had to be replaced by a new system that reduced processing time to hours. Reengineering and benchmarking are forms of innovation to replace a flawed system rather than try to fix it. Innovation requires a learning environment. Barriers to creating a learning environment may take the form of internal pressures to focus on profits or production quotas or negative criticisms and remarks that induce employees not to express an opinion or offer a suggestion. A learning environment:

- encourages employees to talk with others, customers, and internal and external suppliers,
- establishes long-term goals to extend the time horizon of employees beyond their immediate concerns,
- organizes a formal training for managers to learn how to lead the creative process,
- incorporates innovation into an organization's business strategy,
- inaugurates a recognition program to reward team and individual efforts in innovation, even if not successful,

- develops cross-functional collaboration to encourage creative thinking across functional boundaries,
- encourages employees to participate in team efforts and conflict resolution,
- provides training in the process of creating new ideas and in enhancing problem-solving skills, and
- takes steps to overcome barriers to innovation, including treating TQM as the only solution.

THE LOADED GUN

The enormous change in basic attitudes by both managers and workers is usually accomplished under a threat: the threat of bankruptcy. For Xerox, the threat faced by its chief executive officer David Kearns was Canon's selling a superior-performing copier for less than Xerox's manufacturing costs. Xerox was forced to critically examine every facet of its operation from top to bottom to ensure its survival. The company originated benchmarking and shifted to single-sourcing as part of the overall effort to reinvent itself.

Likewise, Mack Trucks was having financial difficulties in the 1980s. This forced the company to search for an alternative way of doing things to stay in business. Failure to change meant going out of business. The loaded gun with the bullet of bankruptcy pointed at the head of top management can be a strong motivating force. Change started with a corporate communication to all managers and employees on the urgency of the company's financial state. The board of directors appointed a new management team whose first course of action was to end restricted access to the executive floor and sell the private corporate jet. Then the new management team led efforts to unify the company to improve quality and productivity. They started training programs to enable workers to get involved with the process of manufacturing trucks utilizing TQM techniques. Warranty claims were examined to identify causes of problems with the intent of eliminating them. In only a few years, Mack Trucks turned itself around by increased sales of higher-quality trucks built at a lower cost through gains in worker productivity.

Harley Davidson dominated the motorcycle market until the 1980s, when superior-quality Japanese motorcycles captured the market. The choice facing Harley Davidson management was simple: change or go under. Fortunately, management selected the former and originated the productivity triad consisting of employee involvement, just-in-time inventory, and statistical operator control. Employees were trained in new skills and new ways of thinking about their jobs, enabling them to make timely decisions on the production floor. They were taught how to solve problems and improve quality. Employee involvement led to a higher degree of job satisfaction and productivity.

A just-in-time inventory system was set up to deliver small quantities of parts to the assembly line as needed. Push manufacturing gave way to pull manufacturing where parts were grouped into families requiring similar machines set up in cellular manufacturing units. Batch processing of large numbers of parts gave way to flow processing where only parts needed for assembly were manufactured. Production was controlled through *kanban* where an empty container of parts returning from the assembly line was the authority to manufacture or purchase another container. This significantly reduced work-in-process inventory in addition to exposing hidden operating problems that had been previously covered over by just-in-case inventory. These problems, once exposed, were rectified, further reducing production costs. The introduction of JIT manufacturing reduced inventory, scrap, rework, and space requirements and greatly improved worker productivity.

The third component of the productivity triad was statistical operator control, where all employees were trained in statistics from the standpoint of being able to measure the quality of their output. Operators recorded data from each manufacturing process in order to be able to measure variation. Then actions could be taken to improve quality by reducing variation. Machine operators were also given responsibility for preventive maintenance and simple repairs to instill a sense of ownership. The productivity triad set in motion the revitalization of Harley Davidson. The company did not just achieve parity with its Japanese competitors in terms of quality, cost, and productivity but also restored itself to its former position of world dominance. The company became a model for others to emulate.

INTERNAL QUALITY AUDITS

Quality audits are a means for a company to uncover problems that impede quality and to discover opportunities that can lead to improvements in quality. These audits encompass:

- management involvement and leadership in pursuing high standards of quality,
- product and process design considerations in meeting customer needs,
- product control to prevent defects,
- communication with customers and suppliers,
- quality improvement plans and programs,
- employee involvement with quality improvement,
- managerial and worker education and training in quality improvement, and
- information feedback from internal and external customers.

In addition to internal audits, external audits are available to ensure that a company has an effective quality improvement program in place. The most common external audit for quality is the International Organization for Standardization (ISO) 9000 series standards. U.S. companies applying for the Malcolm Baldrige National Quality Award must complete its associated external audit.

ISO 9000 QUALITY STANDARDS

The ISO was organized in 1947 to establish a universally accepted set of standards for buying and selling products and services. Its purpose is to promote standardization in order to facilitate the global exchange of goods and services. The first ISO covered steel to ensure that buyers and sellers had common expectations. In 1987 ISO developed a series of standards (ISO 9000-9004) for quality management and quality assurance in the manufacturing process from design, development, production, inspection, and testing, to installation and servicing. A manufacturing company becomes registered for compliance with ISO 9000 series standards by passing an audit performed by a certified independent provider. The audit includes a review of:

- the nature of a company's quality system and requirements,
- contract terms for proper definition and satisfaction of quality requirements,
- product design to ensure satisfaction of quality requirements,
- documentation control,
- procedures to ensure that purchased material and purchaser-supplied products conform to quality requirements,
- a company's ability to identify and trace products through the production and delivery process,
- inspection, labeling, measuring, and testing to ensure agreement with quality requirements,
- means to avoid use of nonconforming product and to correct problems leading to nonconforming product,
- product handling, storing, and delivery,
- quality records and internal quality audits,
- training of employees,
- servicing of customers, and
- statistical control procedures over processes, products, and services.

A buyer is assured that quality is part of the manufacturing process when a firm complies with ISO 9000 series standards. A company not in compliance is at a competitive disadvantage in the global marketplace.

MALCOLM BALDRIGE NATIONAL QUALITY AWARD

The U.S. government established this award to promote the adoption of the TQM philosophy and to stimulate U.S. companies to improve quality and productivity through pride of recognition. Not only does the award recognize the achievements of a company, but the recipient is also expected to guide others in achieving higher levels of quality and productivity. The award standards also provide guidelines that can be incorporated into an internal quality audit. A company is judged in seven major categories listed on the following page:

1. senior executive leadership in fostering a corporate culture to promote quality;
2. data management concerning quality from source to analysis, use, and accessibility;
3. role of quality, customer service, and market leadership in a company's strategic plan;
4. human resource development and management role to involve, train, and recognize employee efforts to achieve quality;
5. management of the manufacturing process for continuous improvement of quality, including supplier participation,
6. results of quality initiatives with regard to manufacturing, product design, and suppliers; and
7. company commitment to customer focus and satisfaction including communication with customers, dissemination of such information within the company, and follow-up on customer service complaints.

The Malcolm Baldrige Award is to some extent modeled on the Deming Prize instituted by the Union of Japanese Scientists and Engineers in 1951. The Deming Prize can be awarded to an individual for accomplishments in statistical theory and to companies for recognition in applying statistical theory to improving quality standards on a company-wide basis. Quality awards have also been established in Europe, Canada, and elsewhere.

DEMING'S FOURTEEN POINTS

Nothing better epitomizes the various aspects of making a quality product or providing a quality service than Deming's Fourteen Points.

1. Create constancy of purpose toward improvement of product and service with a plan to become competitive, stay in business, and provide jobs.

The Deming chain reaction described in Chapter 2 best covers this point.

2. Adopt the new philosophy of a new economic age where there can no longer be the commonly accepted levels of delays, mistakes, defective material, and defective workmanship.

In Chapter 2, the purchasing manager insisted on the maximum use of 11¢ recycled zinc rather than 40¢ virgin zinc in manufacturing the company's plumbing fixtures. To the purchasing manager, this minimized costs and hence maximized the bottom line. To the assistant production manager, this locked the company into a mediocre product line where discounting prices failed to halt the slide in sales. As revenue declined, so, too, did profits that could be plotted on a graph to predict the company's demise. The assistant production manager desired to improve the quality of the company's product line by reducing the amount of recycled zinc. He was thrown out of the purchasing manager's office for maximizing, rather than minimizing, costs. Although the assistant production manager sensed the company's downward spiral into oblivion, he was too junior in the organization to promote change.

As time went on, the purchasing manager advanced in position until he was promoted to president. In that position, he realized he would be sending out résumés in about six months' time. The résumé would state that soon after taken over the reins of a company as president, it went bankrupt. His chances of finding another opportunity to ruin a company would be nil. Sensing that the company could not survive much longer, the same individual most responsible for the company's predicament received a heavy dose of quality religion. Out went the recycled zinc and in came consultants to remove delays, mistakes, defective material and workmanship. The company was turned around and actually developed a niche market for its products in Japan, demonstrating the truism that the first prerequisite for transforming a company is top management commitment.

3. Cease dependence on mass inspection. Require statistical evidence that quality is being built into the product to eliminate the need of mass inspection.

In his book *Out of the Crisis*, Deming gave an example of inspection. The reader is instructed to count the number of Fs in the following statement where each F is considered a defect. How many Fs do you count?

Finished files are the result of years of scientific study combined with the experience of many years.

My experience in doing this in class is a variety of responses normally ranging between three and six. The variety of responses alone illustrates the unreliable nature of mass inspection. My original count was three. Deming mentioned six, and my recount was still three. Deming mentioned six again, and my recount steadfastly remained at three. I finally concluded that Deming could not have this defect in his book, so I did a letter by letter count and arrived at the correct answer of six. In my case and frequently with the students, the Fs in the three occurrences of the word "of" are missed.

Deming maintains that adding inspectors worsens the situation. A single inspector will make a decision, right or wrong, but three inspectors will tend to defer the decision of whether a marginal product should be rejected to one another. This dispersal of responsibility for making a decision normally ends up with a marginal product's slipping through the inspection process. More importantly, inspection is too late, ineffectual, and costly—too late in that the defect is already in the product, too ineffectual in that nothing is being done to remove the cause of the defect, and too costly because the product will have to be reworked or scrapped. These factors led to Feigenbaum's hidden factory, which added 30 to 50 percent to manufacturing costs.

Quality does not come from inspection but by improving the process to eliminate the causes of defects. This concept predates Deming. H. Dodge, a quality guru in the 1920s, maintained that quality could not be inspected into a product. Building quality into the process by eliminating the causes of defects was institutionalized in Japan to ensure its economic survival. Feigenbaum extended this process from the factory floor to suppliers, customers, investors, employees, and the community as part of total quality control.

Another example Deming used in his campaign against inspection was the colored bead experiment. Participants were invited to draw a sample of 50 beads with a specially designed paddle from a container holding 800 red beads and 3,200 white beads. The participants were instructed to withdraw as many white beads as possible since red beads represented defects. Try as they may, the participants could not help but withdraw some red beads. Deming then applied the traditional management reactions to the existence of defects from cajoling, to threatening the livelihoods of the participants, all to no avail. The fact that the frustrated participants were withdrawing red beads was not their fault but the fault of a system that produced the red beads.

This experiment can be done as a simulation where each cell in an array, $A(100,100)$, represents the output of 10,000 items. A 20 percent defect rate can be established by randomly assigning a value of 1 to 2,000 of the array cells, representing defects, and a value of 0 to the remaining 8,000 cells. An item can be withdrawn for inspection by randomly selecting two values between 1 and 100 and examining the associated array cell. Thus, the simulation program can take a random sample of 50 from the 10,000 array cells and total the "1's" in the sample to obtain the number of defects and the defect rate. In Table 10.5, 20 sequential sample results were assigned to four shift supervisors over a five-day period. Students are asked to review the results and explain their reaction if they managed the four shift supervisors. They soon identify that Tom's performance is superior to Jim's. They recommend that Tom should be rewarded for his superior performance. Some suggest that Tom should set up a training session to disseminate the secrets of his success to the other shift supervisors. Others suggest that Jim should be informed that if his performance does not improve with or without Tom's tutelage, perhaps he should look for a new job.

The students are shocked to realize that the performance of each shift supervisor is identical. They are each producing precisely 2,000 defects out of a total output of 10,000. Sampling error, not performance, is responsible for the variation in the results. A larger sample would reduce the magnitude of the sampling error, but the "luck of the draw" would still result in falsely upbraiding one supervisor and wrongly praising another. Rather than a spurious ranking of supervisor performance, perhaps a manager should concentrate on reducing the defect rate.

Table 10.5
Supervisor Performance Results

SHIFT NUMBER	SHIFT SUPERVISOR	PERCENT DEFECT
	Day 1	
1	Bertha	16
2	Tom	12
3	Agatha	20
4	Jim	24
	Day 2	
5	Bertha	28
6	Tom	12
7	Agatha	14
8	Jim	24
	Day 3	
9	Bertha	14
10	Tom	24
11	Agatha	10
12	Jim	26
	Day 4	
13	Bertha	26
14	Tom	18
15	Agatha	24
16	Jim	22
	Day 5	
17	Bertha	24
18	Tom	14
19	Agatha	18
20	Jim	34

Deming is not a proponent of acceptance testing as espoused by the American Society of Quality Control, one of whose founding members was Deming's mentor Shewhart. Acceptance testing leads to the uncomfortable position that as quality improves, the need for inspection, reflected in the size of a sample, increases. To illustrate this phenomenon, suppose that a sample of 100 is drawn from a population of parts whose defect rate is 2 percent. Does this mean that the number of defects in the sample would necessarily be 2? No, there would be a distribution of results. Using the Poisson distribution to model the sampling results, there are associated probabilities for drawing out anywhere from 0 to 8 defects. Multiplying these by their associated probabilities does yield a weighted average of 2 defects. For a sample size of 100, selecting 4 defects as a decision point would yield a correct decision 95 percent of the time. In other words, for a population defect rate of 2 percent, there is only a 5 percent chance of drawing out 5 or more defects from a sample of 100. Thus alpha, the risk of rejecting a good shipment, is 5 percent. Suppose that a bad shipment is defined as one with a 3 percent defect rate. A sample of 100 ought to have 3 defects, but it won't. In fact, the chance of drawing 4 or fewer defects from a bad shipment is 82 percent. Since the decision point for a good shipment is 4 or fewer defects, then beta, the risk of accepting a bad shipment, is a whopping 82 percent. The sample size has to be increased to reduce beta, keeping alpha at 5 percent. For a sample size of 2,000, the hypothetical number of defects for a good shipment is 40. If the decision point is 40 defects, then there is a 45 percent chance of drawing a sample with greater than 40 defects. This means that alpha, the risk of rejecting a good shipment, would be 45 percent. Using 50 defects as a decision point would reduce alpha to an acceptable 5 percent. For the defined bad shipment with a defect rate of 3 percent, a sample of 2,000 would have an expected 60 defects. But there would be an 11 percent chance of a sample's having 50 or less defects. Thus, there is an 11 percent chance of accepting a bad shipment, which is a reasonable value for beta.

Suppose that quality has been improved, and the standard for determining a good shipment is now 1 percent, and a bad shipment is now defined as 1.5 percent. The size of the sample to maintain a value of 5 percent for alpha, the risk of rejecting a good shipment, and 11 percent for beta, the risk of accepting a bad shipment, is 4,000. Thus, the better the quality, the larger the sample size and the greater the inspection effort. For Motorola's defect rate of 3 in 1 million, the sample size would be the population of the shipment to ascertain such a low defect rate. Thus, 100 percent inspection is necessary in order to verify that Motorola meets its specifications of being virtually defect-free. This makes little sense to Deming. As quality improves, there should be less effort in inspection.

Deming proposed that an incoming shipment should either be wholly inspected or not at all. The criterion for selecting either 100 or 0 percent inspection is based on a comparative economic analysis. For 100 percent inspection, there are the costs of the test and repairs if a defect is found and corrected before the part is installed in the product. For no inspection, the cost is the repair when the defect is found after installation. Both equations for 100 and 0 percent inspection costs contain the defect rate and the breakeven defect rate can be obtained by equating the two. If the defect rate is above the breakeven rate, then there should be 100 percent inspection; otherwise, no inspection.

Even if the analysis supports 100 percent inspection, the buyer and supplier are expected to work together to reduce the defect rate. At some point, shipments arrive with a defect rate below the breakeven rate, calling for no inspection. This may make the buyer a little uncomfortable. Deming's suggestion is to require statistical evidence that quality is being built into the product. The evidence is the statistical process control charts. If the charts are stable–that is, the mean and variance are not changing–then there is no reason to believe that the underlying defect rate has changed. As long as the statistical control charts are stable, no inspection is necessary. If the charts are no longer stable, then incoming shipments should be 100 percent inspected because the defect rate is no longer known.

4. End the practice of awarding contracts to suppliers on the basis of price. Depend on meaningful measures of quality, along with price. Move toward a single supplier on a long-term relationship based on loyalty and trust.

The Xerox experience in Chapter 7 illustrated that the traditional American approach of an adversarial relationship with suppliers based on minimizing price did not actually minimize price. All it did was minimize the 5¢ of profits without attacking the 95¢ of costs. Xerox reduced the number of suppliers by 90 percent when it switched to single sourcing. Xerox cut the price of purchased parts by about half by enabling the supplier to utilize the latest technology through a high-volume, multiyear contract with sharing of further cost savings. Xerox worked with the remaining suppliers to reduce their defect rates to the point where it was no longer necessary to inspect shipments. Some suppliers succeeded in virtually eliminating defects. In addition, Xerox made its material requirement plan available to its suppliers to allow them to manufacture and deliver according to the MRP. This substantially reduced parts and components inventory both at the suppliers' and Xerox's plants, generating savings in inventory carrying costs.

Outside suppliers are becoming more important as companies focus on their core competencies, that is, do what they do best and buy the rest. Close alignment of the mutual interests of suppliers and buyers is part of supply chain management, which involves:

- selecting suppliers who can provide quality parts and components,
- ensuring that purchase orders clearly define quality requirements,
- building a long-term relationship based on trust for the mutual benefit for both parties (win-win),
- improving the quality of supplier's products through training encouraged or provided by the buyer, and
- maintaining a close relationship between buyer and supplier to deal with technical problems, quality issues, and product design changes.

Supplier certification audits are a means to manage the member companies of a supply chain. The purpose of the audits is to improve quality and delivery, reduce costs and the number of suppliers, end inspections, and reward suppliers for superior performance. Certified suppliers are expected to control manufacturing processes to minimize nonconformance to product specifications, provide a means of linking inspection data with lot identification, and develop feedback systems for prompt and effective correction of problems.

5. Improve constantly and forever the system of production and service using PDCA (plan-do-check-act) cycle.

The Deming PDCA cycle is described in Chapter 5 as part of the blue-collar contribution to the first step in the Deming chain reaction of making a better product.

6. Institute modern methods of training, including statistical methods and thinking.

This is the cost for the benefit of manufacturing a better-quality product or providing a better-quality service. In the Taylor system, training is minimized when a task is broken down into its simplest elements and an individual is assigned to each element. Workers on Ford's Model T assembly lines could be "trained" in a few minutes of observation. Some of Ford's workers spent 30 years in his plant without knowing a word of English. Workers in Volvo's plants where automobiles are assembled by teams require months of classroom and on-the-job training. The economic benefit of having a superior quality product must and does justify the cost of training and education.

7. Institute modern methods of supervision where the goal is continuous and never-ending improvement.

Supervisors must step back from being bosses and become leaders. They must learn to facilitate, rather than intrude, and to lead, rather than direct. Supervisors must create a positive environment whereby the workers are willing to contribute to the process of continuous improvement by thinking about what they do and offering helpful suggestions.

8. Drive out fear from the workforce.

There are all sorts of fear. One is the fear of change described by Niccolò Machiavelli in 1514 in his book *The Prince*:

It should be borne in mind that there is nothing more difficult to arrange, more doubtful of success, and more dangerous to carry through than initiating change. The innovator makes enemies of all those who prospered under the old order, and only lukewarm support from those who would prosper under the new.

Yet continuous improvement, *kaizen*, is continuous change. While Deming stands for incremental change to improve the existing system, benchmarking and reengineering stand for radical change incorporating a new system and abandoning the old. Continuous improvement, benchmarking, and reengineering have institutionalized change and accelerated the rate of change. Companies have learned that they can ensure competitive advantage by hastening change, leaving their competitors in the backwaters with an obsolete technology or product. A few decades ago, a worker, having learned a technology, would not have to learn another for the rest of his or her working lifetime. This is no longer true. Technological processes are in a constant state of flux for blue-collar workers, as are career patterns for white-collar managers. The world has become a very unsettling place regardless of the color of the collar brought about by the accelerating rate of change.

There are other forms of fear. There is the pervasive fear among managers of giving up control that is necessary for a boss to become a leader. There is the fear of failure when a worker suggestion fails to correct a problem. Leaders of work teams have to expect that most suggestions do not work. Suggestions that do work are discovered by continuous experimentation with the Deming PDCA cycle. Criticizing workers for offering suggestions that do not work is one sure way to stop the flow of worker-inspired suggestions. A manager's withholding vital information from the workers fosters the fear of not knowing. Workers sensing that they are not trusted will withhold vital information from management. An intimidating management style instills the fear of reprisal. This results in a "please the boss" attitude among workers, leading to problems not being brought to management's attention and suggestions not being made.

Perhaps the greatest fear of the workers is the fear of being laid off. Why should any worker contribute intellectually to a company if job security is continually in jeopardy? The success of Japanese corporations up to the late 1980s depended on providing job security and bonuses based on corporate profits. The vaunted Deming chain reaction of making a better product leading to a greater market share, greater profits, and job security has become unhinged in the late 1990s. The secret to making a superior quality product is no longer a secret. It is no longer a valid assumption that making a better product leads to greater job security when every company is making a better product. In the late 1990s the Japanese began laying off workers. If the fear of layoffs pervades the Japanese economy, Japan may lose its greatest competitive advantage–the willingness of workers to participate by making helpful suggestions.

9. Break down organizational barriers and promote teamwork.

The benefits of breaking down organizational barriers are best seen in concurrent or simultaneous engineering, the white-collar contribution to making a better product, described in Chapter 5. By removing the organizational barriers between research, product and process development, and manufacturing, cycle time between conceiving an idea and having an improved, or new, product on the shelf was cut in half. Another benefit was fewer parts in a product, resulting in fewer failures and enhanced quality. Still another was the remaining parts being easier to manufacture and assemble, lowering manufacturing costs.

There is also a natural barrier between managers and workers in the United States based on the historical hostility between labor and management, which does not make for pleasant reading. There is no legacy of antagonism in Japan. In the aftermath of World War II, Japanese labor and management cooperated to resuscitate the economy. The bonus system aligns workers' goals with those of management. Japanese unions ensure an effective link of communication between workers and management to avoid misunderstandings. Thus, management and labor are basically sitting on the same side of the table. Japanese managers do not reside in private offices separated from the workers. They are normally found on the factory floor. They wear short-sleeve white shirts without jackets. They share the same cafeteria and parking lot with the workers. They are genuinely interested in the welfare of their workers, even to the point of assuming the responsibility of finding suitable mates! The organizational barrier between Japanese management and labor does not have to be torn down as in the United States; it was never built.

10. Eliminate arbitrary numerical goals, posters, and slogans for the workforce that seek new levels of productivity without providing means.

In *Out of the Crisis*, Deming described a visit to a railroad car repair facility where the walls were plastered with posters urging the workforce to increase their productivity. A great deal of managerial attention had apparently been paid to creating these posters. Deming asked a worker how long he spent getting a part to repair a railroad car and was told six hours out of an eight-hour workday. Deming pointed out that if the worker had to wait "only" four hours, his productivity would double. Therefore, management could better enhance the productivity of the workforce by improving the process of obtaining parts rather than creating posters. In Deming's eyes, if managers are not doing their part to improve the process, they become part of the problem.

For this reason, Deming is against management by objective (MBO), where success is measured in financial terms. Obtaining a desired financial goal may have been accomplished not by improving the process but by cutting costs in areas where costs should not be cut, in letting performance or quality suffer in order to inflate short-term profits, and other acts that can lead to long-term, adverse consequences. Rather than MBO, managers should roll up their shirt sleeves and become part of the process to enhance quality and productivity. This is the way to improve profits, not games and gimmicks with financial figures.

According to Deming, managers should possess "profound knowledge." They should appreciate the nature of the system producing revenue from the customer, to product design, to manufacturing, to service after sales. They should realize the link between quality, worker productivity, and corporate profitability. Managers should understand variation and be able to distinguish between common and special cause. They should possess the requisite knowledge, not just experience, to make intelligent decisions. Experience can describe a situation but cannot make a prediction. Knowledge is obtained by systematically analyzing objective data. Knowledge enables a manager to forecast and make sound business decisions. Managers should understand human behavior, appreciate the differences in personalities, and be able to lead a diverse group of individuals to achieve a desired goal. Managers should realize that employees are not going to be productive if they do not enjoy their work. Whether workers enjoy their work depends on management's approach to work design and the nature of managerial leadership.

11. Eliminate work standards and numerical goals.

This is the death of Taylor. Deming advocates making work meaningful, giving the workers the proper tools to do a job, making them responsible for performing a task, and holding them accountable for their performance.

12. Remove barriers that rob employees of their pride of workmanship, particularly, performance appraisal systems.

The Taylor system creates barriers to pride by taking a task and breaking it down to its simplest elements and assigning a worker to each element. It is ironic that work teams are a return to the nineteenth-century method of organizing work before Taylor. The difference is that work teams can achieve a high degree of productivity through modern manufacturing technology.

13. Institute a vigorous program of education and training.

This goes without saying; it is the cost side of the cost benefit analysis of switching from total control to total quality management.

14. Create an organizational structure that will push the prior 13 points every day.

Deming is generally silent on organizational structures, but initiating just-in-time manufacturing and work teams does encourage an organizational structure that supports continuous improvement.

SUMMARY

TQM is basically an inward-looking activity to reduce defects and enhance quality and conformance to meet customer needs. A company establishes strategic targets with regard to satisfying customer needs and ensures that its internal processes and suppliers satisfy these targets. Customer needs are linked through the quality function deployment (QFD) to product design and specifications. Design specifications are aligned with performance measures to ensure customer satisfaction. Appropriate process technology is put in place to meet product design specifications.

An organizational culture and structure are nurtured capable of responding to continuous improvement, innovation, and creativity. Thus, an organization becomes flexible and amenable to the flow of new ideas and information. The organizational chart is flattened, made lean but not necessarily mean. Managers have multidisciplinary backgrounds with cross-functional experience. Work teams are responsible for work-related decisions and are properly motivated, trained, and encouraged. A benchmarking system is in place in order for a company to establish targets to continuously improve all functional areas, including information technology, human resources, supplier relations, and marketing.

Product design and manufacturing technology are integrated in order to create high-quality products at a low cost. Satisfying varying consumer desires in a global marketplace may require more simply designed products made from a smaller number of standardized parts that are easily manufactured and assembled. Modular design allows different products to be manufactured and assembled using common processes. Manufacturing technology is a determining factor for corporate success. By taking advantage of computer-controlled equipment and processes, flexible and flow manufacturing systems save time and money by integrating production activities and tying production closely to market demand. Evaluating manufacturing technology may be misleading if performed by traditional measures of profit and labor savings without taking into account savings in throughput time, in-process inventory, materials handling, quality consistency, and flexibility in responding to changing market conditions. These are the real benefits of modern manufacturing technology, not reducing direct labor costs. Continual review of product design and manufacturing technology is necessary to ensure that the firm maintains a cost advantage over its competitors.

IS TQM SUFFICIENT TO ASSURE SUCCESS?

Up to 1990 TQM was both sufficient and necessary to assure success. This was best seen by Japanese ascendancy to a world economic power by incorporating the principles of TQM. But the 1990s have not been kind to Japan. TQM may be necessary to be globally competitive but may no longer be sufficient. In today's world, globally successful companies must produce high-quality products as a necessary precondition for survival, but this no longer necessarily guarantees success.

Success seems to be moving away from an emphasis on producing quality products to managing a corporation in a complex and fast-changing business environment. In recent decades, oil companies have lost control of oil resources and oil prices. Governments have lost control over currency exchange rates. Banks have lost control over interest rates. Barriers to trade used to protect inefficient industries, but no more. Large areas of the world operate as free trade zones where borders are becoming transparent to the movement of goods. Formerly, the pace of technological and market change was slow and to some degree controlled. Decades past, IBM and Boeing decided on the timing of when to introduce a new model, not the competition. This is less true today. Change not only has been accelerated by continuous improvement, benchmarking, and reengineering but also has become a way to ensure competitive advantage.

Managing complexity and rapid change is not the same as managing the quality of a product or service. A high-quality product that has become technologically obsolete or no longer satisfies consumer tastes has little value in ensuring a company's survival.

One of the strengths of Japanese companies was the wherewithal of the *keiretsu* to provide internal support to its member companies. This was a competitive advantage when an individual U.S. company was up against Japan, Inc. Mergers and strategic alliances in all fields of commerce are eroding that advantage. These mergers are partly a reaction to worldwide excess production plant capacity, partly a means for companies to protect themselves from the ravages of competition, and partly a means to deal with increasing chaos in markets and technology.

Just as boundaries between independent nations are permitting a freer movement of goods, the same is happening between independent companies where mutual rather than competitive interests are being pursued in the form of mergers, joint ventures, and strategic alliances. In supply chain management, a manufacturer must carefully orchestrate the activities of many suppliers and purchasers to efficiently get a product on a shelf. Supply chain management entails a manufacturer dealing with suppliers and purchasers who are also conducting business with a manufacturer's competitors. The lines of distinction between cooperation and competition are becoming blurred. The same is happening within a company where organizational boundaries are becoming more permeable to the flow of ideas. Companies with highly ordered hierarchical structures are not able to respond as rapidly to changes in the market environment as are less-structured and less-ordered companies.

Five- and 10-year strategic plans are giving way to some sort of agreed, but not well-defined, corporate aspiration. This allows companies to better deal with challenges from emerging competitors and changing markets than a fixed strategic plan embedded in yesterday's world. Standard operating manuals containing procedures approved by management and expected to be adhered to by employees are giving way to a system consisting of minimum rules to more effectively deal with ever-changing conditions. Information resources are no longer the proprietary property of certain groups or individuals within a company but are shared among all who have a need to know. The same is true for all corporate resources: access can no longer be restricted to a privileged few. Permanent committees established to handle all problems are giving way to ad hoc task forces organized with the required expertise to handle a specific problem. Whereas a permanent committee presumably lasts forever, an ad hoc task force is disbanded when its objective has been accomplished.

Corporations were once organized around physical assets; now they are organized around intellectual resources, core competencies, and niche markets. Corporate strategy is more concerned in preserving and enhancing a company's core competencies as a source of competitive advantage than in simply maximizing shareholder wealth. Strategic alliances and supply chain management harness core competencies of several or many companies for their mutual advantage. This interest in the mutual well-being of a group of companies is in opposition to the concept of an independent company pursuing its own interests, and in many ways, is reminiscent of the Japanese approach to business.

Thus, an operations manager cannot just be competent on the factory floor but should be knowledgeable on how operations on a factory floor contribute to the core competencies and competitive advantage of his or her company. Through supply chain management and strategic alliances, an operations manager may become involved with the inner workings of upstream and downstream companies rather than concentrating his or her efforts in the interests of a single company. This requires a broad background of experience. An operations manager should seek a variety of assignments, both staff and line, to become a more valuable member of an operations team. Specialization may not be in the long-term career interests of an individual.

Aligning core competencies through supply chain management and strategic alliances is the wave of the future. This may be the greatest challenge facing operations managers: how to corral the diverse activities of suppliers and users of a firm's products into an integrated whole to construct a competitive advantage. Competitive advantage built around the core competencies of a group of companies may be the solution posed by the challenge of continual change in technology, markets, and competition. The days of idyllic comfort of resting on one's oars and enjoying the fruits of past accomplishments are long gone. In the world of tomorrow, intellectual resources are going to be taxed to their fullest just to enable a company to survive the vicissitudes of the commercial world.

ENDNOTES

1. See Web site: mu.motorola.com
2. See Web site: dfca.larc.nasa.gov/dfc/snt.html

Bibliography

Aft, Lawrence S. *Fundamentals of Industrial Quality Control*. Boca Raton, FL: St. Lucie Press, 1998.

Ammerman, Max. *The Root Cause Analysis Handbook—A Simplified Approach to Identifying, Correcting, and Reporting Workplace Errors*. New York: Quality Resources, 1998.

Ansari, A. and Modarress, B. *Just in Time Purchasing*. New York: Free Press, 1990.

Anupindi, Ravi, Chopra, Sunil, Deshmukh, Sudhakar D., Van Mieghem, Jan, and Zemel, Eitan. *Managing Business Process Flows*. Upper Saddle River, NJ: Prentice-Hall, 1999.

Asaka, T. and Ozeki, K. *Handbook of Quality Tools: The Japanese Approach*. Portland, OR: Productivity Press, 1997.

Balm, Gerald J. *Benchmarking: A Practitioner's Guide for Becoming and Staying Best of the Best*. Schaumburg, IL: QPMA Press, 1992.

Barrett, D. and Bodek, N. *Fast Focus on TQM: A Concise Guide to Companywide Learning*. Portland OR: Productivity Press, 1994.

Barsky, Jonathan D. *World-Class Customer Satisfaction*. New York: Irwin Professional, 1994.

Bass, Bernard M. and Avolio, Bruce J. *Improving Organizational Effectiveness through Transformational Leadership*. London: Sage, 1994.

Becker, Franklin and Steele, Fritz. *Workplace by Design: Mapping the High-Performance Workscape*. San Francisco: Jossey-Bass, 1995.

Bennis, Warren and Mische, Michael. *The 21st Century Organization: Reinventing through Reengineering*. San Francisco: Jossey-Bass, 1997.

Bodek, Norman. *Today and Tomorrow: Henry Ford*. Portland, OR: Productivity Press, 1988.

Bogan, Christopher E. and English, Michael. *Benchmarking for Best Practices: Winning through Innovative Adaption*. New York: McGraw-Hill, 1994.

Bothe, David R. *Measuring Process Capability: Techniques and Calculations for Quality and Manufacturing Engineers*. New York: McGraw-Hill, 1997.

Boxwell, Robert J. *Benchmarking for Competitive Advantage*. New York: McGraw-Hill, 1994.

Brocka, Bruce. *Quality Management: Implementing the Best Ideas of the Masters.* Burr Ridge, IL: Irwin, 1992.

Brown, Mark Graham, Hitchcock, Darcy E., and Willard, Marsha L. *Why TQM Fails and What to Do about It.* Burr Ridge, IL: Irwin, 1994.

Burns, Clarence. *Building Your Organization's TQM System: The Unified Total Quality Model.* Milwaukee: ASQC Quality Press, 1997.

Camp, Robert C. *Business Process Benchmarking: Finding and Implementing Best Practices.* Milwaukee: ASQC Quality Press, 1995.

Camp, Robert C. *Benchmarking: The Search for Industry Best Practices That Lead to Superior Performance.* Milwaukee: ASQC Quality Press, 1989.

Carr, David K., Hard, Kelvin J., and Trahant, William J. *Managing the Change Process: A Fieldbook for Change Agents, Team Leaders, and Reengineering Managers.* New York: McGraw-Hill, 1996.

Chang, Richard Y. *Process Reengineering in Action: A Practical Guide to Achieving Breakthrough Results.* Irvine, CA: Chang Associates, 1996.

Chang, Richard Y. and Niedzwiecki, Matthew E. *Continuous Improvement Tools: A Practical Guide to Achieve Quality Results.* Irvine, CA: Chang Associates, 1994.

Chase, Richard B., Aquilano, Nicholas J., and Jacobs, F. Robert. *Production and Operations Management.* New York: Irwin/McGraw-Hill, 1998.

Cheng, T.C.E. and Podolsky, S. *Just in Time Manufacturing: An Introduction.* Amsterdam: Kluwer Academic Press, 1996.

Claunch, Jerry W. and Claunch, Jerry C. *Set-Up Time Reduction.* New York: Irwin, 1996.

Creech, W. *The Five Pillars of TQM: How to Make Total Quality Management Work for You.* New York: Plume, 1995.

Crosby, Philip B. *Quality and Me: Lessons from an Evolving Life.* San Francisco: Jossey-Bass, 1999.

Crosby, Philip B. *The Absolutes of Leadership.* San Francisco: Jossey-Bass, 1997.

Crosby, Philip B. *Quality Is Still Free: Making Quality Certain in Uncertain Times.* New York: McGraw-Hill, 1996.

Crosby, Philip B. *Quality Is Free: The Art of Making Quality Certain.* New York: Mentor Books, 1992.

Damelio, Robert. *The Basics of Benchmarking.* New York: Quality Resources, 1995.

Damelio, Robert and Englehaupt, William. *An Action Guide to Making Quality Happen.* New York: Quality Resources, 1995.

Davenport, Thomas H. and Prusak, Laurence. *Working Knowledge: How Organizations Manage What They Know.* Cambridge, MA: HBS Press, 1997.

Davidow, W. and Malone, M. *The Virtual Corporation.* New York: HarperBusiness, 1993.

Delavigne, Kenneth T. and Robertson, J. Daniel. *Deming's Profound Changes: When Will the Sleeping Giant Awaken?* Englewood Cliffs, NJ: Prentice-Hall, 1994.

Deming, W. Edwards. *The New Economics: For Industry, Government, Education.* Cambridge: Massachusetts Institute of Technology Press, 1995.

Deming, W. Edwards. *Out of the Crisis.* Cambridge: Massachusetts Institute of Technology Press, 1986.

Dettmer, H. William. *Goldratt's Theory of Constraints: A Systems Approach to Continuous Improvement.* Milwaukee: ASQC Quality Press, 1996.

Dettmer, H. William and Dettmer, William H. *Breaking the Constraints to World-Class Performance.* New York: McGraw-Hill, 1998.

Dorf, Richard C. and Kusiak, Andrew. *Handbook of Design, Manufacturing, and Automation.* New York: John Wiley, 1994.

Drucker, Peter F. *Management Challenges for the 21st Century*. New York: HarperBusiness, 1999.

Drucker, Peter F. *Managing in a Time of Great Change*. New York: Plume, 1998.

Edosomwan, Johnson Aimie. *Organizational Transformation and Process Reengineering*. Delray Beach, FL: St. Lucie Press, 1996.

Evans, James R. and Lindsey, William M. *The Management and Control of Quality*. St. Paul, MN: West, 1996.

Fabrycky, Wolter J. and Blanchard, Benjamin S. *Life-Cycle Cost and Economic Analysis*. Englewood Cliffs, NJ: Prentice-Hall, 1991.

Feigenbaum, A. V. *Total Quality Control*. New York: McGraw-Hill, 1991.

Fisher, Kimball. *Leading Self-Directed Work Teams: A Guide to Developing New Team Leadership Skills*. New York: McGraw-Hill, 1992.

Friesen, Michael E. *The Success Paradigm: Creating Organizational Effectiveness through Quality and Strategy*. Westport, CT: Quorum Books, 1995.

Fry, Michael. *Adam Smith's Legacy: His Place in the Development of Modern Economics*. London: Routledge, 1992.

Fusfield, Daniel R. *The Age of the Economist*. Reading, MA: Addison-Wesley, 1993.

Gabor, Andrea. *The Man Who Discovered Quality: How Deming Brought Quality to America*. New York: Penguin, 1992.

Gerlach, Michael. *Alliance Capitalism: The Social Organization of Japanese Business*. Berkeley: University of California Press, 1997.

Gitlow, H. S. *A Comparison of Japanese Total Quality Control and Deming's Theory of Management*. The American Statistician, Vol. 48. Washington: American Statistical Association, August 1994.

Gitlow, H. S., Oppenheim, A. J., and Oppenheim, R. *Quality Management: Tools and Methods for Improvement*. Burr Ridge, IL: Irwin, 1995.

Goldratt, Eliyahu M. *Critical Chain*. New York: North River Press, 1997.

Goldratt, Eliyahu M. and Cox, Jeff. *The Goal: The Process of Ongoing Improvement*. New York: North River Press, 1994.

Gray, C. D. and Landvater, D. V. *MRP II Standard System: A Handbook for Manufacturing Software Survival*. New York: John Wiley, 1995.

Gryna, Frank M. and Juran, Joseph M. *Quality Planning and Analysis: From Product Development through Use*. New York: McGraw-Hill, 1993.

Hammer, Michael. *Beyond Reengineering: How the Process-Centered Organization Is Changing Our Work and Our Lives*. New York: HarperCollins, 1997.

Hammer, Michael. *The Reengineering Revolution*. New York: HarperCollins, 1995.

Hammer, Michael and Champy, James. *Reengineering the Corporation: A Manifesto for Business Revolution*. New York: HarperBusiness, 1994.

Handfield, Robert B. *Reengineering for Time-Based Competition*. Westport, CT: Quorum Books, 1995.

Harrington, H. James, Esseling, Eric K.C., and Van Nimwegen, Harm. *Business Process Improvement Handbook: Documentation, Analysis, Design, and Management of Business Improvement Process*. New York: McGraw-Hill, 1997.

Harrington, H. James and Harrington, James S. *Total Improvement Management: The Next Generation in Performance Improvement*. New York: McGraw-Hill, 1994.

Harrington, H. James, Hoffherr, Glen D., and Reid, Robert P. *Statistical Analysis Simplified: The Easy-to-Understand Guide to SPC and Data Analysis*. New York: McGraw-Hill, 1998.

Hirano, Hiroyuki. *5S for Operators: 5 Pillars of the Visual Workplace*. Portland, OR: Productivity Press, 1996.

Hodgetts, Richard M. *Implementing TQM in Small and Medium-Sized Companies: A Step-by-Step Guide*. New York: AMACOM, 1995.

Hunt, V. Daniel and Hunt, Daniel. *Quality in America: How to Implement a Competitive Quality Program*. Burr Ridge, IL: Business One Irwin, 1995.

Imai, Masaaki. *Gemba Kaizen: A Commonsense, Low-Cost Approach to Management*. New York: McGraw-Hill, 1997.

Imai, Masaaki. *Kaizen: The Key to Japan's Competitive Success*. New York: Random House, 1989.

Ishikawa, K. *What Is Total Quality Control?* Englewood Cliffs, NJ: Prentice-Hall, 1985.

Jablonski, Joseph R. *Implementing Total Quality Management: Competing in the 1990's*. Albuquerque, NM: Technical Management Consortium, 1994.

Juran, J. M. *Managerial Breakthrough: The Classic Book on Improving Management Performance*. New York: McGraw-Hill, 1995.

Juran, J. M. *A History of Managing for Quality*. Milwaukee: ASQC Quality Press, 1995.

Juran, J. M. *Juran on Quality by Design: The New Steps for Planning Quality into Goods and Services*. New York: Free Press, 1992.

Kearns, David T. and Nadler, David A. *Prophets in the Dark: How Xerox Reinvented Itself and Beat Back the Japanese*. New York: HarperCollins, 1992.

Knouse, Stephen B. *The Reward and Recognition Process in Total Quality Management*. Milwaukee: ASQC Quality Press, 1995.

Krajewski, Lee J. and Ritzman, Larry P. *Operations Management*. Reading, MA: Addison-Wesley, 1996.

Landvater, D. V. *World Class Production and Inventory Management*. New York: John Wiley, 1997.

Lawson, Ron and Stuart, Bob. *Measuring Six Sigma and Beyond: Continuous vs Attribute Data*. Schaumburg, IL: Motorola University Press, 1997.

Levine, David I. *Reinventing the Workplace: How Business and Employees Can Both Win*. Washington: Brookings Institution, 1995.

Lindsay, William M. and Petrick, Joseph A. *Total Quality and Organization Development*. Delray Beach, FL: St. Lucie Press, 1997.

Louis, Raymond S. *Integrating Kanban with MRPII: Automating a Pull System for Enhanced JIT Inventory Management*. Portland, OR: Productivity Press, 1997.

Lu, David J. *Kanban Just-in-Time at Toyota*. Portland, OR: Productivity Press, 1989.

Madu, Christian N. *Strategic Total Quality Management: Corporate Performance and Product Quality*. Westport, CT: Quorum Books, 1995.

Mahoney, Francis X. and Thor, Carl G. *The TQM Trilogy: Using ISO 9000, the Deming Prize, and the Baldridge Award to Establish a System for Total Quality Management*. New York: AMACOM, 1994.

Main, Jeremy. *Quality Wars: The Triumphs and Defeats of American Business*. New York: Free Press, 1994.

Manz, Charles C. and Sims, Henry P. *Business without Bosses: How Self-Managing Teams Are Building High-Performing Companies*. New York: John Wiley, 1993.

McLaughlin, Gregory C. *Total Quality in Research and Development: Achieving High Performance in the Public and Private Sectors*. Delray Beach, FL: St. Lucie Press, 1995.

Milakovich, Michael E. *Improving Service Quality*. Delray Beach, FL: St. Lucie Press, 1995.

Miyashita, Kenichi. *Keiretsu: Inside the Hidden Japanese Conglomerates*. New York: McGraw Hill, 1996.

Mizuno, Shigeru. *Management for Quality Improvement: The Seven New QC Tools*. Portland, OR: Productivity Press, 1988.

Munro-Faure, Lesley and Munro-Faure, Malcolm. *TQM: A Primer for Implementation.* Burr Ridge, IL: Irwin, 1994.

Nakajima, Seiichi. *Introduction to TPM: Total Productive Maintenance.* Portland, OR: Productivity Press, 1994.

Neave, Henry R. *The Deming Dimension.* Knoxville, TN: SPC Press, 1990.

Nelson, D., Moody, P. E., and Mayo, R. *Powered by Honda: Developing Excellence in the Global Enterprise.* New York: John Wiley, 1998.

Northey, P., Southway, N., and Bodek, N. *Cycle Time Management.* Portland, OR: Productivity Press, 1994.

Ohno, Taiichi. *Toyota Production System: Beyond Large-Scale Production.* Cambridge, MA: Productivity Press, 1988.

Orlicky, Joseph and Plossl, George W. *Orlicky's Material Requirements Planning.* New York: McGraw-Hill, 1994.

Ouchi, William. *Theory Z: How American Business Can Meet the Japanese Challenge.* Reading, MA: Addison-Wesley, 1981.

Pike, Wilbur L. *Leading the Transition: Management's Role in Creating a Team-Based Culture.* New York: Quality Resources, 1995.

Porter, L. J. and Tanner, S. J. *Assessing Business Excellence: A Guide to Self-Assessment.* Boston: Butterworth-Heinemann, 1996.

Proud, John F. *Master Scheduling: A Practical Guide to Competitive Manufacturing.* New York: John Wiley, 1999.

Rao, A., Carr, L. P., Dambolena, I., Kopp, R. J., Martin, J., Rafii, F., and Schlesinger, P. F. *Total Quality Management.* New York: John Wiley, 1996.

Roberts, Harry V. and Sergesketter, Bernard F. *Quality Is Personal: A Foundation for Total Quality Management.* New York: Free Press, 1993.

Roberts, Lon. *Process Reengineering: The Key to Achieving Breakthrough Success.* Milwaukee: ASQC Quality Press, 1994.

Ross, Joel E. *Total Quality Management: Text, Cases and Readings.* Delray Beach, FL: St. Lucie Press, 1995.

Russell, J. P. *Quality Management Benchmark Assessment.* Milwaukee: ASQC Quality Press, 1995.

Saskin, Marshall and Kiser, Kenneth J. *Putting Total Quality Management to Work.* San Francisco: Berrett-Koehler, 1993.

Schonberger, Richard J. and Knod, Edward M. *Operations Management: Continuous Improvement.* Burr Ridge, IL: Irwin, 1994.

Sekine, K., Arai, K., and Bokek, N. *Design Team Revolution.* Portland, OR: Productivity Press, 1994.

Shewhart, W. A. *Economic Control of Quality of Manufactures Product.* Milwaukee: ASQC Quality Press (reprinted), 1980.

Shingo, Shigeo. *A Study of the Toyota Production System from an Industrial Engineering Point of View.* Cambridge, MA: Productivity Press, 1989.

Shingo, Shigeo. *Zero Quality Control: Source Inspection and the Poka-Yoke System.* Portland, OR: Productivity Press, 1986.

Shingo, Shigeo and Dillon, Andrew P. (trans.). *A Revolution in Manufacturing: The SMED System.* Portland, OR: Productivity Press, 1985.

Singer, Charles Joseph. *A History of Technology.* Oxford: Clarendon Press, 1958.

Smith, Janice L. and Russell, J. P. *The Quality Audit Handbook.* Milwaukee: ASQC Quality Press, 1997.

Snyder, Neil H. *Vision, Values and Courage: Leadership for Quality Management.* New York: Free Press, 1994.

Snyder, Neil H. and Clontz, Angela P. *The Will to Lead: Managing with Courage and Conviction in the Age of Uncertainty.* New York: Irwin, 1996.

Spendolini, Michael J. *Customer Satisfaction Measurement.* New York: Amacom, 1996.

Spendolini, Michael J. *The Benchmarking Book.* New York: Amacom, 1994.

Stamatis, D. H. *Total Quality Service: Principles, Practices, and Implementation.* Delray Beach, FL: St. Lucie Press, 1995.

Stevenson, William J. *Production Operations Management.* New York: Irwin/McGraw-Hill, 1999.

Sumanth, David J. *Total Productivity Management: A Systemic and Quantitative Approach to Compete in Quality, Price, and Time.* Boca Raton, FL: St. Lucie Press, 1997.

Suzaki, Kiyoshi. *The New Shop Floor Management: Empowering People for Continuous Improvement.* New York: The Free Press, 1993.

Swanson, Roger C. *The Quality Improvement Handbook: Team Guide to Tools and Techniques.* Delray Beach, FL: St. Lucie Press, 1995.

Swift, J. A., Omachonu, Vincent K., and Ross, Joel E. *Principles of Total Quality.* Delray Beach, FL: St. Lucie Press, 1998.

Tague, Nancy R. *The Quality Toolbox.* Milwaukee: ASQC Quality Press, 1995.

Taylor, Fredrick Winslow. *The Principles of Scientific Management.* Norcross, GA: Institute of Industrial Engineers, 1998.

Terninko, John. *Step-by-Step QFD: Customer-Driven Product Design.* Boca Raton, FL: St. Lucie Press, 1997.

Terninko, John, Zusman, Alla, and Zlotin, Boris. *Systematic Innovation: An Introduction to Triz (Theory of Inventive Problem Solving).* Boca Raton, FL: St. Lucie Press, 1998.

Todorov, Branimir. *ISO 9000 Required: Your Worldwide Passport to Customer Confidence.* Portland, OR: Productivity Press, 1996.

Togo, Yukiyasu and Wartman, William. *Against All Odds: The Story of the Toyota Motor Corporation and the Family That Created It.* New York: St. Martin's, 1993.

Vollmann, Thomas E., Berry, William L., and Whybark, D. Clay. *Manufacturing Planning and Control Systems.* New York: McGraw-Hill, 1997.

Wallace, Thomas F. *M.R.P. II: Making It Happen: The Implementers' Guide to Success with Manufacturing Resource Planning.* Gloucester, UK: Oliver Wight, 1994.

Walton, Mary. *Deming Management at Work.* New York: G. P. Putnam, 1990.

Watson, Gregory H. *The Benchmarking Workbook: Adapting the Best Practices for Performance Improvement.* Portland, OR: Productivity Press, 1994.

Wellins, R. S., Byham, W. C., and Dixon, G. R. *Inside Teams: How Twenty World-Class Organizations Are Winning through Teamwork.* San Francisco: Jossey-Bass, 1996.

Wheeler, Donald J. *Understanding Variation: The Key to Managing Chaos.* Knoxville, TN: SPC Press, 1993.

Wight, Oliver W. *Executives Guide to Successful Mrp II.* Gloucester, UK: Oliver Wight, 1994.

Wilson, Paul F. and Pearson, Richard. *Performance-Based Assessments: External, Internal, and Self-Assessment Tools for Total Quality Management.* Milwaukee: ASQC Quality Press, 1995.

Wind, Jerry Y. and Main, Jeremy. *Driving Change: How the Best Companies Are Preparing for the 21st Century.* New York: Free Press, 1998.

Wrege, Charles D. and Greenwood, Ronald G. *Frederick W. Taylor-The Father of Scientific Management: Myth and Reality.* Burr Ridge, IL: Irwin, 1991.

Index

About the Author

ROY L. NERSESIAN is Associate Professor of Management at Monmouth University's School of Business Administration. He is the author of several books, including *Managing a Global Enterprise* (Quorum Books, 1999).

ISBN 1-56720-225-X

9 781567 202250

HARDCOVER BAR CODE